Holiday Yugoslavia

Katharine Wood-de Winne was born in Edinburgh in 1960 of Belgian and English parents. She was educated there, reading Communications, then English language and literature at Edinburgh University. Following a period as a freelance public relations consultant she entered the world of travel journalism. An eighteen-month spell touring Europe and North Africa resulted in the book *Europe by Train* (published by Fontana) which is one of the UK's top-selling guidebooks. As well as working on this series of Holiday Guides, she is currently involved in several projects encompassing every aspect of the travel industry – from backpacking students to round-the-world first-class tours. In the course of her work she travels extensively and has so far clocked up 46 countries, having spent a considerable part of her working life in the last couple of years in Yugoslavia. She is married and lives in Perth, Scotland, with her husband and young sons, Andrew and Euan.

George McDonald was born in Dumfries, Galloway, in 1955 and was educated at Fettes College and Edinburgh University. Following a spell on the family farm he toured Europe and North Africa to help research the guidebook *Europe by Train*. He continues to travel for a living, researching for the various guidebooks he is involved in with Katie Wood, and is rarely in one place for more than three weeks at a time. Home, when he's there, is Guernsey in the Channel Islands.

Holiday
YUGOSLAVIA

Compiled and Edited by
Katie Wood

Head Researcher: George McDonald

Fontana/Collins

To Andrew

First published in 1987 by Fontana Paperbacks
8 Grafton Street, London W1X 3LA

Copyright © Katie Wood and George McDonald 1987

Set in Linotron Plantin

Maps by Ken Lewis

Made and printed in Great Britain
by William Collins Sons & Co. Ltd, Glasgow

Contents

Part Two – HOW TO GO 66

Part Three – WHEN YOU'RE THERE 123

Part Four – GUIDE TO THE COUNTRY

ACKNOWLEDGEMENTS

Thanks are owed to the following people: the Yugoslavian Tourist Authority in London; Yugotours of Regent Street, London, notably Alex Winkley for proof reading; Syd House for his helpful criticism, tireless research and additional historical contributions; Leo, our guide in Slovenia, for showing us the sights of his beautiful home territory; Mariette, for the excellent babysitting service which allowed me to get the book written at all; and the team of valiant researchers who helped bring it all together.

WHAT THIS GUIDE IS ABOUT

For too long now there has been a gulf in the guidebook market. On the one hand there are the 'heavies' – books which, though good in their way, assume the holidaymaker wants a stone-by-stone description of all the ancient remains in the country of their choice, and, what's more, assume that their readership is middle-aged, middle-class and predominantly American with a lot of cash to splash about. At the other end of the scale are the backpacking, student-orientated, 'rough it on $10 a day' guides which assume the traveller wants to cover the maximum amount of ground possible and spend the absolute minimum doing so (even if this does mean surviving on one bowl of vegetable rice a day and no baths for two weeks).

But in the middle of these poles lies the vast majority of tourists: normal, fun-loving people who go on holiday to unwind from a year's toil, and who, though not able to throw cash about indiscriminately, are willing to spend enough to enjoy themselves. Predominantly these people fall into the under-40 age group – the 'young ones' keen to see the countries they visit and have a good time in their own way. This guide is written for this sort of person.

It does not wade into pages of history – it just gives you the basics to enable you to make sense of the monuments and places you'll see while on holiday. It does not pretend to be a specialist guide for one group of people (watersports enthusiasts, nature lovers, archaeologists, etc.), but it does point you in the direction of where to pursue these type of hobbies once you are in the country. If any one 'hobby' is highlighted more than most it is that of 'sun worshipping' and where best to do it, as time after time surf, sea 'n' sand still come top of most people's priorities for a good holiday.

With Yugoslavia's increasing popularity as a holiday destination we look at the options open to would-be travellers and at the pros and cons of all the different packages offered by tour operators. But the guide is not aimed only at the package travellers. Independent travellers are remembered too, and we look in great detail at the crucial decision whether to opt for a package or independent holiday. All the relevant up-to-the-minute info is in Part One – Before You Go.

Our recommendations for restaurants, nightlife, hotels, etc. start at the lower end of the market, since we believe the art of using money when on holiday lies in saving it without sacrificing the holiday spirit.

We hope this guide will help you to have a rewarding time in Yugoslavia – a country whose amazing holiday potential is only now being recognized. Much space is devoted to the Dalmatian and Istrian coastline, for there lies the centre of Yugoslavia's tourist market. If you feel we've missed anything out, let us know. This is a different type of guide: informal and chatty, not academic and definitive. We are not setting ourselves up as *the* authority on Yugoslavia. We know a lot and have travelled there extensively, but our knowledge is more on where the best places for different types of holidays are, than on Yugoslavian history. If any of our recommendations fails to come up to the mark, or if you find a super undiscovered beach which you are willing to share, or a new lively taverna, write and tell us about it. After all, we all want the same in the end – the memory of at least two glorious, fun-filled weeks to sustain us through the long, dark, winter nights.

Part One

BEFORE YOU GO

ENTRY REQUIREMENTS British visitors with a full passport are allowed a 90-day stay without a visa (for longer stays, apply to the police within seven days of your arrival). Those on a British Visitor's Card will be issued with an identity card on arrival.

POPULATION 22,500,000

CAPITAL Belgrade (pop: 1,850,000)

CURRENCY Dinar (£1 = 4690D)

POLITICAL SYSTEM Socialist Federal Republic

RELIGIONS Serbian Orthodox, Muslim, Catholic, Protestant

LANGUAGES Serbo-Croat, Slovenian, Macedonian (some German, English and French understood)

PUBLIC HOLIDAYS   1, 2 January
1, 2 May
4 July
29, 30 November

Additional regional holidays are:

Serbia	7 July
Montenegro	13 July
Slovenia	22 July
Bosnia-Herzegovina	27 July
Croatia	27 July
Macedonia	2 August and 11 October

What to Expect

Yugoslavia offers cheap, simple holidays in attractive settings. Most of its tourist industry is based on packages on the Dalmatian, Istrian and Croatian coasts. The air of commercialism which pervades the package holiday industry in Spain and Greece has not penetrated Yugoslavia, with the result that Yugoslavia is more a place in which to unwind by the coast than to indulge in the high life. The vast majority of hotels (most of which have been built in the last thirty years, since mass tourism hit the country) are not, as is the case in Spain, built cheek by jowl along the coast, but are grouped together in holiday complexes leaving the coastline and surrounding towns and villages largely unspoilt. Grouping hotels together often results in the sharing of facilities, sports and nightlife being the obvious areas for the overlap. Cooperatively owned hotels and less private enterprise in the restaurants and shops will result in a subtle difference to the 'feel' of your holiday, but don't imagine that because you are in a (non-aligned) Socialist (Communist) state it's all queues for food and nothing in the souvenir shops. Yugoslavia may not be the South of France, but it's hardly distinguishable from Western Europe in most ways and there's certainly no feeling of being in the Eastern bloc for package holidaymakers.

The most spectacular parts of the country are the Transylvanian Alps of Montenegro, the Julian Alps in Slovenia, the resorts on the Istrian coast, and the medieval city of Dubrovnik. All down the coast, though, with the exception of the Zadar–Split section, the mountains act as a spectacular backdrop to the resorts, and you are unlikely to be disappointed in the scenery. The best beaches are right down in the south, in the area beyond Budva. Roughly speaking, the 3823 miles of coastline divides itself into three main sections: Istria and the Croatian coast in the north (major resorts: Opatija, Rovinj and Portoroz); the Dalmatian coast and islands in the middle section of Yugoslavia's coastline (Tučepi and Brela are the major resorts, while Split is the major city and it's from there that the ferries leave to the islands); and the third section of the coast encompasses the city of Dubrovnik and the area to its south – Montenegro (Cavtat and Miločer are the major resorts; this can really be subdivided into five sections, but we go into more detail later in the book).

Once you turn away from the coast it hits you that, in fact, this is one of Europe's, and indeed the world's, most complex and culturally diverse countries. Away from organized tourism it's quite possible to transport yourself back a century or more. Life goes on in the region of Macedonia, for instance, pretty much how it used to one hundred years ago, yet only a few hours away, in Belgrade, there's hardly one building in the city centre more than thirty years old.

This diversity is due to the country being an amalgam of six republics – Bosnia-Herzegovina, Montenegro, Croatia, Macedonia, Slovenia and Serbia – and inhabited by as many as *eight* different nationalities, speaking *three* separate languages, using *two* different alphabets and practising *four* separate religions! If nothing else, this makes Yugoslavia one of the world's most interesting and colourful countries to visit.

The major historical influences which shaped present-day Yugoslavia were, in the north, the domination of the Austro-Hungarian Empire and, in the south, the Turks and the rule of the Ottoman Empire. The main influence on the coastal region was that of the Venetians, hence Dubrovnik's Venetian-style architecture. Yugoslavia as such only came into being after the First World War (and if you remember your history lessons, this is where it all started, too, with old Archduke Ferdinand in Sarajevo, etc.), and during the Second World War she suffered terribly with as much as one-fifth of her population being wiped out, partly by the war and partly by the bloody civil war which developed from it. Marshall Tito emerged on the scene in the 1940s and continued to rule the country until his death in 1980, managing, against all odds, to keep the country non-aligned to either superpower (though undoubtedly its centralized economy gives it more similarities to the USSR than to the USA).

Tourism is a growth industry in Yugoslavia. In just the past ten years the annual number of tourists to the country has increased by as much as 60 per cent and the trend looks set to escalate. Mainly this is due to the fact that Yugoslavia is one of the cheapest countries currently on offer for Northern Europeans, with a virtual guarantee of summer sunshine. Unlike Spain and some of Greece, she is making determined efforts not to spoil her main asset – the coastline – and the major industrial centres such as Rijeka and Split are kept well away from the mainstream of organized tourism. There are literally hundreds of islands (approximately a thousand) in the Adriatic, only a few of which could possibly be described as commercialized, so the potential for future expansion is great. For many years only hotel-based full-board holidays were being offered, but now half-board and self-catering deals are provided as well. Independent travel is also becoming more of a feature, though travel in many inland regions is not for inexperienced first-timers as facilities can often be very basic. Bear in mind that the picture you get on the coast of Yugoslavia is not representative of the whole country. In the past couple of years the 'Club' holidays have been moving into the Dubrovnik region. The combination of low prices, hot sun, an exotic destination and reasonable facilities for sports and nightlife is making Yugoslavia an increasingly popular destination for the under-35s – a trend likely to continue in future years.

When to Go

July and August are the busiest and the hottest months and they constitute the 'peak season' as far as all tour operators are concerned. You'll pay most for your holiday at this time of year however you do it, but in return you'll find everything open and the nightlife and social scene at its peak.

April and May are good compromises for those who want the sun but not in such burning proportions, and to escape the crowds and inflated peak season prices. At the beginning of the season you will also find people have more time for you (by the end of October they do not want to see any more tourists; ever) and as a result service is often better.

If you travel right at the beginning of the season (particularly if it's before Easter) you may still find certain restaurants, museums and tourist-related shops are not open yet.

June is a happy medium for all these considerations and is one of the most pleasant months to visit Yugoslavia.

September finds the tourist season still in its swing, though the crowds are less and the nights are getting dark earlier; and by October you're entering the off-season rates (and cooler temperatures, particularly in the evenings). Reductions can be as much as 40 per cent on July room rates, so it's worth considering for those on a tight budget. By late October you are into temperatures not worth the sunbathing effort, so bear this in mind.

Winter Yugoslavia

SKIING

Yugoslavia offers some very good skiing in the winter months. Again, the big attractions are the lower costs and fewer crowds than in most other major European countries.

The best skiing can be found near Sarajevo, on the plateau of JAHORINA – the area which was revamped and developed for the 1984 Winter Olympics. Other resorts worth considering are BOHINJ and KRANJSKA GORA in the north of Slovenia; PLANICA, which boasts a 525-feet ski jump, and the ŠAR PLANINA in Macedonia which rises at Titov Vrh to 660 feet and has Popova Sapka as its main resort. Winter sports begin in December and last through until April or May. Contact the Yugoslavian Tourist Board, 143 Regent Street, London W1, for further details and a current list of tour operators.

WINTER SUN?

No, not really. Despite efforts by some tour operators to persuade you to the contrary, Yugoslavia's winter weather is not much better than our own. It can be extremely cold, particularly in the mountains. True, the hotels virtually pay you to stay in them during the winter months, but there's no point going for a winter tan. If it's not the sun you're after, though, there's sound logic behind going at this time of year, particularly if you're interested in visiting some of the attractive coastal towns which are mobbed in the summer. If this is your intention, consider the centres of Poreč, Opatija, Rijeka, Zadar, Split, Makarska, Dubrovnik, Sveti Stefan or, right down close to the Albanian border, Ulcinj. Many of the hotels in these resorts have indoor seawater pools and thermal baths, and concentrate on health cures. The prices for an out-of-season break on full board can often work out less than the heating bills you'll incur by staying at home!

The Climate

Coastal Weather

In summer the coast is as hot as most Mediterranean destinations. July and August are the hottest (and busiest) months, with temperatures up around 29°C or the mid-80s°F. Although it's usually dry at this time of year, you can still expect a couple of overcast or wet days or the odd short-lived thunderstorm. The season for predictably good weather starts mid-April with pleasant mid-60s°F temperatures. By May it's really acceptable – in the low 70s°F – and from June until late September it's more or less guaranteed sunbathing weather. October is getting cooler, though you'll still get on the beach, but thereafter until April you can forget serious sunbathing.

Noted for their particularly mild climates are Opatija and Lovran in Istria which enjoy the shelter of Mount Ucka, and the islands of Korčula and Hvar. In the height of summer it hardly cools down at all at nights here, which is not the case for the rest of the coast.

Average maximum daily temperatures, based on Split:

	JAN	FEB	MAR	APR	MAY	JUNE
°F	50	52	57	64	73	81
°C	10	11	14	18	23	27

	JULY	AUG	SEP	OCT	NOV	DEC
°F	86	86	79	68	59	54
°C	30	30	26	20	15	12

There's an appreciable difference in climate between the north and the south of Yugoslavia. If you're really keen on the heat and sun and don't want to risk any wet days, stick to the area around Dubrovnik, for even the Dalmatian islands are noticeably wetter than the southern stretch of the coast.

The heat is tempered by cooling breezes on the coast (Split is the only obvious exception as it is sheltered by the mountains and can become stiflingly hot), and the strong winds – the cold, dry 'bura' and the warm 'yugo' – have been known to create havoc with the weather, though these don't usually make an appearance until the winter. More often felt is the maestral, which blows in from the sea. Don't worry, though, the chances are 90:10 in favour of you returning home with a disgusting tan!

Inland Weather

Summers can be very hot and airless inland, with no cooling sea breezes to help you. The Slovenian mountain resorts have warm, wet summers (warmer than in neighbouring Austria, or in Switzerland), but wetter even than in Britain. Spring is really the ideal time to see the interior, particularly the mountain areas when the countryside looks its lushest. Winter sports have a season from December to April/May.

Average maximum daily temperatures, based on Belgrade:

	JAN	FEB	MAR	APR	MAY	JUNE
°F	37	41	52	64	73	79
°C	3	5	11	18	23	26

	JULY	AUG	SEP	OCT	NOV	DEC
°F	82	82	75	64	52	41
°C	28	28	24	18	11	5

Where to Go for What

People often spend weeks deliberating which country to choose for their holiday destination, then leave the final choice of where they stay within the country to either a photo and brief, optimistic write-up in a travel brochure, or to the discretion and persuasive talk of a travel agent (many of whom haven't actually visited the country). This lottery results, not surprisingly, in people having a disappointing holiday simply because they got the facts wrong on this crucial decision. If anything, the decision about which part of the country you base yourself is more important than the choice of country itself, for there is good and bad in every country – Britain, for example, offers the tourist a superb holiday destination, but if the visitor were to opt for two weeks in Sheffield when he really wanted a 'get away from it all' type of break, he would be sadly disappointed. Don't think that the Yugoslavian equivalents of Sheffield aren't on offer. They are, but unless you're careful you will not know if you've landed it until you've paid your hundreds of pounds and arrived at the resort.

In order to match your needs to the most suitable resorts we have divided holidaymakers into certain stereotypes. Doubtless most of you fall into several of the categories, but the idea is to find which resorts crop up under the headings which interest you, and match your needs accordingly.

The following symbols representing the various interests appear throughout this book as an easy guide to the places likely to be of interest to you:

The Sun Worshipper

The Naturist

The Sightseer

The Socialite

The Sportsman

The Nature Lover

The Recluse

Family Holidays

 The Sun Worshipper: *Surf, Sea and Sand*

The best beaches are undoubtedly in the extreme south, in the area south of Budva in Montenegro. The beaches further north are not all bad, but generally they are man-made and have more in the way of rocks and pebbles than miles of golden sand. Fortunately an increasing number of hotels are cementing over stretches of rocks and pebbles to provide access to the sea and sunbathing platforms without inflicting permanent damage to your tender, white, Northern European feet. It is possible to find the odd attractive rocky bay backed by pine trees and the mountains, but you'll have to do some investigative work first. Most hotels have loungers and provide showers, but public beaches rarely have any facilities; and where bathing is off the rocks, be on your guard for sea urchins. As you've probably heard, Yugoslavia is one of the world's leading centres for 'naturism' or nudist bathing, and more about this is said under the Naturist section. The area to concentrate on if your main aim is to flop on a beach, admire the talent and pick up a good tan is the southern Adriatic. Professional sun worshippers should look out for the following resorts:

BEČIĆI – the 'mosaic beach' is thought to be the best on the Montenegrin coast (therefore in all Yugoslavia). It has attractive, pinkish coloured, coarse sand and gently shelving slopes into the water and it's a long enough expanse of sand to accommodate many serious sun-worshippers. The only drawback is it can lack shade, but there is an abundance of water sports and a young, lively crowd.

SVETI STEFAN – a purpose-built tourist village with good beaches on the fringes of the narrow artificial causeway which links the town with the mainland (it used to be an island but is now connected to the mainland). This is one of the showpieces of Yugoslavia's tourist industry and therefore it aspires to more up-market facilities and prices than other resorts.

MILOČER – once the location of the summer palace of the royal family, Miločer is now a thriving resort with several stretches of good, pink sandy beaches within its vicinity. If anything, Miločer should be regarded as the best beach in Yugoslavia, for it combines a beautiful setting with a naturally fine beach.

ULCINJ – right in the south by the Albanian border, is like entering a different world, for now you are into the Muslim part of Yugoslavia, and the mosques and minarets will add that extra exotic touch to a holiday here. The 1979 earthquake unfortunately resulted in Ulcinj resembling a builder's yard for a long time, but the main tourist area of Velika Plaza is far enough removed for you not to worry about that. It is located two and a half miles from the main town and boasts a huge beach of fine sand. In fact, the grey sand here is radioactive and is reputed to offer remarkable results to rheumatics sufferers, so don't be too surprised when your next-door neighbour digs a hollow in the sand and lies covered to the neck in the stuff! The only snag about this otherwise fine beach is that it is rather exposed and can suffer from winds. In July and August this needn't worry you too much as the heat can be quite unbearable and you'll welcome the wind; outside the hottest months it can occasionally be a nuisance.

Outside the Montenegrin coast the only other area worth seriously considering by a professional sun worshipper is the Makarska riviera –

the area wedged between the Dalmatian riviera and the Dubrovnik riviera. Although the beaches in this region are not sandy, they are still very attractive, and ideal for those who enjoy the beach and all its pleasures without the nuisance of sand in awkward places. The beaches here are of white pebbles and set in beautifully scenic surroundings: pine trees, olive groves and vineyards, with the Biokovo mountains as their backdrop.

BASKA VODA and BRELA – the names to watch out for. Baska Voda, just around the headland from Brela, has a long pebble beach, backed by a promenade of shops, cafes and bars. It is quite commercialized, and Brela is a more attractive proposition – a small resort with attractive bays of white-pebbled beaches. Some of the hotels have their own secluded beaches, and water sports are on offer.

MAKARSKA itself has a mile-long pebble beach called DONJA LUKA close at hand, but it is quite busy and crowded; PODGORA's beach is picturesque but not terribly big, and the maestral wind particularly affects this beach and that at TUČEPI, though this is often a blessing as the area can become unbelievably hot. The Tučepi beach is attractive and spacious and offers a range of water sports. For a secluded beach in this region your best bet is to try some of the bays around Brela, or in the area south of Makarska the little fishing villages on the foothills of the Biokovo mountains such as IGRANE, ZAOSTROG or ZIVOGOSCE.

As far as the islands are concerned, many of them are a bit disappointing on the beach front. The best of the bunch are: LOPAR (ten miles from Rab town on the island of Rab); the island of LOPUD; and SUPETAR on the island of Brač.

 # The Naturist

Yugoslavia pioneered the cause of naturist holidays long before other holiday destinations got in on the act, and today it remains one of the leading countries in this field. There are naturist centres all down the Adriatic coast and on the islands, and their number is increasing. The point should be made that these special beaches and centres are for serious naturists only, and every effort is made to keep out the peeping-Tom, cheap-thrill set. (For example, males unaccompanied by females must have an International Naturist Membership Card before being able to book a holiday at one of these special resorts. Apply to the General Secretary, The Central Council for British Naturism, Assurance House, 35–41 Hazelwood Road, Northampton NN1 1LL.)

Photography is prohibited on all naturist beaches, except for taking pictures of your own party with their permission (though wide-angle lenses could foul this up!). Anyway, the point is the whole naturist ideology is very much based on the German *Freikorperkultur* idea (that's what the FKK you'll see posted on these beaches stands for: unfortunately, most Slavs assume all tourists are German!), so it's all very healthy and above board, in theory. It is in practice, too (most of the time).

There are two ways to enjoy a naturist holiday. Either you can stay in a 'normal' hotel which caters for everybody, and just visit a local naturist beach, as and when you want to (often these are islands just off the shore) or you can stay at an enclosed naturist centre where nudism is the order of the day (except for mealtimes, dances, etc., when it could be slightly inconvenient). Everyone staying at a naturist centre is pretty well devoted to the cause and you'll find intense German-types here in vast numbers.

Enclosed naturist centres and hotels can be found near to the following places: VRSAR, POREČ, ROVINJ, MEDULIN, PUNTA SKALA, PRIMOŠTEN, STARIGRAD, OMIS, ULCINJ and SLANO. And on the islands: PUNTA KRIŽA on Cres, PUNAT on Krk, and NOVALJA on Pag. The centres and hotels are all located a few miles outside these main resorts but you'll find them easier to trace under these resort names. Among the best of the naturist beaches are the ones at Umag and Rovinj on the Istrian coast, MALI LOSINJ on the isle of Losinj, and ULCINJ in Montenegro. Others are available at the following resorts: Bol, Cavtat, Dubrovnik, Hvar, Jelsa, Korčula, Lopud, Mlini, Rab, Srebreno, Supetar, Tučepi, Umag, Vela Luka and Vrbroska.

The Sightseer: *Sights, historical monuments and archaeological remains*

Fortunately, many of the best of Yugoslavia's sights are located on the coast, within reach of the resorts, thus allowing you to enjoy a beach holiday with the added advantage of interesting excursions. To be frank, Yugoslavia is not the sort of country you would ideally choose for an intensive sightseeing holiday. There is no Yugoslavian equivalent to Paris, London or Rome in terms of impressive monuments and buildings outside Dubrovnik, so it's just as well that you can combine your sightseeing activities with the country's main tourist asset – the coast and its attendant pleasures.

Most of the coastal towns have an old quarter, often dating back to medieval times, and narrow winding streets and a picturesque harbour. These are the areas to concentrate on, for modern Yugoslavia invariably means endless concrete buildings and indistinguishable high-rise blocks.

The old churches are always worth a visit, but the museums are generally a poor show, with amateur displays, erratic opening hours and descriptions only in Serbo-Croat, so you have got to be really keen on your subject. By far the best place to base yourself if you're a keen sightseer is Dubrovnik, for here you have an interesting city with plenty to see and do and an ideal base for daytrips. The beach is even thrown in for days to recuperate.

Most of the resorts on the coast run excursions to Dubrovnik, so it's not strictly necessary to stay in the city or its immediate resorts, but obviously the closer you are the more you'll see. Other good bases for sightseeing are Split, Zadar, Trogir and Šibenik on the Dalmatian riviera; Pula on the Istrian coast. These towns offer not only old quarters worth a visit but also impressive Greek and Roman remains.

POREČ, OPATIJA and MAKARSKA are the resorts best located for excursions (bear in mind, though, that excursions in Yugoslavia are relatively expensive, therefore it's cheaper to stay in one of the main sightseeing centres).

From many of the Istrian resorts it's possible to make a daytrip to Venice, which, for the keen sightseer, will undoubtedly be the climax of the holiday.

As far as the islands are concerned, the towns of Korčula, Rab and Hvar on the islands of the same names offer the most, with walled towns and several interesting sights.

Excursions particularly worth taking in are:

THE POSTOJNA CAVES – from several resorts in northern Yugoslavia (the mountain resorts and many of the Istrian bases) you get an opportunity to visit this twelve-mile labyrinth of caves which contain incredible stalagmite and stalactite rock formations. You travel by mini-railway through the first 13 miles, then by foot for a mile or so (take a jacket, it's very cold and damp).

THE PLITVICE LAKES – again, accessible from Istria and the mountain and lake resorts, the Plitvice Lakes excursion constitutes a visit to sixteen lakes lying like terraces on different levels, linked by numerous underground caves and waterfalls. The result is quite spectacular as they are in an attractive National Park. Wear sturdy shoes with a good grip.

DUBROVNIK – definitely worth a daytrip to see this medieval city, which was one of Europe's leading centres in the fifteenth century. There are numerous buildings to see, Renaissance palaces and churches, the Doge's Palace, old city walls, etc., etc. Even for tepid sightseers, this is one excursion worth making.

GULF OF KOTOR and CETINJE – the Gulf of Kotor lies at the northernmost edge of Montenegro, close to the 'border' with the Dubrovnik riviera. It is an incredible fjord of dramatic scenery, and will provide you with some superb photos even if you don't get out of the coach, which, if you suffer from vertigo, is quite likely as the winding road you take round the steep mountain often leaves you with the impression that there is nothing between you and the sea (there isn't). Spectacular scenery, though, and well worth the tummy flips.

Also included in the organised trips here is a visit to some of the twelfth century churches in the medieval town of Kotor, including the Cathedral of St Tryphon. Most of the buildings in this interesting town suffered badly in the 1979 earthquake, but are now restored.

The historic buildings of Cetinje, the old capital, suffered the same fate, but are now open to visitors and provide an interesting final part to this varied daytrip, which can be taken from most of the resorts on the Montenegrin riviera.

Obviously, these suggestions merely scrape the surface of what can be seen, but they are the vital excursions which should not be missed. More details on all the sights of the regions are given under the relevant sections.

The Socialite: *Man-watching, Nightlife, etc.*

Undoubtedly the classiest way to visit Yugoslavia would be to sail around the islands on a luxury yacht, stopping off at various points on the coast and at a few of the more sophisticated islands. Most of us, however, settle for a couple of weeks based in one place or region. For the person who is concerned with 'seeing' and 'being seen in' the right places, Yugoslavia, to be honest, isn't the right country to choose. While there are a few swankier resorts on the coast and islands, it's all relative, and if you're hoping to bump into the Mykonos or Côte d'Azur set you'll be disappointed. Yugoslavia is not really the place for that.

Man-watching is, however, a different story and if it's just this innocent, enjoyable hobby you're keen to indulge in, you're in for a treat. The Slavs are very keen on it themselves, as can be seen by watching them on their evening *korzo* (promenade/stroll). After work and on Sundays when the weather is fair, they change into their latest fashions and walk out in true Mediterranean style, aiming to see and be seen. The town squares are the main gathering points for this mutual scrutinization, or on the coast it's often down on the waterfront. It usually takes place around dusk, with the peak time between 7 and 8 p.m. If you're keen to size up the local talent, this is your best opportunity.

Other good chances for man-watching arise by sitting at pavement cafés and bars. Yugoslavia rates quite highly in these stakes as most of the major tourist centres and towns have a selection of suitably located establishments, and they're quite used to people passing a few hours this way for only the price of two or three drinks (which are cheap anyway). Promenade or harbour cafés are obvious choices, and have the added advantage of affording you the opportunity to see people on their way to the beach. If you're in a resort which is quite a distance from the main town, you'll have to resort to the pool-side gaze or the bar venue. The benefits of beach posing are obvious, but be warned: the naturist beaches in Yugoslavia are predominantly for the serious nudist, not the voyeur, and clichéd as it is – once you've seen one. . . . By the second and third day on a naturist beach you'll hardly notice the nudity any longer, and at the end of a week you'll wonder what all the fuss was about. However, in all seriousness, don't go to a naturist beach and sit there smugly in your trunks expecting a cheap thrill. You'll be the one everyone's looking at and at some resorts you'll either be told to 'get them off' or clear off.

As regards nightlife, again, to be quite honest, Yugoslavia is not the first choice if you're the nightclubbing disco-king type whose main enjoyment on holiday is getting sloshed and raving through the small hours. There are discos and nightclubs, but they're pretty tame by Northern European standards, and unless you're desperate to chat-up the stunning redhead you eyed up on the beach earlier, they are a bit of a waste of time and money (though it must be said that all nightlife in Yugoslavia is cheap, discos coming in at about £2 a head). Most discos wind up around 1 a.m. (despite claims to go on till much later) but unless you're under twenty-one you're likely to get the 'oldest swinger in town' syndrome.

Most of the big hotels have dancing to live music which is open to non-residents (generally no entrance fee but drinks prices are higher than normal), and 'local entertainment' is often provided in the form of folk dancing and musical evenings. If you're into these sorts of things, aim to stay at one of the bigger hotels and travel with a tour operator who offers these facilities. Increasingly resorts are erecting purpose-built 'nightlife centres' which offer discos, bars, nightclubs and restaurants all under one roof, and larger resorts often have cinemas showing English-language films. If you base yourself near a major town or city you can even find classical concerts and opera on offer, particularly if you travel at the time of one of the festivals of music and drama. The times these are held are:

Split	mid-July to mid-August
Ohrid	12 July to 20 August
Opatija	June to September
Ljubljana	July to August
Zagreb	June to August
Belgrade	mid-October
Dubrovnik	10 July to 25 August

(More details under individual sections.)

The *korzo* is a national phenomenon which you will experience to some degree or another wherever you base yourself, though obviously the bigger the resort the better the *korzo*. For café and bar-posing the best places are ROVINJ and PORTOROZ in Istria; TROGIR and PRIMOŠTEN in Dalmatia; TUČEPI, BASKA VODA and PODGORA on the Makarska riviera; DUBROVNIK, CAVTAT and MLINI on the Dubrovnik riviera. As far as the islands go, the town of HVAR and SUPETAR on Brač.

For details of naturist beaches, see the separate section on 'The Naturist'. For nightlife, the best resorts are concentrated on the Istrian riviera: POREČ, with its Zelena Luguna entertainments complex and the casino at Hotel Perentium; PORTOROZ, with the Hotel Metropole casino and many large hotels offering entertainment; and ROVINJ, which has the Monvi Entertainment Centre and the Hotel Eden casino.

Further down the coast: OPATIJA on the Kvarner riviera boasts an open-air theatre and several clubs and discos; and in the south DUBROVNIK and SPLIT are the two main cities for nightlife – the resorts have nothing out of the ordinary as yet. Dubrovnik caters for the tourist better than Split does, and if you are a restless type who wants to be on the go – sightseeing during the day and swinging away the nights – this is probably your best destination in Yugoslavia.

RECORDING YOUR HOLIDAY

The true socialite these days will be seen with nothing less on the beach, to capture those happy holiday moments, than a full-blown video recorder. Conventional cameras are decidedly passé, and if you aspire to the heights of social acceptance in the highest circles a video is a must.

Video cameras are taking over as *the* new form of home movies. The trend is set and each year an increasing number of people discover the delights of taking their holiday on film, to be played back on their telly and watched from the comfort of their armchair in the dark winter months ahead. Though a video rig-out is still an expensive business, it's the sort of equipment which once you've had you feel you can never do without. Photos, slides and cine films just aren't the same after a full colour and sound film, and on holiday where the sky and sea are so blue, and the colours so much more vibrant, a video camera really comes into its own.

When researching this series of guides we made extensive use of one of our researcher's video cameras – a Ferguson Videostar C-Auto-Focus CCR – which, if you're thinking of investing in an outfit, is an ideal one to choose with travelling in mind. It is incredibly light and portable, weighing only 5 lb including the battery, and it's virtually idiot-proof. There is an auto focus on it and it comes in a small carrying case, ideal to slip over your shoulder wherever you go.

If you feel around £1300 is a bit too much to splash out, consider hiring. That way you can have the fun of taking a film of your holiday for not much more than the equivalent you'd spend on conventional films, processing etc. Hiring is widely available in all areas of the UK and is becoming, like the video camera itself, very much a thing of the future.

 The Sportsman/*Spa Holidays*

A wide range of sports is on offer because hotels have recognized this is one very effective way of enticing the young affluent market. As with nightlife, they represent very good value for money – at no point will you feel you are being ripped off for sports facilities, which comes as a refreshing change compared to most Mediterranean destinations.

Among the sports on offer at resorts are: tennis, table tennis, horse-riding, jogging on set tracks, mini-golf, bowls and a wide variety of water sports – canoeing, sailing, rowing, windsurfing, waterskiing, pedaloes, sub-aqua diving and, of course, swimming.

Away from the main resorts **fishing** is on offer around the lakes and on the Adriatic, but there are stringent regulations governing what can be caught and where. For further information keen fishermen should contact the Sportsski Neadorica, 19–23 Belgrade, or ask the Yugoslavian National Tourist Office in London for further information.

Sailing is another possibility. Sarajevo is one of the main bases from which excursions can be arranged, one of the most exciting and scenic being a canoe trip down the River Drina. From Budva through Montenegro it is possible to arrange a trip on a raft down the River Tara, or if that's not adventurous enough, how about a kayak trip over the rapids of the Soco or Sava rivers of Slovenia? Further information about these trips and general info for salt-water sailors can be found in the 'Nautics' leaflet, available from the Yugoslavian National Tourist Office in London.

There are ample opportunities for **hunting** wild game, including brown bear, wild boar, chamois, ibex and the hart. Game hunting, however, is not cheap, and can hardly be said to fit in nicely with a resort-based beach holiday. If you're keen, though, write to the Yugoslavian National Tourist Office and ask for further details.

The healthier pursuit of **mountaineering**, however, could conceivably be combined with a beach holiday as the Dinaric Alps run parallel to the Dalmatian coast. Other options include the Julian Alps in the north, the inland range of the Durmitor in Montenegro and the Šar Planina in Macedonia. There are impressive mountains within reach of most of Yugoslavia's major cities, and the heights to be conquered should provide enough of a challenge for even the most serious climbers (Triglav in the Julian Alps stands 9393 feet high, the Durmitor range goes up to 8301 feet, and the Šar Planina 6560 feet). For summer climbs you really must start at dawn as the temperatures after noon make for problems.

Back at the resorts, where gentler activities are pursued, the best places for water sports are concentrated in Istria: POREČ, RABAC, UMAG or PULA. Outside Istria the only other places seriously worth considering for keen water sports fanatics are MALINSKA on the island of Krk, VRBROSKA on Hvar, and for sailing MALI LOSINJ on the island of Losinj. For non-water-based sports, one of the best resorts is the 'lively' holiday complex (i.e., best for the very young and active, not mums and dads) of BABIN KUK on Lapad peninsula, a couple of miles from Dubrovnik. Water sports are cheaper in Yugoslavia than in most other countries, with waterskiing averaging £3 for 10 minutes and board-sailing £2 an hour (1988 prices).

Serious walkers, fishermen, golfers and horse-riders should consider the lakes and mountains of Yugoslavia as opposed to the coast for their holiday destination. BLED in the mountains of Slovenia is a superb resort, surrounded by wonderful scenery and ideal for walkers, golfers, horsemen and water sports enthusiasts. There is even a beach here (though it's pebbly, not sandy) and a holiday here need not be at the expense of nightlife, for this is quite a lively resort, even out of high season. Other mountain and lakeside resorts worth considering for outdoor types are BOHINJ in the Julian Alps; KRANJSKA GORA, a winter ski resort; and PLITVICE, the National Park, ideal for fishing and walking.

SPA HOLIDAYS

Yugoslavia has a surprising number of mineral and thermal springs where holidays and health cures can be combined. The Balkan Spa is a well established and remarkably sophisticated affair and 'cures' can range from the relatively inexpensive in a modest rest home to very luxurious in a grand hotel. The spa resorts are principally found in Slovenia, Croatia, Serbia and Bosnia. A complete list of the types of disorders which can be treated by the spas and springs in Yugoslavia can be had from the Yugoslavian National Tourist Office in London.

Among some of the better known spas are the following: ROGASKA SLATINA, DOBRNA and SLATINA RADENCI in Slovenia; LIPIK and TOPUSKO in Croatia; ILIDŽA in Bosnia-Herzegovina; IGALO in Montenegro; NIŠKA BANJA and BUKOVIČKA BANJA in Serbia; and KATLANOVSKA BANJA in Macedonia.

For more detailed information contact the Yugoslavian National Tourist Office.

The Nature Lover

With over 34 per cent of Yugoslavia covered in forests and areas rich with fauna and flora, there's a good selection for the nature lover's holiday.

Obviously the areas to concentrate on are those in the mountains of inland Yugoslavia. INLAND SLOVENIA has many possibilities and is equally acceptable for those wishing an organized holiday and for independent travellers. Resorts such as BLED in the Julian Alps offers fine scenery and walking and water sport opportunities; while BOHINJ at the foot of Triglav, Yugoslavia's highest mountain, gives you access to beautiful alpine pastures with spectacular wild flower displays in the spring. KRANJSKA GORA is another village which now caters for the tourist (and is available through several tour operators), and within a day's trip from here you can visit the Botanical Gardens of the Julian Alps where you can see every kind of flower which is indigenous to the Slovenia mountains. The KAMNIK ALPS and POHORJE MOUNTAINS will offer the visitor an even quieter holiday, while still enjoying magnificent alpine scenery, and the caves of POSTOJNA and ŠKOCJAN make interesting visits for those keen on geology.

 The Recluse

For those who like an 'away from it all' holiday Yugoslavia offers many possibilities, for away from the big resorts on the coast Yugoslavia remains one of Europe's least explored and exploited countries. The mountain resorts offered by several tour operators are where to concentrate your attentions, although if you choose carefully there are still plenty of coastal beach resorts to enjoy away from the madding (maddening!) crowds.

Even at its 'worst', the tourists in Yugoslavia are better distributed and less concentrated than in other major tourist countries. You won't get the sardine syndrome *à la* Torremolinos on many beaches since quite a lot of planning has gone into the location of resorts, and as many holidays are hotel-pool-based rather than beach-based, you need never come into contact with most of the tourists.

For the real recluse the answer is to travel independently to avoid the 'one of a crowd' feeling. Independent travel is not particularly easy or cheap in Yugoslavia, but it's one of the few places left which can guarantee you a 'different' type holiday where you'll feel like an individual. There are countless places in the mountains of Slovenia, Bosnia-Herzegovina and Montenegro where you'll find yourself the only tourist for miles around and have difficulty believing you're in twentieth-century Europe.

With three quarters of this large country comprising mountains and plateaux, there's no shortage of ideal bases for a quiet, simple, restful holiday in attractive surroundings.

The lesser known islands around Lake Ohrid in Macedonia, almost anywhere in Bosnia-Herzegovina, and travels into the depths of the mountains of Slovenia will reward you with the type of holiday you are looking for, but even the busy islands such as Brač, Hvar and Korčula can be havens of peace and quiet off season, which can mean as late in the year as mid-June. The secret for the independent traveller to remain truly independent of package tourists is to scan through all the tour operators' brochures before going, note down all the names of major resorts and destinations, and make sure you completely *avoid* them on your travels. (For further details on independent travel within Yugoslavia see the 'Package v. Independent' section on page 67 and the relevant points of the text for the area of the country you are interested in.)

If you've no objections to having some of the hard work done for you, at the price of being lumped in with other people, take a package with a tour operator but make sure it's at one of the quieter resorts and preferably out of peak season (July and August) not just to avoid any chance of crowds but also to miss the worst of the dry inland heat at this time of year.

Some suggestions for quiet package destinations are VRSAR on the Istrian coast; MOSCENICKA DRAGA on the Kvarner riviera; BRELA on the Makarska section of the coast; the villages outside Supetar on BRAČ, particularly BOL, JELSA on Hvar; and VRBROSKA SLAN and MLINI on the Dubrovnik riviera.

Other areas of Yugoslavia worth considering are TJENTISTE on the River Sutjeska in a National Park in BOSNIA, from where you can visit Europe's only virgin forest at Peručica, the Skakavac waterfall (240 feet) and the seven glacier lakes of the Zelengora mountains. Or, in MONTENEGRO, there are ŽABLJAK or CETINJE as bases from which to explore the spectacular Gulf of Kotor and the gorges of the Tara and Piva rivers. Žabljak is really your best bet for keeping away from crowds and, being set in the Durmitor National Park, it allows you the opportunity to see a wide range of alpine flowers and to get in some fine days of walking.

Serbia's main contribution is the resort of KOPAONIK in the south of this region, though unless you're keen on mountaineering-type walks it has less to offer than its competitors. In MACEDONIA it's LAKE OHRID where you want to concentrate your attentions, though again, if you're a keen botanist or wildlife-watcher there's more to see in Slovenia than here.

And in Yugoslavia's final region – CROATIA – it's the area south of Zagreb, towards the coast, where your interests lie: at the PLITVICE LAKES, to be exact. The Plitvice National Park is one of the best places you can base yourself for a holiday. There's ancient woodland, the sixteen Plitvice lakes which extend for six miles linked by waterfalls, limestone caves, etc., etc. Beautiful scenery and sufficient tourist facilities to ensure a comfortable stay.

So you can see Yugoslavia has a lot to offer in the way of unspoilt scenery. Again, one of the main advantages is that holidays here are so much cheaper than their equivalents over the border in Austria.

 ## The Family Holiday

With safe sandy beaches and suitable hotel facilities as the main criteria for a family holiday, the implication is that most attention should be concentrated in the area south of Budva. This is in fact the case and among some of the best resorts with suitable facilities are SLANO, a few miles north of Dubrovnik, which has a children's playground and sheltered bay; BEČIČI, just south of Budva, which has a long, safe, coarse-sand beach and children's pool and playground; and LOPAR, on the island of Rab, which has shallow, safe beaches.

ULCINJ, on the Montenegrin riviera, at the very end of the Yugoslav coastline where it borders Albania, is the ideal resort for a holiday involving young children. Here there's a large grassy area adjacent to the long sandy beach where children can safely play. Increasingly in the larger resorts babysitting services are on offer – though it's always wise to check with your tour operator first (generally the larger companies will have more in the way of these types of facilities). Children's pools are also becoming more commonplace, but not all of them are particularly safe or well designed, so check out these points before paying over your money. If in doubt, go for package holidays which say they're specifically recommended for family holidays – that way you have a come-back if the resort does not come up to scratch from the children's facilities' point of view. As for the 'one child free' offer on some hotels and resorts, don't be too keen as invariably the costs are included in some other way, or else there is a reason why they have to offer this extra concession to fill up the hotel.

Away from the coast, some other places to think about are the lakeside resorts of BLED, ŽABLJAK and BOHINJ. The 'great outdoor' possibilities in these resorts would appeal to older children and teenagers, and many of the hotels in these more isolated locations put on a good show of games such as mini-golf, table tennis, tennis, etc.

For absolute babies, useful info is that disposable nappies are now quite widely available in most resorts, though the choice of size and types is limited, but babyfood is not, so bring your weaning products from home. Prams cannot be hired in Yugoslavia so again bring your own.

Most Yugoslavians are dotty about babies, and they are certainly *the* way to meet the locals and start up conversations. (As someone who has travelled in Yugoslavia with a three-month son, I can vouch for it!) For advice on coping when travelling with babies and young children, see pages 52–7.

Practicalities

Red Tape

British visitors holding a full passport are allowed to stay up to 90 days without a visa. (American, Australian and Canadian citizens are issued automatically with free entry visas on arrival.) If you are staying more than 90 days, apply for an extension on your stay by contacting the police within your first seven days in the country. British visitors travelling on a Visitor's Passport, as opposed to a full passport, will be issued on arrival with a Tourist Permit valid for 30 days. If you plan on staying longer than 30 days, either apply for a visa before departure or get a full ten-year British passport.

Embassy Addresses

Visas can be obtained from the Yugoslavian Embassy, Consulate Section, 5–7 Lexham Gardens, London W8 5JU.

In the USA there are six Yugoslavian Consulate Generals:
In *New York* – Consulate General of the SFR of Yugoslavia, 767 Third Avenue, NYC 10017.
In *Chicago* – Yugoslavian General Consulate, 307 N. Michigan Avenue, Suite 1600, Illinois 60601.
In *Cleveland* – Yugoslavian Consulate General, 1700 East 13th Street, Suite 4R, Ohio 44114.
In *Pittsburgh* – Consulate General of the SFR of Yugoslavia, 625 Stanwix – Apt 1605, Pa. 15222.
In *San Francisco* – Yugoslavian Consulate, 1375 Sutter Street, Suite 406, California 94109.
In *Washington* – Yugoslavian Embassy, 2410 California Street NW, Washington DC 20008.

In *Canada* there are two sources:
The Yugoslavian General Consulate, 377 Spadina Road, Ontario M5P 2V7.
The Yugoslavian Embassy, 17 Blackburn Avenue, Ontario K1N 8A2.

Health Formalities

No health certificate is needed for entry to citizens of the British Isles, continental Europe and North America. If you're coming from elsewhere, check first – you may require the international smallpox certificate.

Customs

There are no real hassles with customs in Yugoslavia particularly for package tourists. The formalities are got over with as quickly as possible in general. Here are the allowances to which each adult is entitled.

Tourists over fifteen years of age may import free of duty up to 200 cigarettes or 50 cigars or 250 grams of tobacco; 1 litre of wine; 1 litre of spirits; ¼ litre of eau de cologne and 25 grams of perfume; goods to the value of 2500D.

You may bring in unlimited sums of foreign currency, but you may not carry more than 5000 dinars (in denominations no larger than 1000 dinars) in one calendar year across the border in either direction. If this is your second or more trip to Yugoslavia within the space of one year, you can only import or export a maximum of 2000 dinars.

Personal effects such as clothes, gifts, luggage, etc. are not questioned provided they are not carried in obviously excessive amounts.

For photographic equipment the allowance is two cameras with up to five rolls of film; a cine camera (not professional) with two rolls of film and a pair of binoculars.

Other pieces of equipment you might just be carrying – such as a typewriter, tape recorder, radio, musical instrument, calculator or sports gear – will be allowed, but if you possess a full range of photographic equipment or a hunting weapon with ammunition you must declare these on entry and receive a customs document which you will present again on departure.

Money

There is no limit to the amount of foreign currency you can take with you but the import and export of more than 5000D is illegal. You can change back your surplus dinars before leaving provided you can produce your official exchange receipts at the bureau de change.

The monetary unit of Yugoslavia is the dinar, which appears abbreviated to 'din'. It is divided into 100 'para' and comes in the following denominations:

Coins: 5, 10, 20, 50 paras; 1, 2, 5 and 10 dinars.
Notes: 10, 20, 50, 100, 500, 1000 dinars.

The dinar was recently devalued substantially which should, in general, mean that Yugoslavian holidays remain pretty competitive in cost terms.

Sometimes you'll hear the Yugoslavians referring to 'stari dinar' which means 'old dinar'. There are 100 old dinar to one new dinar (novi dinar). Generally, though, and certainly in all shops and restaurants where a tourist is likely to go, the new dinar is the unit of currency referred to.

HOW TO TAKE YOUR MONEY

Invariably you can get a better rate of exchange by buying dinars in your own country (as much as 15 per cent). You have the choice of buying dinars either in cash (up to a given limit) or in traveller's cheques. Because of the lower rate of exchange on offer in Yugoslavia you'd be foolish not to take in your full allowance in dinars, even if it is only worth a few pounds. Hard currency in cash form gets you just about anything – particularly useful to take are US dollars.

Dinar cheques are widely accepted and entitle you to a 10 per cent discount on tourist-related facilities, i.e. restaurant meals, but not on anything which can be construed as non-tourist-related. They are particularly advantageous for independent travellers as virtually all hotels and restaurants will accept them. The only exceptions you may find are in private restaurants where they're not always too keen to take them. Any difference between the value of the dinar cheque and the item purchased is made up in change, and unused cheques can be changed back in banks before leaving Yugoslavia. To do this you need your original receipt from the bank or bureau de change where you purchased them.

Traveller's cheques made out in your own currency are another alternative. No discounts will be offered on cheques made out in sterling, dollars, etc., and it's best to cash them for dinars, as lower rates are usually given if you pay with them in their own currency. They may be cashed at banks, hotels and travel agencies. Bear in mind that once cashed, unless you have your official receipts you cannot reconvert cash to your own currency, so don't overdo your purchase of them. Your passport will almost always be required when cashing traveller's cheques, and it's advisable to have the cheques made out in smaller rather than larger amounts. Always go for a well known bank or credit card company, i.e. American Express, Thomas Cook or Bank of England, otherwise you could have problems in some of the more rural parts of the country.

Credit cards are one of the best ways of taking money on holiday assuming you're heading for one of the larger resorts where they are accepted. American Express and Diners Club are the most widely accepted cards in Yugoslavia. Visa is less so, and no credit cards will find favour in small villages or remote areas.

Personal cheques With a Eurocheque Encashment Card and Eurocheques (available from your bank) you may cash cheques anywhere abroad just as you would with your ordinary cheque book at home. This is a safe way to take your money on holiday.

Where to exchange Traveller's cheques, foreign currency and personal cheques can all be exchanged at the fixed tourist rate at official exchange offices (e.g. 'Putnik') which will be found in travel bureaux, hotels, railway stations and, of course, banks. Banks do not charge commissions so they are the best places to exchange there and the exchange rate is the same everywhere. Remember to keep the certificate of exchange you will receive each time you receive dinars. If you do not, and you don't spend all your dinars, you will not be able to exchange them back when you leave the country: you can only take 5000D out, and duty-free shops will not accept dinars.

To summarize, then, the best advice would be to take a mixture of the following: some dinar cheques (bought at home), a current cheque book and Eurocheque Encashment Card (allow a few weeks for your bank to issue this to you if you don't have one already) and some ready cash in dinars (your dinar allowance) and your own currency. If you have a widely known credit card, take it as a backup. This way you combine security with flexibility and convenience. Traveller's cheques are not strictly necessary for this country as, apart from the fact that the crime rate in Yugoslavia is still refreshingly low, there are no real advantages to taking them – the dinar cheques represent better value. Inflation is high, so bear this in mind when comparing prices listed in this guide which were collected in 1986.

Banking

Opening hours fluctuate wildly, depending on location. At major resorts they can be open 7 a.m. to 7 p.m. Monday–Friday. In more remote areas their opening can be 7 a.m.–11.30 a.m., but 7 a.m.– 3 p.m. Monday–Friday, 7 a.m.–1 p.m. Saturday, is the norm. They will be closed on all the public and regional holidays listed on page 15 of this guide.

Insurance

It really is foolhardy to cut back on holiday insurance, yet each year thousands of people make this false economy and live to regret it. Increasingly if you're taking a package holiday you'll have no say in the matter and insurance will be added on to your final bill, whether you like it or not. While this at least makes sure you get some sort of cover, remember you are not obliged to take this policy.

Note, then, that you are under no obligation to accept the insurance policy offered by your travel agent. In some instances these are not as detailed as policies bought from large reputable companies, and all too often the package policies mean long delays in the settlement of claims as they're snowed under at the peak of the tourist season. On their plus side is the fact that the rep at the resort will have been trained in how to handle claims under these policies and that will take some of the strain off you. If you are not happy with the inclusive package insurance, the best advice is to go to an insurance broker, tell him what you're taking (remembering photographic equipment, etc.), what you envisage doing (i.e., if you plan spending a lot of time doing water sports or, more specifically, skiing), and how long you'll be away. He can then give you the ideal policy tailor-made to your needs. This is particularly sensible if you are taking a lot of new, expensive equipment (many package policies put a limit of around £200 per item on your valuables), or if your chances of ending up requiring medical treatment are higher than average. Also check out the liability clause for flight delays if it's imperative you get back home by the date stipulated.

Lloyds of London are particularly good for travel insurance and will even provide cover for people who normally find it difficult, e.g. disabled people and just-pregnant lady skiers. For most people, a basic insurance package deal costing £15 to £20 will suffice, but the onus is on you to tell your insurance broker or travel agent if you are not just an average holidaymaker for one reason or another. Independent travellers to Yugoslavia are particularly advised to procure a good insurance policy before going as they have no one (such as ABTA or a travel agent) to haggle for them.

As regards medical assistance, the need for insurance is not so vital because British citizens, on production of their passports, are entitled to free medical treatment in out-patient or in-patient hospitals (though if you take ill in a remote part of Macedonia, for example, you may well choose to go private under the auspices of your travel insurance). Some dental treatment is also provided free under Yugoslavia's reciprocal agreement with Britain, but prescribed medicines are charged.

North American travellers and those from further afield are strongly advised to procure good travel insurance cover before leaving home.

Yugoslavia does not really require any specific type of additional insurance cover. Its crime rate is lower than at most other major tourist destinations and unless you're accident-prone or of a particularly delicate disposition the medical side is pretty well covered, which only leaves flight problems to consider, and most of the tour operators going to Yugoslavia are reliable with a good track record. Remember, though, to go entirely without insurance cover would be foolhardy.

Health

Yugoslavia does not present any major health hazards to the average holidaymaker. No particularly nasty diseases are prevalent there, and generally the standard of medicine practised is acceptable to Northern Europeans. Once you're away from the major centres, however, things alter somewhat, and in remote rural areas of Serbia, Macedonia and Montenegro particularly, you may find some of the locals' hygiene customs a bit close to the bone (i.e., take your own loo paper and soap with you). This will obviously affect independent travellers more than package holidaymakers, so if you think it's likely you'll be venturing to untouristy parts, be prepared with your own first-aid kit and consider taking out some health insurance.

British citizens are at an advantage because they come in for free medical care (against payment of a purely nominal fee) on production of any valid travel document. Basically this means that unless you have a very serious accident or illness and wish to be flown back home immediately for treatment, you're unlikely to use your medical insurance. If you're keen to get yourself medically insured (say, for a skiing holiday) check out the AA, RAC and Lloyds, who all do good deals. The cheapest medical insurance Britons can get, and probably one of the best, is given by Europe Assistance Ltd, 252 High Street, Croydon, Surrey CR0 11NF.

For a small premium (average £20 per person travelling by car) you get a 24-hour advice telephone link with the UK and a guarantee of on-the-spot cash for emergency services. This insurance also covers the expenses that can arise from a car accident (hiring another car, flying out spare parts, etc.).

No specific health certificates or certificates of vaccination are required by Britons for entry to Yugoslavia.

Pre-planning and Free Info

The more you know about a country before going, the more you'll get
out of your holiday once you're there. Not only can you then locate
where the things that interest you are, but you'll be able to plan ahead
to make sure you get to see them and don't waste any precious time
waiting in tourist information queues. It's amazing how many people
still leave on holiday with the picture of their hotel from the travel
brochure as their only image of the country they're going to.

Virtually every country imaginable has a National Tourist Office in
London, and Yugoslavia is no exception. Write to them ahead of your
holiday (well ahead, as they can take literally weeks to reply) asking
for general tourist literature and, if you have any specific hobby or
pursuit you're keen to indulge in on holiday, ask them their advice on
where best to pursue it and to send you any literature they might have
on it (fishing, hunting, sailing and skiing are some examples). You've
nothing to lose as their service is free and if nothing else it'll whet your
appetite for what to expect. Request a map if you're considering
touring, and accommodation listings if you are travelling independently. A publication well worth requesting is *Yugoslavian Travel
Information*. The address to write to is: The Yugoslav National
Tourist Office, 143 Regent Street, London W1 (tel: 01-734 5243 or
01-439 0399).

An extremely useful source of information (free and impartial)
comes from the travel agent Hogg Robinson. They produce resort
reports on all the hotels used by tour operators. These can be
consulted free of charge in any of their agencies. Thomas Cook
produce resort reports which can be taken away by the public. These
contain condensed info on the main resorts and give a good idea of
how expensive items such as drinks and meals will be once you're
there.

Another source of free info on Yugoslavia is your local library.
Admittedly it's likely to be in the form of heavy reading, but if you've
any specific interest, such as the country's history or flora and fauna,
this can be a rewarding search. As far as other bought sources go,
there are a few other guidebooks on the country worth considering if
you have specific interests: Collins' *Companion Guide to Yugoslavia* is
a very detailed, fairly dry account of the country, worth considering

for the serious-minded independent traveller intent on touring the country in depth; *Fodor's Yugoslavia* (Hodder and Stoughton) is the usual middle-aged, middle-class American guide to the country, but in fairness it is comprehensive, informative and well researched. For most young(ish) Brits, however, it concentrates too much on history, archaeology and expensive recommendations.

Baedeker's Yugoslavia (AA) is very good for those attempting a massive tour of the country, but otherwise it dissipates its energy too much on large chunks of the country where few tourists venture. And finally, in the Berlitz series there are three pocket guides: *Istria and Croatian Coast*, *Split–Dalmatia*, *Dubrovnik and Southern Dalmatia Coast*. They tend to be a bit out of touch with the market and a bit too American to be really useful, but if you don't mind all the clichéd colour pics and can stand the purple prose, they can pad out your knowledge of the region.

And you are, of course, already reading the best guide on the market!

Budgeting

Despite raging inflation, Yugoslavia is still reasonably cheap in comparison with most other European holiday destinations – there's no denying that, and it's precisely for that reason that it's becoming so popular. Prices for food, drink and entertainment are reasonable by any standards, so you needn't structure your holiday round your budget to any large extent. Unless you're really doing it on a shoestring you won't need to be constantly converting dinars to pounds and watching every coffee or ice-cream.

Obviously, how much spending money you take will largely depend on what basis, if any, you've booked your accommodation. In the early years, virtually all package tourists to Yugoslavia were travelling on a full-board basis. Now half-board and even bed and breakfast are taking over in popularity. This obviously places a larger emphasis on you digging in your pocket for meals, but as an average meal with wine will cost in the region of 8500 dinars per person, it's no real drawback. If you are really budget-conscious, consider a full-board package. This is undoubtedly the way to get the best value out of Yugoslavia as there is rarely any great difference in price between these packages and their half-board counterparts. Alternatively, opt for a 'budget' holiday such as those offered by Yugotours, where you leave the final choice of destination up to the tour operator and don't know where you'll land until you arrive. The compensation of this is a greatly reduced price.

The independent traveller faces an interesting dilemma as, although food and drink will not knock a tight budget out, accommodation of any decent standard can. More is said of this situation on pages 113–4, but suffice to say here that careful planning is required to offset the cost of decent hotels on an independent basis, and unless you're prepared to accept local standards (which in rural areas will not be of a Northern European equivalent), your wallet will soon tell you Yugoslavia is not a cheap holiday destination. (Double rooms in basic hotels start around 17,000D.)

Eating out can range from as little as 4000D to 25,000D. Drinks are also cheap, providing you're prepared to drink the local brews and not insist on British brands (the local vino is perfectly acceptable, so this is no hardship). Bottled fruit juices (Fructal is good), local spirits and beers cost around 800–2000 Din. Wine is around 2400 Din a bottle (double in hotels). Imported drinks will be at least double. Coffee costs around 1200 Din but in the south this is likely to be strong Turkish coffee, which is an acquired taste. (A good tip is to take a small jar of instant coffee with you to Yugoslavia and just ask for hot water in your hotel. When having a coffee in a bar or café the word 'Nescafé' usually gets over the message that you don't want Turkish. In the north and on the Dalmatian coast cappuccino is widely available.)

Another item definitely worth taking from home is a camera film. Not only does it cost twice as much in Yugoslavia but the quality there is very suspect.

Other items of expenditure you'll need to budget for are the hire of sun loungers on most beaches (average 2000 Din a day), and still on the beach, the cost of water sports if you're keen. Again, you'll find prices in Yugoslavia relatively low, windsurfing coming in around 5500 Din an hour, and water skiing costing about 8000–9000 Din for a ten-minute session. As far as nightlife goes – again it won't break the bank – a disco costs around 4500 Din and an evening concert of folk will be anything between 2000 Din and 12,000 Din.

Your biggest expense will undoubtedly be moving around the country when you're there. Both main options – car hire and organized excursions – are expensive in comparison with other Yugoslavian prices, though excursions are on a par with most other European destinations. A small car, however, will cost you a minimum of 60,000 Din a day, and petrol – costing 3600D per gallon – can only be bought with coupons available for foreign currency through tourist agencies and banks (see 'Moving Around the Country' section on page 133 for better details). Given the price of car hire and the condition of many Yugoslavian roads, you may feel happier taking the prearranged trips laid on by tour operators which average 20,000D for a half-day excursion and double that for a full day. They are, therefore, not cheap either and some are of questionable quality, so consider the independent options carefully.

The only people who qualify for discounts on travel, museum entrance fees etc. are students. Holders of a valid International Student Identity Card qualify for 10 per cent discounts on domestic flights on JAT, the Yugoslav National Airline, and train tickets to Eastern Europe can be bought in Belgrade with a 20–50 per cent reduction on prices. If you are still a student, write ahead of your holiday to Naromtravel, c/o Karavan Student Travel Agency, Takovska 2, Belgrade, Yugoslavia, requesting further information on your student discount entitlements.

Finally, when calculating the amount of spending money to take with you, remember that it's easier to take too much than to have money sent on or transferred to your account. An extra £100 or so in your current account or taking a credit card will not go amiss in case of emergency. The average holidaymaker on a half-board two-week coastal holiday should be able to make it through comfortably in Yugoslavia on a budget of around £200. And don't change too much at one time. You'll be surprised how far it can go, and remember you can't change it back.

As a footnote – duty-free is good at most of the Yugoslavian airports, but don't keep back a stash of dinars for the duty-free shop as they only accept foreign currencies. Of them all, the best range of goods is at Split, Dubrovnik, Ljubljana and Pula airports but if you're after a specific brand of goods you're best to get it at the British end before you leave, or buy it on the plane. The price of duty-free alcohol is particularly good given the favourable rate of exchange. And again, a final reminder, you can't pay for duty-free in dinars.

Getting Yourself Organized

What to Take with You

Package holidaymakers should simply take the minimum of light casual clothes and accessories plus a showerproof raincoat, just in case. Dress is not formal in hotels, in fact the atmosphere in Yugoslav holiday resorts is particularly relaxed, so there's no need to pack a suit or evening dress, unless you're heading for a 5-star Grand Hotel.

For those going on naturist holidays the choice is that much easier, but do take some clothes for the evenings when the temperatures may require a little dressing up. Always take the absolute minimum. Think back to previous years when you returned with half the clothes unused and remember you'll need to allow a bit of extra room in your luggage for any items you buy over there or for your duty-free. Try to travel with just hand luggage. If you're going for a two-week sea, sun and sand holiday there's no reason why you shouldn't manage to get all you need into a lightweight bag which you can take on the flight as hand luggage. Think of the advantages of not having to wait in baggage collection queues wondering if what you checked in will actually reappear.

If you're travelling independently in Yugoslavia, however, the picture is not so rosy, particularly if you're the brave type determined to camp or hostel your way round the country. Apart from taking the absolute minimum of lightweight kit, some things you might find useful to take would be an empty plastic water bottle (jerry-can idea) to fill up whenever you get the chance of drinking water; a padlock for hostel lockers; a travelling alarm clock (handy for morning calls if you've train connections etc. to catch); and a money belt to keep your valuables safely on you. Bring all your camping gear with you as the range in Yugoslavia is not terribly impressive, and if you're doing any serious walking in the mountains look out for maps in Britain before you go – they're often better than the ones you can buy locally. A good first-aid kit is a must for independent travellers heading off to remote parts, and a phrase book would not go amiss either.

The vast majority of holidaymakers to Yugoslavia, however, need not equip themselves for an overland expedition, and should take as little as possible. There are some items which definitely merit packing:

(1) Take with you all photographic equipment you're likely to need. This includes all films for your camera. The Yugoslavian equivalent films (which you'll be presented with even if you ask for brand names such as Kodak or Agfa) are of poor quality and are expensive. (Their developing techniques also leave much to be desired, so don't be tempted to get your film processed while you are there.)

(2) Any English-language books or magazines you're likely to want for beach reading, again bring from home. Some of the larger resorts do carry a stock of British and American books but they're overpriced and generally of a poor quality.

(3) If you're not keen on strong, sweet Turkish coffee and are heading for a destination in the south of Yugoslavia (i.e., on the Dubrovnik or Montenegrin coasts) consider taking a small jar of instant coffee with you. The hotels are quite used to people coming down to breakfast clutching a jar of Nescafé and asking for only hot water. After a few days of Turkish coffee for breakfast you'll begin to see why.

(4) Toiletries and medicines should also be brought with you (and this includes suntan preparations, which are more expensive in the resorts than back home). There are few countries which offer cheaper toiletries than Britain, and even if you do find some, the quality could well be questionable. Any prescribed medicines should definitely be brought from home as often the equivalent drug will not be available abroad.

(5) Loo paper and soap are two things not to be overlooked. There really is no substitute for them when you need them, unless you're

prepared to resort to some of the more ethnic local habits of the south. Even if you're on a package, it's not a bad idea to pack a roll or packets of tissues as once you're away from the hotels and larger resorts you can't be sure that every bar or restaurant will be equipped.

(6) If you're planning on visiting any of the churches in the country it's still frowned upon (and in some cases insisted upon) if women don't have a shawl or something to cover their heads. Take a light scarf for this purpose and make sure you don't do your sightseeing tours when you're clad in shorts and T-shirt.

Travelling with Babies and Young Children

The addition of babies and children to the travelling duo *does* make a difference, there's no point denying this, but with a bit of careful preplanning and the purchase of a few items, taking your youngsters on holiday abroad can be a relatively easy experience, and there is certainly no need for the commonly held belief that foreign travel has to stop with the arrival of tiny feet.

Today a whole range of well designed products is on the market, specially for the travelling and holidaying parent. The recent introduction of these goods has revolutionized family travelling, and with the ever increasing awareness on the tour operator's part that families make up a sizeable part of their market, the situation is improving each year.

Invariably, in southern Europe your children will be the best introduction to the locals you can have. Babies, particularly, are a passport to conversations, for even without being able to speak the language your brood will be adopted by the local mamas and grandmas, and you'll find pleasant little surprises like your ice-creams are that bit bigger; your service friendlier. The major holiday destinations are, after all, still places where the family unit is a very strong binding force.

Babies under six months generally make excellent holidaymakers. They are not yet mobile, tend to be up late anyway, and will not be too upset about being out of their normal environment. Also, before they are weaned feeding is a lot simpler, and you don't yet need to transport a plethora of favourite toys. Three months is a particularly good age, as, if you're lucky, they're just about sleeping through the whole night; are still easily fed; still take daytime naps; and are at the stage when the bustle and activity in places like airports will keep them entertained and quiet. Under three months it is still perfectly possible to go on holiday, but obviously they are that bit more prone to infection, etc.

Between six months and a year, as every parent will tell you, it gets slightly harder. A crawling baby is not the best passenger, but if you're sensible about your flight timings and the transfer times from airport to hotel, it can still work. Feeding is more of a problem, but this can be overcome by taking instant dried babyfoods and relevant supplies of milk and juice granules. Products such as Milupa Herbal Drink Granules, or Boots dried baby foods, and SMA ready-to-feed UHT Baby Milks, which come in cartons are ideal. The latter was new on the market in 1988 and makes travelling with bottle-fed babies far easier as there is no need to find sterile water. At this stage, if your child is difficult, you may find it easier to go for a self-catering holiday based in a villa away from other people.

Toddlers and young children need constant amusement, so choose your resort carefully. Regular bedtimes are important too, so somewhere with a reliable babysitting service should be on your list of priorities unless you want it to be a real home away from home.

Our 'family researchers' have tested all the products they could find on the market for travelling babies and children, and recommend the following items. In every case the cost was more than justified by the added convenience and peace of mind.

FOR BABIES

A lightweight buggy from home is an essential piece of equipment for all children under two and a half. If the one you have is heavy or cumbersome, try to borrow a lighter one, or, if you're planning on doing a lot of travelling, or are buying one for the first time with travelling in mind, the best thing to do is look at the *MacLaren* range. They have several lightweight buggies which are easily steered, quick to fold into an umbrella shape, and have all the weatherproof attachments you need, and a useful playtray which helps at feeding times. For a very young baby the lie-back multi-position MacLaren

Dreamer is a good alternative.

In some holiday destinations it is technically possible to hire prams, but in our experience this is not a good idea as foreign makes tend to be less well designed and sometimes do not meet with British safety standards. Also it does not get round the problem of how to transport your baby from home to your holiday destination.

Do not check-in your buggy with your other luggage at the airport. Instead tell the airline that you require it until the last minute and hand it to the baggage handlers on the tarmac as they load the plane. This way you have your hands free for duty-free shopping etc. (An alternative would be to take a papoose.)

The business of cots on holiday can present unforeseen problems if you are not aware in advance of the cost involved, or you are going to a small hotel or villa where a cot cannot be supplied. Most tour operators will endeavour to get a cot for you if you stipulate this on your booking form but costs vary dramatically (anything from £5 to £25 a week), so do check first. Again, check with your tour operator that the cot you are hiring meets British safety standards.

The alternative to hiring is to take your own travel cot with you. For a very young baby a Moses basket is best, but after six months a full-size travel cot is necessary. *Mothercare* has two very good designs: one smaller and lighter, and one sturdier model, suited to the older child. Either of these could easily be taken as luggage on a plane, and mattresses are included in the price. They retail around £45 and £65 respectively but obviously their usefulness is not restricted to foreign holidays alone, and if you are being charged a comparable sum merely for the hire of a cot in your hotel the purchase of a travel cot would make a lot of sense. The weight of the smaller cot is 7kg; the larger is 11kg (15.4lb and 24.2lb respectively). An alternative for an older child is the *Boots Bed Barrier* which secures the child from rolling out and allows any conventional bed to be used.

Other pieces of equipment to bring from home are portable seats to make mealtimes easier. Two very well designed, low-priced and highly portable models are the *Babydiner* and the *Tota Portable High Chair*. Both slip on to most conventional tables (the Babydiner will not fit on tables with any substantial structure below the worktop such as farmhouse-style tables) and are invaluable for feeding babies in restaurants and places where highchairs are not available.

The Tota product is more expensive, but is sturdier, and fits on to more styles of table. It is heavier, takes a child up to five stone, and is likely to last longer.

Both these products are available from leading baby stores, or through the John Lewis Partnership.

Another useful product suited to toddlers and young children is the *Tamsit Baby Chair Harness* – a cloth harness which fits over any chair and restrains the child while eating. This folds into the size of a scarf and can be used in any location: a café, restaurant, etc.

One item found to be useful when coping with 'little emergencies' was the *Bubble Potty*, produced by Babydiner. This plastic, blow-up potty with disposable liners fits in a corner of a suitcase and is very useful for virtually potty-trained youngsters, for one thing's for sure – if they're going to 'forget', you can be sure it'll be at the airport, in the heat of the moment! For around £3 this little piece of additional luggage could save a lot of problems.

Feeding babies on holiday

Young babies still on a milk diet are far easier to travel with than older ones. Obviously breastfeeding is the perfect answer in that no equipment is necessary, and it doesn't matter where you are (nursing babies is a common sight in all major holiday destinations).

Bottle feeding is possible abroad with a bit of pre-planning and the purchase of a few essential items. Sterilizing tablets are easier than liquid, and to immerse the bottles and teats try an old ice-cream carton, rather than taking a big sterilizing unit. Your bottle brush and formula, obviously, cannot be cut down, but there are alternatives to provide the sterile water needed. Unless you can be certain that a constant supply of *sterile* water will be available at your hotel/villa (and that means it must have boiled for at least ten minutes to kill off the bacteria), you do best to take one of the following from home: either a 'mini-boiler' – a heating element which is immersed in the water to be heated (for which you can easily ask for a cup from the hotel) – or a jug kettle.

The former is obviously far smaller and more convenient. Pifco make an ideal model which has a universal voltage. Traveller International also make two alternatives: *Hot Rod*, an immersion heater which can boil water in two minutes, and *Travel Jug* which acts as a mini-jug kettle, making cuppas for Mum and Dad as well as boiling water efficiently for Junior's feed. If you are on a driving holiday, they also produce a car jug called 'Pit Stop', which you plug into the cigar lighter socket. This way you can brew up in a lay-by and feed baby *en route*. One final alternative is to buy bottled mineral water, but the problem there is heating up the milk once made if your baby will not take it cold.

You would be best advised to take your normal formula from home as a foreign-bought one could easily upset your baby's digestive system for a few days.

Weaning babies require more equipment. Although weaning foods are available in all the major holiday destinations, again you would be better to bring from home products which your baby is used to and you know he will eat. The 'instant' dried varieties are lightest and most convenient to carry. Also available now are granules to make up drinks for babies, which are better for them than syrupy juices and far easier to carry. Lightweight plastic feeding equipment (such as the Boots Red Range) is a good idea to bring from home. A bowl, beaker and spoon are the absolute basics not to leave the UK without. If you'll be away for a period of time, or are self-catering, the *Moulinex Babychef* will come in very useful and be worth its space in the suitcase as it allows you to purée your own food. The screw-lid jars it comes with allow prepared foods to be taken with you on outings.

Changing, washing, emergencies

Disposable nappies are available now in almost every major holiday resort, but the quality and sizing systems vary enormously. Again, it's really better to bring your own from home. They don't weigh much, so won't affect your baggage allowance; it's just the bulk involved.

Disregard any thought of terry nappies and daily washings. Even in self-catering it isn't a good idea. Washing machines are not generally provided, and after all it is your holiday too!

For washing babyclothes, take a little container of soap flakes from home. Invariably you cannot find a small enough packet of soap powder in the shops, and if you resort to using the local soap you will often find that it leaves colour and scum on the fabrics. A small plastic bottle filled with soft rinse wouldn't go amiss either, to counteract the hard water, if you have any space left.

To clean baby at change times, Baby Wipes of some sort are a good idea. Baby Lotion Wipes were the ones our researchers found best. They do the job of both soap and water and are easy to carry and convenient. At bathtimes a bath additive which doubles as a shampoo will save duplicating. Don't count on baby baths being available, even in high-grade hotels. You'll have to make do with the hand basin for tiny babies, or the big bath for older ones.

Apart from a range of baby toiletries, pediatric medicines are definitely best brought from home. British pharmaceutical products are better than any you're likely to get abroad, and cheaper too. Don't leave home with a baby or child without a first-aid kit which includes gripe water, paracetamol, pain relief syrup and nappy rash cream.

Remember the effect which the sun has on babies. If your child seems especially grumpy, tired and miserable it may just be that you have had him in the direct sun for too long. Be very careful about the length of exposure a young baby gets. Put on a protective sun block/screen at all times, and give plenty of drinks to counteract dehydration. (This is when the drink granules come in handy, rather than giving milk which is not as thirst-quenching and is a food as well.)

CHILDREN ON HOLIDAY

Keeping young children amused on a journey and while on holiday can be a problem. If yours are the restless type, bear this in mind when choosing your resort and choose a hotel where special children's facilities are laid on and which have something like 'Recommended for Families' in the write-up. Check beforehand exactly what this means, as this vague statement can mean anything from 'a full range of games, toys and a professional childminding service', to 'a small dirty paddling pool is available', depending on the tour operator.

Try buying a new toy which is only brought out on the journey to keep him/her preoccupied, and also pack a couple of old favourites from home so they have a familiar face for night-times.

There is a whole range of well designed toys on the market today. The Early Learning Centre and Boots are just two places which stock toys ideal for travelling: lightweight and durable. Firm favourites for travelling are pop-up storybooks, novelty rattles and similar toys for babies; small Lego toys and a double-sided playboard which can occupy two children at a time. Other favourites seem to be the Turn 'n' Learn Key Sorter; Lift-Out-Shape Puzzles; Toddler's Puzzle Sets; and Fisher-Price's Activity Centre (for car travel). Giant snap lock beads are also good. Obviously each child has its own special favourite, but these all worked out a treat on all the travelling toddlers we tried them on, and as they're available from the Early Learning Centre, they're easy to locate.

Don't be too ambitious about the amount of nightlife you will be able to get in during the first few days. Young children are often upset enough being in a strange place without having 'funny-looking' (in their eyes) babysitters thrust upon them right away as well. It's best to give it a few nights until they're used to their surroundings before leaving them in care.

With older children, the hardest thing is to keep them from getting bored. If your brood are of this nature consider a two-centre holiday, or an activity or touring type. Before leaving, try to instil into them a little background knowledge of the country you are travelling to. Once interested in their destination, they will make their own discoveries and will amuse themselves to a far greater extent when they are there.

The Holiday Industry

Tourism is big business these days, and realizing the vast potential market which exists in holidaymakers each year, more manufacturers are entering the business of catering for the holiday industry, designing and marketing products specifically for the traveller. Photographic goods, electrical gadgets, luggage, clothing, toiletries . . . the list goes on, all being produced with the annual two weeks in the sun in mind.

Some travel products are excellent; some do not merit the expense involved, and some are just plain awful. As full-time professional travellers, we have had the opportunity to try out many products in this category, and here we bring you a list of only the very best items which we found genuinely useful and worth investing in.

TOILETRIES

On the toiletries side Boots have two first-aid kits which are exceptionally well packed, nicely presented and good value. *The Trip Kit* is a survival kit for those attempting an adventurous holiday, such as skiing, mountaineering, etc. It has the equipment to cope with sprains, pains and general nasties. The *Holiday Kit* is for your average two-weeks-in-the-sun-holidaymaker and provides you with the basics for the sort of things you're likely to be stricken with. At only £7 each, you'd be hard-pressed to put a first-aid kit of your own together for their price.

At holiday time you will also find ranges of travel toiletries available in Boots: small, plastic bottles containing just enough for a couple of weeks. Despite their slightly inflated prices, these products are a good idea and save you carrying surplus or dangerous glass bottles.

ELECTRICAL GOODS

Turning to electrical goods: if you're on the point of buying a shaver, hairdryer, iron, electric toothbrush, alarm clock etc., just bear in mind that for very little extra cost one can buy an appliance which will operate abroad, on a different voltage, and can therefore be used on holiday. Granted, an International Adaptor (Traveller International do one for around £5) will allow you to use any appliance anywhere in the world, but if you're buying a new electrical appliance of a personal nature it is a good idea to consider the following, which are all designed specifically for travelling and using abroad:

Shavers Braun, Boots, Carmen and Black & Decker are the names to look for. The Braun System 1-2-3 Universal comes out tops on all scores. This rechargeable shaver can be used anywhere and performs extremely well. Once charged, it will last for about a week's use. The Braun Battery 200i is another ideal travelling shaver. Being battery operated it can be used anywhere, and as battery shavers go, this is one of the best available. The Philips Battery Ladyshaver is another good model. The Boots Rechargeable 1500 is another option.

Battery and rechargeable shavers are a decided asset when travelling, and are well worth the few extra pounds for the convenience.

Panasonic's Wet and Dry Shavers give you the best of both worlds and their ES862 rechargeable is recommended.

Black & Decker, a name previously associated with the other end of the electrical market, have now launched a range of travel products under the collective name of 'Stowaway'. Included in the range are travel irons (dry or steam, the steam model being particularly recommended); two travel hairdryers – the 1000 with a folding handle, and 1500 in a travel bag and with the capacity to dry even the longest hair in record time after a day at the beach; curling tongs, and a battery-operated ladyshaver.

Travel irons entered the small electrical appliance market only a few years ago and in that time around a dozen manufacturers have started to produce them. At first they may strike you as an unnecessary luxury, but once you've had one you'll wonder how you ever managed without. Clichéd as that sounds, they really are very useful little items, particularly if you're staying in a plush hotel where dressing for dinner is the norm, or if you travel on business a lot. The ability to press the creases from your clothes as they emerge from the suitcase looking as if you've slept in them, and to be able to launder and wear again what you bring, is a great asset, and considering travel irons sell around the £12 mark, they are a good long-term investment. Worth considering are: Travellers' International Smoothie Steam Iron, the Pifco Travel Iron, the Prestige Travel Iron, the Black & Decker Travel Iron, and the Braun Travel Iron attachment to the Compact 1200 hairdryer. This latest model (collectively known as the Travelcombi PGI 1200) is an ingenious device which actually clips on to this model of Braun hairdryer and gives you an efficient dry or steam (separate spray provided) iron.

Travel hairdryers The basic difference between an ordinary hairdryer and a travel model is the dual voltage which the latter has, enabling it to be used abroad without fear of it blowing up, fusing, or taking an age to heat up. A continental plug adaptor must, of course, be used with all appliances brought from home with a British 13 amp plug, but these are widely available. Travel adaptors can be bought almost everywhere, and Traveller International is a reliable make. Travel hairdryers are also smaller and neater to pack, and as there is no real price difference involved, and the level of efficiency is just as high on a travel model, it does make sense to choose one if you're planning on doing any globetrotting at all.

There are numerous models available. Out of the extensive range on offer we have singled out the following models as being particularly well designed and cost effective: The Boots 1200 Travel represents very good value; the Braun Silencio 1200 Travelair with its folding handle and quiet performance travelled well, performed well, and was small enough to be carried in a handbag; the Philips Voyager 1200 is an excellent folding dryer; the Carmen Romany is neat and powerful; the Black & Decker range proved very popular – the 1000 Foldaway is the most compact dryer on the market, and the 1500 Fastdry one of the most powerful; and the Braun Compact 1200 has the added advantage of doubling up as a power source for the travel iron attachment (see above).

Hair stylers and tongs have also been given the travel treatment of late. The breakthrough in this field has got to be the Braun Independent Styler GC 2 – using butane gas for power, this styler allows complete freedom of use and is small, compact and extremely efficient into the bargain. It is ideally suited to the traveller, the only point to note – and it is extremely important – is that it is strictly illegal to take refills of butane gas on to an aircraft for reasons of combustion. What this means is that you can pack a styler containing a gas unit in your luggage which must be checked in and travel in the hold, but you must not take a refill. As a full styler gives you about a week's average use, or two weeks' sparing use, this should suffice for an average holiday anyway.

Alternative hair stylers for travelling are the Carmen Heatwave, which has dual voltage and retractable bristles, and the Black & Decker Stowaway Styler, again with retractable bristles and universal voltage. Carmen are also introducing travel heated rollers.

Other useful appliances for the holidaymaker include the new Braun voice control AB 312 vsl travel alarm and the Traveller International equivalent alarm which is even smaller. For those who, like me suffer from mosquitoes making life miserable on holiday, you could try a new product I certainly feel has helped: it's called Spira-No-Bite and is distributed through Travel Accessories, 10 Shelley Drive, Lutterworth, Leics. It's available either as an electrical device with tablets, or fuelled by meths for situations where no electricity exists (i.e. camping).

Another product of theirs of interest to those whose mental

arithmetic isn't up to much is the X-Changer – a tiny calculator which you programme with the current rate of exchange, then all you have to do is feed in the price in the foreign currency and, hey presto, you know how much that beer's costing you. You may have seen these in Scotcade's catalogue – they cost around £6, but for a regular foreign holiday-goer, they can soon pay their way.

Another very interesting product if you suffer from travel sickness is 'Sea Legs' – two wristbands which work to relieve nausea by applying pressure to the relevant acupuncture points on your arms. The makers report an 80 per cent success rate. Send £7.95 to NOVAFON Ltd, 3 Atholl Road, Pitlochry, Perthshire PH16 5BX.

If you were thinking of getting an electric toothbrush be sure to go for either a battery model or a rechargeable one. The Braun Travel d3t is a very good system and comes complete with travel case.

A couple of interesting little travel gadgets are made by Allcord Ltd, Ilford Rd, Newcastle-upon-Tyne and are available by post. One is a knife and spoon set which would double up for feeding children or camping; the second is a miniature camera tripod. This is of good design, weighs only 90g and folds into 5″ × 1″. Another new product to make life easier for the traveller is 'washaway' detergent tablets. For around a pound you get twelve foil-wrapped tablets of detergent, which are light and easy to carry and work well. Most major chemists, including Boots, sell these.

THE LUGGAGE REVOLUTION

For most travellers packing a suitcase for a holiday is a chore – rushed and often frustrating. It needn't be, however, if you follow a few simple guidelines and choose your cases carefully in the first place. In recent years there has been something of a revolution in luggage design. Pull-out handles and cases on wheels are just two of the innovations which have taken much of the strain out of travelling; cabin cases, which fit neatly under the seat in an aircraft, are another. The advantage of these is you miss out the bother of having to check-in your luggage and wondering if you'll see it again at the other end of the journey. In Britain there are numerous luggage manufac-turers offering a whole range of goods, from the craftsman-made goods to plastic cases, which after only a couple of trips will be falling to bits. Buying cheap luggage is a false economy which many people make. Luggage is one area where you definitely get what you pay for.

Three reliable, widely available manufacturers are Delsey, Samsonite and Antler. They produce a wide range of cases, from luxury executive models to basic yet sturdy cases aimed at the annual foreign holidaymaker market. The *Delsey Club, Delsey Helium*; *Antler Stag, Airlight* and *Shires*; and *Samsonite Scope, Rhapsody,* and *Transit,* all fall into this category. The more expensive ranges, such as *Antler's Harrier* and *Signature,* and *Delsey's Airstyle Deluxe,* do however look better at the end of it, and if you travel a lot or want to make a good investment for the future then consider these ranges. Cheaper cases (especially those bought from magazine offers, i.e. three cases for £50), are unfit to travel after only a month or so's continual use.

When it comes to deciding between hard-shell and soft-top luggage, bear in mind that hard-shell cases (such as Delsey Club) stand up better to the rigours of baggage handling than cheaper soft tops, but if you don't fill them you will find the contents rattling around the case. More can be crammed into a soft-top case, particularly if, like the Antler cases, they have a wide gusset. The top-range soft-tops are made out of incredibly strong stuff (Antler use up to 1000-denier nylon), so they will withstand any normal batterings.

When the new Heathrow Terminal 4 was having its luggage equipment tested, the cases to come out best were the Antler Harrier (top of the range due to its double aluminium frame), with the Signature not far behind – a good result for a range which concentrates so heavily on style.

Delsey also produce a most useful item of luggage which they refer to as a 'cabin case'. Basically, these are designed to take on a flight as hand luggage, to hold all that you would need on your flight; or if you're only going on a short trip, to take your quota for a couple of days. These are made to fit exactly under the seat of any aircraft.

When packing for a trip, make a list of what you want to take. Gather all the things together, then halve it. This is a perfectly serious statement as we all take far too much with us, year after year. List what you're left with so you can check it off when packing for the return journey. Try to choose clothes that mix and match so you get maximum use from them, and remember that most of the time you will be wearing very little. Modern-day fabrics mean you don't have to interleave clothes with tissue paper, as you did in the past, but it is still advisable to roll whenever you can to ensure the minimum of creasing. To get rid of residual creasing either invest in a travel iron (see page 59), hang the clothes in a steamy bathroom, or splash out on a new Rowenta product – the *Steam Brush*, which performs the tasks of a valet, steaming and pressing your clothes until they look as good as new. Always pack shoes at the bottom of the case, against the hinge. This will prevent them moving up and squashing clothes. Don't pack large bottles of make-up, perfume or suntain oil (you won't use it all up) – buy small bottles or transfer toiletries into lightweight pots or plastic bottles and pack them all into a safe waterproof bag.

Use the bottom half of the case for jumpers, lingerie, shirts, trousers and accessories and fold everything – except trousers – lengthways, and then roll up. Pack dresses and suits in the top half of the case, and fold them as flatly as possible. These few guidelines will ensure you get as much as possible out of the space available.

For taking one's photographic equipment a proper photographic equipment bag is a good idea. These ensure delicate items, such as lenses are properly buffeted against knocks, and they're handy for keeping all the camera equipment together when you're out and about taking photos. One of the best, in terms of value and quality, is the *Cullmann* brand, available from Boots. It's worth noting that photographic equipment is nearly always cheaper in the UK; a couple of exceptions to this rule are West Germany and Holland. Where possible, buy own-brand goods, such as Boots, which are equally good in terms of quality and represent a considerable saving.

TRAVEL CLOTHING

The past few years has seen several companies set up in the business of manufacturing and designing clothes specifically made for the traveller. Most of these specialist companies have the 'serious traveller' in mind and their clothes are more suited to those heading off on jungle or mountain expeditions than the average holiday. They also tend to be expensive.

There are a couple of firms however, who are worth looking out for as their clothes are no more than average in price, but they do stand up well to the rigours of long flights and car journeys. Mountain Equipment is one. As the name suggests they go more for the cold weather conditions, but they have a range of trousers and jackets equally well suited to the summer traveller, and they are cheaper than the Rohan lookalike equivalents. Their clothing can be found in most good camping and outdoor shops.

Travelling Light aim more for the other end of the travel market – the tropical and high temperature traveller. They sell through mail order, and their clothes are made from special fabrics which stand up well to creasing and staining, and allow the body to breathe no matter how high the humidity. They produce a wide variety of items of clothing: trousers, skirts, shirts, jackets, etc. They're not cheap – none of these specialist companies are – but they are good quality, and their designs are very pleasing. Address for catalogue – Morland House, Morland, Penrith CA10 3AZ.

If all you really want is a light rainproof or a pair of comfortable trousers for the flights and car journeys, a trip to your local camping and outdoor shop will probably suffice and stick to own brand makes.

As more companies enter this market in the next year or two we will be testing and reporting on their merchandise.

Part Two
HOW TO GO

Package v. Independent

There is no doubt that in Yugoslavia package holidaymakers come off the best. This is one country above all major holiday destinations where it's simpler, better value and better fun to take a prearranged holiday. It's not impossible to travel independently, but it does require a good deal of pre-planning to ensure things go at all smoothly and it will work out expensive when you compare the prices that tour operators are offering. There are three main disadvantages for independent travellers: the price to get over there in the first place, the prices asked for reasonable accommodation, and the price, discomforts and general hassles you have to put up with to tour the country. The other side of the coin is, of course, that you are your own boss and you're not made to feel one of the crowd of tourists. You also stand a much better chance of seeing what life in Yugoslavia is actually like, as staying in one of the resorts you are very far removed from the life of the everyday Yugoslavian. The options open to you are discussed in detail later on in this section, but suffice to say that the Yugoslavian tourist market is divided 93.7 per cent in favour of package holidaymakers, for good reason.

The package holidaymaker has a wide choice of tour operators to choose from and on offer are holidays as disparate as two weeks in a busy resort such as Poreč or a break set in somewhere as unspoilt and uncommercialized as the Plitvice National Park. Increasingly tour operators are offering destinations away from the coastal resorts, so you needn't assume that just because it's a package holiday it will necessarily turn out to be a Torremolinos-type experience. The all-inclusive prices of package deals would be impossible to beat as an independent traveller, for tourism, like most things in Yugoslavia, runs on the lines of bulk buying and group arrangements.

This list was correct at the time of going to press, but the operators had not then finalised all their destinations, so the details should be checked before booking.

Package Holidays

Tour Operators in Britain Offering Packages to Yugoslavia

There are over seventy British tour operators who offer holidays in Yugoslavia: some are specialists in that country; some offer only one or two Yugoslavian destinations as part of their overall package programme. By far the biggest operator to Yugoslavia with the biggest share of the British market is Yugotours. They specialize in just this country and offer the most comprehensive set of destinations.

Other tour operators specializing in Yugoslavia and worth checking out are Phoenix, Thomas Cook, Pan Adriatic and Pilgrim. Phoenix are the second largest specialist company to Yugoslavia, and among the many quality tours they offer specialist sailing holidays; horse-riding holidays; villa and apartment holidays; naturist beach holidays and coach tours. Their holiday clubs represent exceptional value for facilities, and their winter skiing packages are definitely worth checking out.

On the following pages are the names, addresses, telephone numbers, and details of the British tour operators who run holidays to Yugoslavia. Some of the firms are relatively obscure and their brochures will not be widely available but if they specialize in the type of holiday you're after, give them a phone and request a brochure. Those not discussed in any of the specific listings on pages 102–109 can be assumed to be offering just general holidays to Yugoslavia. Every effort has been made to ensure this list of operators is comprehensive and accurate, but please remember that we can only publish the details of the tour operators who have their brochures out in time for our publishing deadline, at the end of the calendar year, and in the fluctuating world of the travel business tour companies spring up and go bust with amazing regularity. The Yugoslavian Tourist Board at 143 Regent Street, London W1 keep an updated comprehensive list, and will send you a free copy on request.

ADRIATIC CRUISING CLUB
Orchard House, Potsbridge Rd, Ninchfield, Hants RG27 8BT
(Tel: 025 126 3495)

Bare Boat Yacht Charter
Air: Gatwick and Heathrow *to Dubrovnik*
Stay: 1/2/3 weeks. Variety of six-berth yachts based at Dubrovnik Marina

ANGELA HOLIDAYS
Oaktree Cottages, Lowford, Bursledon, Southampton SO3 8ES.
(Tel: 042 121 4536)
Resort: LOVRAN (Coach Tours)

APPLEGATES SUPREME COACHES
Heathfield Garage, Newport, Berkeley, Gloucestershire GL1P 9PL
(Tel: 0453 810314)

Coach Tours
Resort: BLED

BALKAN SHOOT
36 Kings Road, Chelsea, London SW3 4UD.
(Tel: 01-584 3105)

Shooting Holidays
Air: Heathrow *to Zagreb, Belgrade and Dubrovnik*
Stay: 1/2 weeks
Resorts: Game reserves throughout Yugoslavia; 2–4 star hotels & lodges.
(Waterfowl, bear, wolf, boar, chamois, mouflon and others)

Coach Tours
Air: to Lovran

BEBB TRAVEL
The Coach Station, Llantwit Fardre, Pontypridd, Mid-Glamorgan CF38 2HB.
(Tel: 0443 204211)

Coach Tours to Yugoslavia
Stay: 2 weeks. Visiting Holland, Germany, Austria, YUGOSLAVIA, Italy, Switzerland and France
Resort: POREČ (5 nights)

BEST TRAVEL
31 Topsfield Parade, Crouch End, London N8 8PT.
(Tel: 01-348 8211)

Air
Hotels and Villas
Resorts: MAKARSKA, JELSA, SUPETAR

CLUB ADRIATICA LTD
283 Kenton Lane, Kenton, Harrow, Middx. HA3 8RR.
(Tel: 01-907 1131)

Air: Heathrow *to Dubrovnik*
Stay: 1/2 weeks
Resorts: KORČULA (Park, Korčula, Liburna, Self-catering apartments),
DUBROVNIK (Vis)

2 Centre Holiday
DUBROVNIK (Vis) with KORČULA (Park, Korčula and Liburna)
Bare-boat and flotilla sailing holidays (Dubrovnik Marina)
Skippered Yacht Charter (Dubrovnik Marina)
Children's snorkelling holidays and scuba diving (Korčula)

CLUB CANTABRICA
Holiday House, 146-8 London Road, St Albans, Herts.
(Tel: 0727 33141/66177)

Camping Coach Tours
Resort: POREČ

CLUB MEDITERRANEE
106-8 Brompton Road, London SW3 1JJ.
(Tel: 01-581 1161)

Air: To Club Med Villages at PAKOSTANE, SVETI MARKO

CONSORT TRAVEL
Wickersley House, Bawtry Road, South Yorkshire S66 0BB.
(Tel: 0709 701701)

Coach Tours – Istrian Riviera
Stay: 10 days. Visiting France, Belgium, Germany, Austria and
YUGOSLAVIA
Resorts: SELCE and CRIKVENICA

CONTIKI HOLIDAYS
Wells House, 15 Elmsfield Road, Bromley, Kent BR1 1LS.
(Tel: 01-290 6422)

Coach Tour – *Grand European Special*
Stay: 58 days. Visiting France, Spain, Monaco, Italy, Greece, Turkey, Bulgaria, YUGOSLAVIA, Austria, Liechtenstein, Switzerland, Germany and Holland

COSMOS HOLIDAYS
Cosmos House, 1 Bromley Common, Bromley, Kent BR2 9LX.
(Tel: 01-464 3400)

Air: Gatwick, Luton, Heathrow, Birmingham and Manchester *to Pula*
Gatwick, Heathrow and Manchester *to Dubrovnik*
Stay: 1/2 weeks
Resorts: BLED (Park), RABAC (Narcis), POREČ (Lotos, Albatros, Delfin, Zagreb, Pical, Rubin, Sv. Nikola), NOVIGRAD (Laguna), NEUM, KOTOR, PULA

2 Centre Holidays
BLED (Park) with RABAC (Narcis) or POREČ (Rubin, Delfin)

Coach Tours

Yugoslavia, The Rhineland, Austria and Bavaria
Stay: 2 weeks. Visiting Belgium, Germany, Austria and YUGOSLAVIA
5 nights at OPATIJA (Bellevue), BLED (Jelovica)

Jewels of Yugoslavia
Stay: 10 days. Visiting Belgium, Germany, Austria and YUGOSLAVIA (Postojna, Zadar, Split, Dubrovnik, Sarajevo, Banja Luka, Zagreb and Ljubljana)

Tour and Stay
Itinerary as above plus week at NEUM (Sunce)

Europe in 20 days
Stay: 20 days. Visting Belgium, Holland, Denmark, East and West Germany, Austria, YUGOSLAVIA, Italy, Switzerland and France

Highlights of Yugoslavia
Air: Gatwick, Luton and Manchester *to Pula*
Stay: 1/2 weeks. Visiting Pula, Opatija, Trogir, Split, Dubrovnik, Sarajevo, Plitvice, Karlovac, Novo Mesto, Ljubljana, Postojna and Pula
1 week at your chosen resort POREČ (Lotos-Lila)

Balkan Adventure
Air: Gatwick and Manchester *to Dubrovnik*
Stay: 2 weeks. Visiting YUGOSLAVIA, Greece, Turkey, Bulgaria and Romania

Express Coach – Istrian Riviera
Stay: 10/17 days
Resort: NOVIGRAD (Laguna)

ENTERPRISE HOLIDAYS
6-8 Manor Mount, London SE23 3PZ.
(Tel: 01-699 8833)

Air: Gatwick, Manchester and Glasgow *to Pula*
Stay: 1/2 weeks
Resorts: POREČ (Albatros, Delfin, Diamant), MEDULIN (Mutila), PORTOROZ (Barbara), DUBROVNIK (Neptun), ROVINJ, BLED, KRANJSKA GORA

Lakes and Mountains
Air: Gatwick and Manchester *to Ljubljana*
Stay: 1/2 weeks
Resorts: KRANJSKA GORA (Slavec, Larix), BLED (Kriek, Krim, Park, Golf)

EUROCAMP TRAVEL
Edmundson House, Tatton Street, Knutsford, Cheshire WA16 6BG.
(Tel: 0565 3844)

Self-Drive Camping Holidays
Resort: POREČ

EXPLORE WORLDWIDE LTD
7 High Street, Aldershot, Hants. GU11 1BH.
(Tel: 0252 319448/9)

Air: Gatwick/Heathrow *to Dubrovnik*
Stay: 2 weeks. Visiting Dubrovnik, Zabljak, Sarajevo, Mostar, Kardeljevo, Split, Brac, Hvar, Korčula using local buses, trains and boats

2 Centre Holiday
Italy with KRANJSKA GORA (Prisank)

FLAIR HOLIDAYS
4-6 Manor Mount, London SE23 3PZ.
(Tel: 01-291 7979)

Air: Gatwick, Manchester and Glasgow *to Pula*
Stay: 1/2 weeks
Resorts: POREČ (Parentino, Porec, Lotos Istra 4), RABAC (Girandella), PORTOROZ

FREEDOM TRAVEL LTD
103 High Street, Erdington, Birmingham B23 6SA.
(Tel: 021-384 5111)

Coach Tour – Slovenian Mountains – Night Rider
Stay: 10/17 days (7/14 nights at your resort)
Resorts: KRANJSKA GORA (Alpina, Zrenjanin), CRIKUENICA, SELCE, BLED

GLOBAL CONTINENTAL COACH HOLIDAYS
47 Grattan Road, Bradford, North Yorkshire BD1 2QF.
(Tel: 0274 729739)

Air/Coach Tours
Resort: BLED

3 Country Tour

GLOBERATE HOLIDAYS LTD
7-11 Queensferry Place, London SW7 2DL.
(Tel: 01-584 9792)

Air/Hotel Packages
Resorts: PULA, ROVINJ, TROGIR, MAKARSKA, DUBROVNIK, CAV, KORCULA

HF HOLIDAYS LTD
142/144 Great North Way, London NW4 1EG.
(Tel: 01-203 3381)

Walking/Lakes and Mountains
Air: Heathrow *to Zagreb*
Stay: 9/14 days

Resort: BOHINJ (Pod Voglom) KORCULA, DUBROVNIK, MILANOUAC, DONJI, BOVEC

HOLIDAY CLUB INTERNATIONAL
Broadway, Edgbaston, Five Ways, Birmingham B15 1BB.
(Tel: 021-632 6282)

Air: Gatwick, Manchester, East Midlands and Birmingham *to Pula*
Stay: 1/2 weeks
Resort: POREČ, RABAC, ORASAC, DUBROVNIK

HORIZON HOLIDAYS LTD
Broadway, Edgbaston, Five Ways, Birmingham B15 1BB.
(Tel: 021-632 6282)

Air: Gatwick, Birmingham, East Midlands, Manchester
Stay: 1/2 weeks
Resorts: ROVINJ (Katarina, Rovinj, Montavro, Eden) PULA (Mutila, Brioni, Palma, Park), MEDULIN (Belvedere, Histria), POREČ (Vrisar, Kristal, Pical, Panorama), KRANJSKA GORA, VRSAR

2 Centre Holiday
BLED (Kompasi) with POREČ (Kristal)

INDEPENDENT COACH TRAVEL
Blake House, Admiral's Way, Waterside, London E14 9UJ.
(Tel: 01-538 4627)

Coach Holidays
Resorts: OPATIJA, LOVRAN, RABAC

INGHAMS TRAVEL
329 Putney Bridge Road, London SW15 2PL.
(Tel: 01-785 7777)

Air: Gatwick, Heathrow *to Ljubljana*
Gatwick, Bristol, Glasgow, Luton, Manchester, Edinburgh, Birmingham, Newcastle and Belfast *to Munich*
Stay: 1/2 weeks
Resorts: BLED (Krim, Park, Golf, Savica Apartments, Villa Bled, Toplice), KRANJSKA GORA (Prisank, Larix, Lek)

2 Centre Holidays
KRANJSKA GORA (Larix, Lek, Prisank) with BLED (Park, Krim, Golf, Savica Apartments, Villa Bled, Toplice)

2 Centre 2 Country Holidays
OPATIJA (Paris, Ambasador), BLED (Park, Krim, Golf, Savica Apartments, Villa Bled, Toplice)

Car – Motoring Holidays
Stay: 1/2 weeks
Resorts: BLED (Park, Krim, Golf, Savica Apartments, Villa Bled, Toplice), KRANJSKA GORA (Larix, Lek, Prisank)

INATOURS (UK) LTD
22 Turnham Green Terrace, Chiswick, London W4 1QP.
(Tel: 01-994 9959)

Air/Hotels/2 Centre/Lakes and Mountains/Self-catering/Naturist
Resorts: BLED, KRANJSKA GORA, POREC, NOVIGRAD, UMAG, ROVINJ, CRIKVENICA, KRK, LOSINJ, HVAR, DUBROVNIK and others.

INTASUN
Intasun House, 47 Grattan Road, Bradford, Yorks. BD1 2QF.
(Tel: 0274 760011)

Air: Manchester, Birmingham, Newcastle and Glasgow *to Pula*
Manchester *to Split*
Manchester and Newcastle *to Dubrovnik*
Stay: 1/2 weeks
Villas and Apartments
2 Centre Holidays
Coach and Camping Holidays
2 Centre – 2 Country Holidays
Resorts: PORTOROZ (Bernadin, Grand Palace, Park, Neptun), POREČ (Kristal, Luna, self-catering apartments), VRSAR (Panorama), UMAG (self-catering village), BLED, KRANJSKA GORA.
Coach Express
Stay: 1/2 weeks
Resort: POREČ (Kristal, self-catering apartments, camping at Lanterna)

INTERHOME LTD
383 Richmond Road, Twickenham, Middx.
(Tel: 01-891 1294)

Villa and Apartment Holidays
Resorts: PORTOROZ, UMAG, NOVIGRAD, POREČ, ROVINJ, PULA, OPATIJA, CRIKVENICA, ZADAR, CRES, MALI LOSINJ, KRK, NOVALJA, KORČULA and VELA LUKA

ISLAND SAILING LTD
Northney Marina, Hayling Island, Hampshire PO11 0NH.
(Tel: 0705 466331)

Flotilla and Bareboat Sailing Holidays
Beneteau 25 Beneteau Island 30 yachts
Air: Gatwick *to Split*
Stay: 2 weeks
Resorts: PRIMOSTEN and DUBROVNIK

MARTIN ROOKS HOLIDAYS
204 Ebury Street, London SW1W 8UU.
(Tel: 01-730 0808)

Air: Gatwick and Manchester *to Pula and Rijeka-Krk*
Gatwick, Manchester and East Midlands *to Dubrovnik*
Stay: ROVINJ (Montauro, Eden), RABAC (Apollo, Lanterna), OPATIJA (Grand Adriatic), MEDULIN (Medulin), VRSAR (Pineta), DUBROVNIK (Tirena), SREBRENO (Orlando), POREČ, KRK, SUTEMORE, BLED

NAT HOLIDAYS LTD
Holiday House, Domestic Road, Leeds LS12 6HR.
(Tel: 0532 434077)

Air/Train/Coach Tours/Self-Drive, Camping and Caravans
Resorts: PORTOROZ, POREČ, MALINSKA, OMASALJ, PUNAT

NATIONAL HOLIDAYS
George House, George Street, Wakefield, West Yorkshire WF1 1LY.
(Tel: 0924 387387)

Coach Tours, Camping and Apartments
Resorts: OPATIJA, PULA, MALINSKA

FRED OLSEN LINES
Victoria Plaza, 111 Buckingham Palace Road, London SW1N 0SP.
(Tel: 01-630 8844)

Air/Cruises
Resorts: DUBROVNIK, KOTOR

P&O CRUISES LTD
77 New Oxford Street, London WC1A 1PP.
(Tel: 01-831 1331)

Air: From Gatwick
Resorts: DUBROVNIK

Various Cruise Itineraries

PAGE & MOY LTD
136-140 London Road, Leicester LE2 1EN.
(Tel: 0533 552521)

Air: Heathrow *to Rijeka or Ljubljana*
Stay: 1/2 weeks
Resorts: KRK-MALINSKA (Apartments Lavanda), BLED (Lovec), RAB
ZABLJAK, DUBROVNIK, KORCULA, BOVEC, OREBIC

2 Centre Holidays
Stay: 2 weeks
Resorts: MLJET with OREBIC
Air: Heathrow *to Dubrovnik*
Stay: 2 weeks

2 Centre, 2 Country Holiday with Italy

PALMAIR/BATH TRAVEL
Space House, 2 Albert Road, Bournemouth, Dorset BH1 1BY.
(Tel: 0202 299299)

Air
Hotels, Lakes and Mountains
Resorts: PORTOROZ, BLED, DUBROVNIK, MINI, SREBRENO,
CAVTAT

Resorts: BOL (Bijela Kuca) with TUČEPI (Jadran)
Air: Heathrow *to Dubrovnik*

Stay: 2 weeks
Resorts: MLJET (Odisej) with DUBROVNIK (Vis)
Air: 2 weeks
Resorts: KORČULA (Feral) with DUBROVNIK (Neptun)
2 Centre 2 Country Holidays
Italy with MOSCENICKA DRAGA (Mediteran)

PAN ADRIATIC TRAVEL LTD
2nd Floor, 49 Conduit Street, London W1R 9FB.
(Tel: 01-439 1916/7)

Specialist for Independent Holidays and Business Travel to Yugoslavia
Fly and drive holidays – flexible itineraries
Car hire
Selected holidays – Island of Brioni, Hotel Toplice & Villa Bled at Lake Bled,
Sveti Stefan, Hotel Belvedere at Dubrovnik, Island of Mljet
Hotel reservations – throughout Yugoslavia
Go as you please holidays
Self-catering in private houses
Guest house holidays
Small pension holidays at Makarska and Budva
Farm house holidays
City holidays
Low cost air fares to all destinations in Yugoslavia
Conference arrangements and special interest groups

Cruising Holidays
Dalmatian coast and islands – traditionally built Dalmatian boats 1/2 week
holidays

Coach and Cruise Holidays
Heart of Yugoslavia and Aegean Sea
15 days. Visiting Belgrade, Sarajevo, Dubrovnik, Venice, Piraeus, Rhodes,
Crete and Corfu
Greek and Yugoslav Delights
17 days. Visiting Dubrovnik, Venice, Piraeus, Rhodes, Heraklion, Corfu,
Split, Trogir, Zadar, Plitvice, Postojna, Bled and Zagreb
Danube Dream Cruise
13 days. Visiting Vienna, Budapest, Belgrade, Sofia, Krusevac, Sarajevo and
Dubrovnik

Coach Tours
Grand Tour of Yugoslavia
14 days. Visiting Belgrade, Sarajevo, Dubrovnik, Split, Plitvice, Postojna, Bled and Zagreb
Eastern Rhapsody
15 days. Visiting Zagreb, Budapest, Brasov, Sofia, Belgrade, Sarajevo and Dubrovnik
Byzantine Imperial Odyssey
18 days. Visiting Belgrade, Sofia, Plovdiv, Istanbul, Thessaloniki, Athens, Ohrid, Montenegro and Dubrovnik

Special Interest Tours
Yugoslavian Mountain Trails
8 days. Visiting Dubrovnik, Mostar, Sarajevo, Igman, Zlatibor, Novi Pazar, Zabljak, Durmitor, Montenegro and Sveti Stefan
Tara Canyon Adventure
8 days Coach/Boat. Visiting Dubrovnik, Zabljak, Durdevica, Tara River/ Canyon and Dubrovnik
Yugoslavia for Beginners Tour
Air, Ferry, Coach 8 days. Visiting Zagreb, Split, Island of Hvar and Dubrovnik
Medjugorje and Dubrovnik
5 or 6 days. Visiting Dubrovnik, Citluk/Ljubuski, Medjugorje and Mostar

PANORAMA HOLIDAYS
Panorama House, Church Road, Hove BN3 2BA.
(Tel: 0273 730281)

Rail Holidays
Resorts: PORTOROZ, BLED

PENG TRAVEL
86 Station Road, Gidea Park, Essex RM2 6DB.
(Tel: 0402 71832)

Naturist Holidays and Cruises
Air: Gatwick and Manchester
Resorts: KOVERSADA, SOLARIS, OSMIRE, PUNTA SKALA

Dalmatian Cruises
Air: Gatwick and Manchester *to Split*
Stay: 1/2 weeks

Cruise: Split, Brač, Korčula, Dubrovnik, Mljet, Hvar and Split
Cruise: Split, Trogir, Zlarin, Kornati Islands, Punta Skala, Zadar, Šibenik, Primošten and Split

PHOENIX HOLIDAYS
16 Bonny Street, London NW1 9PG.
(Tel: 01-485 5515)

Air: Birmingham, Edinburgh, Norwich, Glasgow, Heathrow, Manchester and Newcastle *to Pula*
Birmingham, Norwich, Glasgow, Heathrow and Manchester *to Dubrovnik*
Heathrow and Manchester *to Split*
Stay: 1/2 weeks
Resorts: ANKARAN (Ankaran), UMAG (Aurora, Istra, Umag), PORTOROZ (Palace, Grand Palace), POREČ (Lotos-Istra, Delfin, Galiot, Albatros, Kristal, Poreč, Neptun, Parentium, Tamaris, Galeb), ROVINJ (Eden, Villas Rubin, Montauro, Park), PULA (Brioni, Zlatne Stijene, Splendid, Splendid Pavilion), MEDULIN (Belvedere, Mutila), RABAC (Girandella, Narcis), OPATIJA (Slavija, Imperial Atlantic, Ambasador), VRSAR (Funtana), ŠIBENIK (Jura), ZADAR (Kolovare), KASTEL STARI (Palace 1, 11, 111), VODICE (Olympia, Imperial, Imperial Pavilion), PRIMOŠTEN (Zora), SPLIT (Lav), TROGIR (Medena), BRELA (Berulia 1, Soline), MAKARSKA (Meteor, Riviera), TUČEPI (Alga, Pavilions Maslinik, Jadran), OREBIĆ (Rathaneum), SLANO (Admiral), PLAT (Galeb, Ambasador), DUBROVNIK (Argosy, Adriatic, Excelsior, Neptun, Dubrovnik Palace, Belvedere), MLINI (Astarea 1, Mlini), SREBRENO (Orlando), CAVTAT (Croatia, Epidavrus), KOTOR (Fjord), RISAN (Teuta), PERAST (Perast), BUDVA (Avala, Slovenska Plaza), BEČIČI (Splendid, Bellevue), SVETI STEFAN (Sv. Stefan), MILOČER (Maestral, Villa Milocer), PETROVAC (Palas, Castellastva)

Lakes and Mountains
KRANJSKA GORA (Kompas Alpina, Kompas Pavilions), BLED (Kompas, Krim, Jadran, Golf), PLITVICE (Jezero, Plitvice), ŽABLJAK (Jezera, Planinka), BOHINJ (Zlatorog, Kompas), OHRID (Biser, Slavija)

Villa, Apartments, Self-Catering and Pension Holidays
POREČ (Galiot apartments, Citadela apartments, private houses, self-catering apartments), UMAG (Stella Maris, Polynesia Samoa and Tahiti, private houses and self-catering apartments), ROVINJ (Villas Rubin, private houses and self-catering apartments), PULA (Punta Verudela apartments, private houses and self-catering apartments), SPLIT (self-catering apartments), TROGIR (Medena apartments), BRELA (self-catering

apartments), KORČULA (private houses and self-catering apartments, Lumbarda apartments)

Coach Tours

The Best of Southern Europe

Air: Gatwick and Manchester *to Dubrovnik*

Stay: 1/2 weeks. Visiting Dubrovnik, Visegrad, Novi Pazar, Prizina, Skopje, Sveti Stefan, Titovo Uzice

2nd week at your chosen hotel DUBROVNIK (Minčeta, Neptun), CAVTAT (Epidavrus)

3 Countries Coach Tour

Air: Gatwick, Luton and Manchester *to Pula*

Stay: 1/2 weeks. Visiting Pula, Plitvice, Kranjska Gora, Villach, Kobarid and Venice

2nd week at your chosen hotel POREČ (Tamaris, Delfin), ANKARAN (Ankaran)

ISLAND HOLIDAYS

HVAR (Pharos, Amfora, Palace), KOLOČEP (Koločep), KORČULA (Bon Repos, Marko Polo), LUMBARDA (Lumbarda), STARIGRAD (Helios, Arkada), VELA LUKA (Poseidon)

NATURIST HOLIDAYS

ROVINJ (Monsena Bungalows), HVAR, PRIMOŠTEN, MEDULIN, PULA, UMAG

Budget Holidays

Air: Birmingham, Bristol, East Midlands, Edinburgh, Gatwick, Glasgow, Heathrow, Luton, Manchester and Newcastle *to Pula, Split and Dubrovnik*

2 Centre Holidays

There are 27 possible combinations of 2 centre holidays from the resorts listed above, with 2 coastal resorts, one mainland with an island or one coastal resort with one in the mountains.

Special Interest Holidays
Horse Riding Holidays
Flotilla Holidays
Motoring Holidays
Conference and Incentive Trips
Senior Citizens
Golfing Holidays

PILGRIM HOLIDAYS LTD
3 Cork Street, Mayfair, London W1X 1HA.
(Tel: 01-734 9668/9)

Air: Heathrow, Manchester, Birmingham and Glasgow *to Pula and Dubrovnik*
Heathrow *to Split and Ljubljana*
Stay: 1/2 weeks
Resorts: KORČULA (Bon Repos, Marco Polo), OREBIĆ (Bellevue), DUBROVNIK (Adriatic, Pavilion Park, Grand Park), MLINI (Astarea Pavilion), PLAT (Ambasador), HERCEG NOVI (Plaza), TUČEPI (Alga), JELSA (Mina), STARIGRAD (Arkada), PULA (Splendid, Park, Brioni), POREČ (Galeb, Albatros, Rubin), RABAC (Mimosa), ROVINJ (Park, Montauro), OPATIJA (Jadran, Admiral, Kvarner), BLED (Park)

2 Centre Holidays
DUBROVNIK (Adriatic, Pavilion Park) with KORČULA (Bon Repos)
MLINI (Astarea Pavilion) with KORČULA (Bon Repos)
HERCEG NOVI (Plaza) with DUBROVNIK (Adriatic)
PLAT (Ambasador) with KORČULA (Bon Repos)
DUBROVNIK (Adriatic) with OREBIĆ (Bellevue)
JELSA (Mina) with TUČEPI (Alga)
RABAC (Mimosa) with POREČ (Albatros, Rubin)
POREČ (Galeb) with OPATIJA (Jadran)
RABAC (Mimosa) with OPATIJA (Jadran)
POREČ (Rubin, Galeb) with PULA (Park, Brioni)
OPATIJA (Jadran) with BLED (Park)

RAMBLERS HOLIDAYS LTD
13 Longcroft House, Fretherne Road, Welwyn Garden City, Herts. AL8 6PQ.
(Tel: 0707 331133)

Walking Holidays, Lakes and Mountains
Air: Gatwick *to Dubrovnik*
Stay: 2 weeks (13 nights Zabljak, 1 night Dubrovnik)
Resorts: ZABLJAK (Jezera), DUBROVNIK (Petka), KOTOR, OHRID, BOHINJ, KRANJSKA GORA, BLED, SARAJEVO, TRAVNIK, BJELASNICA

RAYMOND COOK HOLIDAYS
118 High Street, Dover, Kent CT16 1EG.
(Tel: 0304 211160)

Air: Heathrow *to Ljubljana*
Stay: 2 weeks
Resort: BLED (Krim)

W. ROBINSON & SONS (TOURS) LTD
Park Garage, Great Harwood, Blackburn, Lancs. BB6 7SP.
(Tel: 0254 889900)

Coach Tour – Slovenian Riviera
Stay: 2 weeks. Visiting France, Belgium, Germany, Austria, YUGOSLAVIA and Italy
Resort: PORTOROZ (Neptun) 7 nights

SAGA HOLIDAYS PLC
The Saga Building, Middelburg Square, Folkestone, Kent.
(Tel: 0800 300600)

Air: Gatwick *to Pula, Dubrovnik, Rijeka, Split and Ljubljana*
Glasgow *to Pula*
Heathrow *to Dubrovnik*
Stay: 2 weeks
Resorts: POREČ (Materada), BLED (Sloboda), HVAR (Delfin), PODGORA (Minerva), TUČEPI (Alga), MAKARSKA (Meteor), DUBROVNIK (Argosy, Tirena, Plakir), SREBRENO (Orlando), PLAT (Ambasador), KUPARI (Goricina), KORČULA (Marko Polo), HERCEG NOVI (Igalo), SUPETAR, MLINI, OHRID

2 Centre Holidays
Coach Tour – Discover Yugoslavia
Air: Gatwick *to Pula or Dubrovnik*
Stay: 2 weeks. Visiting Poreč, Bled, Zagreb, Plitvice, Makarska, Dubrovnik

2 Centre 2 Country Holidays
Air/coach Italy and Yugoslavia
Air: Gatwick *to Ljubljana/one way/coach home*
Stay: 16 nights
Resorts: ITALY with OPATIJA (Adriatic)

Air/coach Yugoslavia and Austria
Air: Gatwick *to Pula*
Stay: 16 nights
Resorts: RABAC (Lanterna) with Austria

SIESTA INTERNATIONAL HOLIDAYS
156-8 Linthorpe Road, Middlesbrough, Cleveland TS1 3RB.
(Tel: 0642 227711)

Coach Tours
Resorts: KRANJSKA GORA, CRIKVENICA

SINCERELY YUGOSLAVIA
36 London Road, Romford, Essex RM7 9RB.
(Tel: 01-597 7628)

Air
Hotels, Self-Catering, Fly-Drive, Low Cost Flights
Resorts: DUBROVNIK, SREBRENO, MAKARSKA, TUČEPI,
CAVTAT, ZATON, IGALO

SKYTOURS LTD
Greater London House, Hampstead Road, London NW1 7SD.
(Tel: 01-387 9699)

Air
Hotels, Apartments
Resorts: NOVIGRAD, VRSAR, TROGIR

SMITHS-SHEARINGS CONTINENTAL HOLIDAYS
Miry Lane, Wigan WN3 4AG.
(Tel: 0942 44264)

Coach Tours
Stay: 14 days
Resorts: OPATIJA, LOVRAN, PULA, MALINSKA

SOVEREIGN HOLIDAYS
4-6 Manor Mount, London SE23 3PZ.
(Tel: 01-291 5000)

Air: Gatwick, East Midlands, Manchester and Glasgow
Stay: 1/2 weeks
Resorts: POREČ, LOVRAN, PULA, SVETI STEFAN, MLINI, DUBROVNIK, BLED

SUCCESS TOURS LTD
42A Roundstone Street, Trowbridge, Wiltshire BA14 8DE.
(Tel: 022 14 64205)

Coach Tours – GROUPS ONLY
Resorts: POREČ, OMISALJ, RABAC

SUNQUEST HOLIDAYS LTD
Aldine House, 9-15 Aldine Street, London W12 8AW.
(Tel: 01-749 9933)

Air: Heathrow, Manchester and Birmingham *to Dubrovnik*
Stay: 1/2 weeks
Resorts: DUBROVNIK, PULA, POREČ

SUPREME TRAVEL
303 London Road, Hadleigh, Benfleet, Essex SS7 2BN.
(Tel: 0702 552995)

Coach Tours
Resort: CRIKVENCIA

SWAN HELLENIC
77 New Oxford Street, London WC1A 1PP.
(Tel: 01-831 1515)

Coach Tour – Art Treasures of Yugoslavia
Air: London Belgrade – Dubrovnik London
Stay: 16 days. Visiting Belgrade, Mataruska Banja, Sopocani, Pristina, Gracanica, Skopje, Staro Nagoricane, Stobi Bitola, Ohrid, Tetovo, Prizen, Decani, Pec, Visegrad, Sarajevo, Travnik, Split, Dubrovnik
Cruises
Various Cruise Itineraries

TAPPINS HOLIDAYS
Station Road, Didcot, Oxon. OX11 7LZ.
(Tel: 0235 819393)

Coach Tour – Express Night Cruiser
Resort: OPATIJA

THOMAS COOK HOLIDAYS
P.O. Box 36, Thorpe Wood, Peterborough PE3 6SB.
(Tel: 0733 502200)

Air: Gatwick, Birmingham, Manchester and Glasgow *to Pula*
Heathrow *to Zagreb*
Gatwick and Manchester *to Split*
Gatwick, Birmingham and Manchester *to Dubrovnik*
Stay: 1/2 weeks
Resorts: POREČ (Mediteran, Materada, Zagreb), ROVINJ (Park), PULA (Park, Brioni), RAB, KORČULA (Park, Liburna), BUDVA (Avala, Slovenska Plaza), CAVTAT (Croatia), DUBROVNIK (Vis, Tirena, Villa Dubrovnik, Excelsior, Argentina), SVETI STEFAN (Sv. Stefan)

2 Centre Holidays
DUBROVNIK (Vis) with KORČULA (Park)
OPATIJA with RAB

Coach Tours
Country and Peoples Tour
Air: Heathrow *to Zagreb and Dubrovnik*
Stay: 1/2 weeks. Visiting Dubrovnik, Split, Zadar, Plitvice, Postojna, Ljubljana, Zagreb, Banja Luka, Sarajevo and Dubrovnik
2nd week at PLAT (Ambasador)

THOMSON HOLIDAYS LTD
Greater London House, Hampstead Road, London NW1 7SD.
(Tel: 01-387 8484)

Air: from Gatwick, Luton, Cardiff, Birmingham, East Midlands, Manchester, Stansted, Newcastle and Glasgow.
Stay: 7/10/11/14 nights.
Resorts: PORTOROZ (Grand Palace, Riviera, Piran), POREČ (Fortuna, Mediteran, Diamant, Zagreb, Albatros, Materada, Tamaris, Pical), OPATIJA (Admiral, Ambassador, Opatija, Grand Adriatic), LOVRAN (Lovran, Excelsior), ROVINJ (Eden, Katarina, Rovinj), PULA (Histria,

Palma, Park, Brioni), MEDULIN (Belvedere, Mutila, Medulin), RABAC (Narcis, Mimosa), DUBROVNIK (Grand Park, Grand Park Annex, Dubrovnik Palace, Vis), BEČIČI (Montenegro, Bellevue), BUDVA (Avala, Maestral), MLINI (Orlando), LOPUD (Lofodra), BLED (Golf, Kompas, Park, Lovec), MALI LOSINJ (Aurora, Vespera, Punta), NOVIGRAD (Maestral), MAKARSKA (Meteor, Dalmacija), TUČEPI (Jadran, Neptun, Labinea), NEUM (Sunce, Neum), CAVTAT/PLAT (Epidavras, Ambasador, Plat).

2 Centre Holidays
BLED (Kompas) with PORTOROZ (Riviera)

Small Hotel and Pension Holidays
Air: Gatwick, Luton, Cardiff, Birmingham, East Midlands, Manchester, Stansted, Newcastle and Glasgow
Stay: 7/10/11/14 nights
Resorts: RABAC (Istra, Fortuna), POREČ/ST NIKOLA (Miramare, Paventino), LOVRAN (Primorka), IZOLA (Marina), DUBROVNIK (Dubravica), CAVTAT (Cavtat, Supetar)

A la Carte Holidays
Air: Gatwick, Luton, Cardiff, Birmingham, East Midlands, Manchester, Newcastle and Glasgow *to Pula*
Gatwick, Luton and Manchester *to Dubrovnik*
Stay: 7/14 nights
Resorts: CAVTAT (Croatia), DUBROVNIK (Belvedere), SVETI STEFAN, PORTOROZ (Grand Metropol), OPATIJA (Kvarner)

Coach Tours
Spectacular Yugoslavia
Air: Gatwick *to Klagenfurt*
Stay: 7/14 nights. Visiting Klagenfurt, Lipica, Rijeka, Zadar, Split, Dubrovnik, Mostar, Sarajevo, Jajce, Plitvice, Ljubljana and Bled
Second week spent at BLED (Park, Lovec)
Scenic Heart of Europe
Air: Gatwick *to Munich*
Stay: 11 nights. Visiting Munich, Salzburg, Salzkammergut, Vienna, Budapest, BLED, Innsbruck and Munich

The new 'Simply Yugoslavia' brochure is well worth getting for budget holidays in the major resorts.

TJAEREBORG LTD
194 Campden Hill Road, London W8 7TH.
(Tel: 01-727 2680)

Air: from Gatwick
Stay: 1/2 weeks
Resorts: MALI LOSINJ, VELI LOSINJ

TOP DECK TRAVEL
131-3 Earls Court Road, London SW5 9RH.
(Tel: 01-244 8641)

Coach Tours and Camping
Maxi Europe
Stay: 10 weeks. Visiting France, Spain, Italy, Greece, Turkey, Bulgaria, YUGOSLAVIA, Italy, Austria, Germany, Liechtenstein, Switzerland and Holland.

Central Europe and Greece
Stay: 7 weeks. Visiting France, Monte Carlo, Italy, Greece, Turkey, YUGOSLAVIA, Italy, Germany and Holland

Europe and Greece
Stay: 4½ weeks. Visiting France, Italy, Greece, YUGOSLAVIA, Italy, Austria, Germany and Belgium

Pace Setters – Camping
Stay: 45 days. Visiting Holland, Germany, Denmark, Austria, Italy, YUGOSLAVIA, Greece and France

TRAFALGAR TOURS LTD
15 Grosvenor Place, London SW1X 7HH.
(Tel: 01-235 7090)

Coach Tours

TRAVELSPHERE LTD
Compass House, Coventry Road, Market Harborough LE16 9BZ.
(Tel: 0858 410456)

Coach Tours
Resorts: BLED, PIRAN

TREND TOURS AND HOLIDAYS
Caxton Hall, Caxton Street, London SW1 0QR.
(Tel: 01-799 1535)

Coach Tours
Resort: PORTOROZ

VOYAGES JULES VERNE
10 Glentworth Street, London NW1 5PG.
(Tel: 01-742 6624)

Air/Hotels – Painting Holidays
Resort: ROVINJ

WALLACE ARNOLD TOURS
107 Hope Street, Glasgow, G2 6LL.
(Tel: 041-221 8921)

Coach Tours
Stay: 2 weeks
Resorts: POREČ, OPATIJA, PORTOROZ, BLED, KRANJSKA GORA, PULA

WAYMARK HOLIDAYS
295 Lillie Road, London SW6 7LL.
(Tel: 01-385 5015 & 01-385 3502)

Walking Holidays
Air: Heathrow *to Zagreb*
Stay: 2 weeks
Resort: MOJSTRANA (Triglav)
Kamniks and Julian Alps hut to hut tour

2 Centre Holiday
LOKVE (Jezero) with MEDVEJA (Castello)

WHITES TOURS
Flint House Garage, Calver, Sheffield S30 1XH.
(Tel: 0433 30401)

Coach Tours
Resort: OPATIJA

WINGS OSL
Broadway, Edgbaston, Five Ways, Birmingham B15 1BB.
(Tel: 021-632 6282)

Air/Hotels, Apartments
Resorts: UMAG, POREČ, PULA, ROVINJ, RABAC

YACHT CRUISING ASSOC.
Old Stone House, Judges Terrace, Ship Street, East Grinstead, Sussex RH19 1AQ.
(Tel: 0324 311366)

Flotilla Sailing Holidays
YCA 30 Yachts (5 berth), Sigma 33 yachts (6 berth)
Air: Gatwick and Manchester *to Dubrovnik and Split*
Stay: 2 weeks
Cruise 1: Visiting Dubrovnik, Makarska, Pucisca, Milna, Trogir, Hvar, Solta, Pakleni Islands, Korčula, Vela Luka and Mljet
Cruise 2: Visiting Split, Veli Rat, Iz Veli, Kornati Islands, Kaprije, Rogoznica, Primošten, Krka Falls, Vodice, Murter, Zlaton and Luka Zut

YUGOTOURS LTD
Chesham House, 150 Regent Street, London W1R 6BB.
(Tel: 01-734 7321)

Air: Birmingham, Bristol, Edinburgh, East Midlands, Gatwick, Glasgow, Heathrow, Leeds-Bradford, Luton, Manchester and Newcastle *to Dubrovnik*
Birmingham, Bristol, Gatwick, Glasgow, Heathrow, Leeds-Bradford, Luton, Manchester and Newcastle *to Ljubljana*
Belfast, Birmingham, Bristol, Cardiff, East Midlands, Edinburgh, Exeter, Gatwick, Glasgow, Heathrow, Leeds-Bradford, Liverpool, Luton, Manchester, Newcastle, Stansted and Tees-side *to Pula*
Edinburgh, East Midlands, Gatwick, Heathrow, Manchester and Newcastle *to Rijeka-Krk*
Birmingham, East Midlands, Gatwick, Glasgow, Heathrow, Manchester, Newcastle and Stansted *to Split*
Heathrow and Manchester *to Titograd*
Gatwick, Manchester and Heathrow *to Zadar*
Stay: 1/2 weeks
Resorts: NOVIGRAD (Laguna, Maestral, Emonia), PORTOROZ (Villas

Park, Slovenija, Bernardin, Emona), UMAG (Koral, Aurora, Kristal, Adriatic, Annexe Jadran, Umag, Istra Pavilions, Punta), POREČ (Sveti Nikola, Tamaris, Lotos-Plavi, Albatros, Galeb, Delfin, Parentium, Diamant, Rubin, Kristal, Turist, Luna, Materada, Zagreb, Pical, Neptun, Riviera, Jadran), VRSAR (Pineta, Panorama, Belvedere, Petalon), ROVINJ (Montauro, Eden, Park, Istra, Annexe Park, Villas Rubin, Annexe Monte Mulin), PULA (Splendid, Punta Verudela Village, Palma, Park, Annexe Park, Pavilions Verudela, Histima, Zlatne, Stijeve, Brioni), MEDULIN (Belvedere, Medulin, Mutila), RABAC (Hedera, Lanterna, Castar Adriatic, Girandella, Marina, Mimosa, Apollo), LOVRAN (Beograd, Excelsior, Lovran, Belvedere), OPATIJA (Palma, Ambasador, Imperial, Kristal, Admiral, Adriatic, Belvedere, Brioni, Istra, Dubrovnik, Kvarner, Villa Amalia, Slavija, Belvedere, Rezidenz), CRIKVENICA (Therapia, Umorika, Esplanad, Crikvenica), PETRČANE (Pinija), BIOGRAD (Adriatic), VODICE (Olympia, Imperial, Punta), SIBENIK (Solaris-Ivan, Solaris-Niko), PRIMOŠTEN (Adriatic), TROGIR (Medena), SPLIT (Lav, Marjan), BRELA (Soline, Berulia, Maestral, Marina), BASKA VODA (Horizont), MAKARSKA (Dalmacija, Meteor), TUČEPI (Alga, Jadran), PODGORA (Aurora, Mediteran, Podgorka, Minerva), DUBROVNIK (Argentina, Excelsior, Imperial, Vis 1 and 2, Minčeta, Dubrovnik-Palace, Belvedere, Villa Dubrovnik, Kompas, Adriatic, Libertas, Lero, Neptun, Lapad, Plakir, President, Tirena), OREBIĆ (Rathaneum, Orsan, Bellevue), SREBRENO (Orlando, Župa Villas Lovorka), MLINI (Mlini, Astarea, Annexe Astarea), PLAT (Ambasador, Plat), CAVTAT (Adriatic, Epidaurus, Albatros, Croatia, Makedonia, Cavtat, Supetar), HERCEG NOVI (Plaza, Topla, Riviera), KOTOR (Fjord), BUDVA (Slovenska Plaza, Avala, Villas Avala, Mogren), BEČIĆI (Montenegro, Montenegro A, Mediteran, Bellevue, Splendid), SUTOMORE (Korali, Bungalows Zlatna Obala), MILOČER (Miločer, Villa Miločer, Maestral, Sveti Stefan), PETROVAC (Palas, Villas Oliva, Castellastva, Riviera, As), ULCINJ (Galeb, Olympic, Bellevue-Borik, Otrant), SUPETAR (Kaktus, Palma), IGRANE (Punta), ŽIVOGOŠCE (Nimfa)

Island Holidays
MALI LOSINJ (Vespera, Aurora, Bellevue), VELI LOSINJ (Punta), MALINSKA (Palace, Tamaris, Triglav, Slavija), NJIVICE (Beli Kamik, Jadran), OMISALJ (Adriatic, Primorka), BASKA (Corinthia), RAB (San Marino, Imperial, International, Padova, Bungalows Suha Punta), LOPAR (San Marino), BOZAVA (Kadulja), BOL (Borak, Pavilions Borak, Bretanide, Bijela Kuca, Annexe Bijela Kuca), HVAR (Amfora, Palace, Bodul, Slcwijg, Dalmacija, Adriatic, Delfin, Pharos), STARIGRAD (Arkada, Adriatic), VRBOSKA (Adriatic), JELSA (Fontana, Mina),

KORČULA (Liburna, Korčula, Marko Polo, Park, Bon Repos, Apartments Bon Repos), VELA LUKA (Adria, Posejdon), KOLOČEP (Villas Kolocep), LOPUD (Lafodia, Grand, Dubrava-Pacat), MLJET (Odisej), ŠIPAN (Sipan)

Lakes and Mountains
BLED (Park, Villa Bled, Toplice, Annexe Jadran, Mlino Inn, Jelovica, Krim, Lovec, Golf, Kompas), BOHINJ (Bellevue, Savica, Zlatorog, Annexe Ukanc, Jezero, Kompas), KRANJSKA GORA (Kompas, Annexe Kompas, Lek, Alpina, Larix, Prisank, Prisank-Garni), BOVEC (Kanin, Alp), KOBARID (Matajur), PLITVICE (Jezero, Plitvice), KOPAONIK (Srebrnac, Baciste), ŽABLJAK (Jezera, Planinka), CETINJE (Grand), OHRID (Metropol, Inex-Gorica), SARAJEVO (Igman, Stojčevac)

Spa Holidays
SMARJESKE TOPLICE (Smarjeske Toplice)

Self-Catering and Camping Holidays
UMAG (Apartments Samoa, Apartments Hawaii, Bungalows Stella Maris, Villa Apartments, Pensions, Umag Caravans), SAVUDRIJA (Apartments Crveni Vrh), NOVIGRAD (Villa Apartments, Pensions), POREČ (Apartments Cervar, Apartments Citadela, Apartments Diamant, Apartments Lanterna, Apartments Pical, Villa Apartments, Pensions, Caravans Poreč), VRSAR (Apartments Belvedere, Apartments Petalon), ROVINJ (Villas Rubin, Villa Apartments, Pensions, Apartments Montauro), PULA (Apartments Punta Verudela, Villa Apartments, Pensions), MEDULIN (Apartments Medulin, Villa Apartments, Caravans Medulin, Camping Medulin), RABAC (Apartments Girandella), MALINSKA (Apartments Lavanda, Villas Haludovo, Camping Njivice), CRIKVENICA (Villa Apartments, Pensions), RAB (Villa Apartments, Pensions), BOL (Apartments Borak), STARIGRAD (Bungalows Trim and Helios), ZADAR (Apartments Novi Donat, Camping Borik), ZATON (Apartments Zaton), SPLIT (Apartments Lavica), OREBIĆ (Apartments Rathaneum, Villa Apartments), KORČULA (Liburna Apartments, Apartments Bon Repos), VELA LUKA (Apartments Posejdon), DUBROVNIK (Pensions, Villa Apartments, Camping Solitudo), BUDVA (Villa Apartments, Apartments Slovenska Plaza), SVETI STEFAN (Villa Apartments, Pensions), ULCINJ (Villas Otrant), BLED (Apartments Savica, Pensions, Camping Zakak, Villa Apartments), TROGIR (Apartments Medina), SUPETAR (Apartments Kaktus), JELSA (Apartments Fontana), TUČEPI (Apartments Afrodita), SREBRENO (Villas Srebreno), KRANJSKA GORA (Apartments Razor)

Naturist Holidays
VRSAR (Koversada Bungalows), MEDULIN (Apartments Kazela), ROVINJ (Monsena, Bungalows), PUNTA SKALA (Punta Skala), STARIGRAD (Alan), PRIMOŠTEN (Marina Lucica), ULCINJ (Bojana Bungalows)

2 Centre Holidays
There are over 200 possible combinations of the resorts listed above, with holidays, in two coastal resorts, or one inland with one on the coast etc.

Coach Tours
Grand Tour of Western Yugoslavia
Air: Gatwick, Belfast, Bristol, Cardiff, Edinburgh, Exeter, Luton, Manchester, Newcastle and Tees-side *to Pula*
Stay: 2 weeks. Visiting Pula, Lipica, Postojna, Nova Gorica, Vršič, Kranjska Gora, Klagenfurt, Bohinj, Bled, Ljubljana, Zagreb, Plitvice, Jajce, Sarajevo, Mostar, Dubrovnik, Montenegro, Split, Trogir, Zadar, Rijeka and Pula
Lakes and Mountains
Air: Gatwick, Belfast, Bristol, Cardiff, Edinburgh, Exeter, Luton, Manchester, Newcastle and Tees-side *to Pula*
Stay: 1/2 weeks. Visiting Pula, Lipica, Trieste, Venice, Udine, Bovec, Tarvisio, Klagenfurt, Kranjska Gora, Bled, Ljubljana, Plitvice and Pula
1 week at your chosen hotel POREČ (Albatros and Galeb), ROVINJ (Montauro), PULA (Park, Splendid)
Three Countries Tour
Air: Gatwick, Birmingham, Glasgow, East Midlands, Luton, Bournemouth, Bristol, Leeds-Bradford, Manchester and Newcastle *to Ljubljana*
Stay: 1/2 weeks. Visiting Ljubljana, Ptuj, Zalaegerszeg, Budapest, Visegrad, Gyor, Szombathely, Graz, Lake Klopein, Slovenj Gradec, Celje, Ljubljana
2nd week at your chosen hotel BLED (Golf, Krim, Park, Jelovica), BOHINJ (Kompas, Bellevue), KRANJSKA GORA (Larix, Alpina)
3 Seas Cruise
Air: Gatwick, Heathrow, Stansted, Tees-side, Aberdeen
Stay: 2 weeks; 1 week cruise, 1 week in chosen hotel
Cruise to: Dubrovnik, Corfu, Heraklion, Kusadasi, Mykonos, Piraeus, Venice, Dubrovnik
Resorts: DUBROVNIK, CAVTAT, BEČIČI, MILOCER, SVETI STEFAN, PETROUAC

Adventure Schooner Cruises
Air: Gatwick, Exeter, Cardiff, East Midlands, Newcastle, Glasgow, Edinburgh
Stay: 7/14 nights

2 Alternative itineraries, 2nd week in hotel of choice

Adriatic Highlights Cruise
Air: Gatwick, Heathrow, Stansted, East Midlands, Birmingham, Manchester, Tees-side, Edinburgh, Aberdeen
Stay: 7/14 nights. Visiting Dubrovnik, Korula, Hvar, Siberik, Venice, Opatija, Kornati Islands, Kotar

Golden Age Holidays
Air: Gatwick, Glasgow and Manchester *to Pula*
Gatwick and Manchester *to Split*
Gatwick, Birmingham, Edinburgh, Luton, Manchester and Newcastle *to Dubrovnik*
Stay: 2 weeks
Resorts: ROVINJ (Park), VRSAR (Petalon), PULA (Brioni), MEDULIN (Belvedere), RABAC (Hedera), OPATIJA (Ambasador, Kristal), VODICE (Imperial Olympia), SPLIT (Lav), BASKA VODA (Horizont), DUBROVNIK (Plakir), CAVTAT (Albatros), BEČIČI (Mediteran), PETROVAC (As), HVAR (Amfora), KORČULA (Marko Polo), MAKARSKA (Biokououra), BUDA (Avala), BLED (Park)

Budget Holidays, Special Budget Holidays and Budget Pensions
Air: To all airports in Yugoslavia, Ljubljana, Pula, Rijeka-Krk, Zadar, Split, Dubrovnik, Titograd and Budua Tivat

Fly and Drive Holidays
Air: From all airports in Yugoslavia, Ljubljana, Pula, Rijeka-Krk, Zadar, Split, Budua Tivat

Naturist Holidays
Air: Most UK airports to Ulcinj, Starigrad, Primošten, Petrčane, Medulin, Rovinj, Vrsar

YUGOSLAVIAN RESORTS 1988/9

This is a list of the main resorts available for holidays in 1988/9 and the tour operators relevant to each resort. Please note that the resorts are grouped as they appear on a map from north to south in various categories:

Coastal Resorts

ANKARAN	Phoenix
IZOLA	Thomsons
PIRAN	Travelsphere
PORTOROZ	Enterprise, Intasun, Interhome, Nat Holidays, Phoenix, W. Robinson, Thomsons, Wallace Arnold, Yugotours
NOVIGRAD	Cosmos, Interhome, Yugotours
UMAG	Intasun, Interhome, Phoenix, Yugotours
POREČ	Bebb Travel, Club Cantabrica, Cosmos, Enterprise, Eurocamp, Flair, Holiday Club International, Horizon, Inatours UK, Intasun, Interhome, Nat Holidays, Pilgrim, Saga, Sovereign, Success, Thomas Cook, Thomsons, Wallace Arnold, Yugotours
SOLARIS	Peng
VRSAR	Horizon, Intasun, Martin Rooks, Phoenix, Yugotours
KOVERSADA	Peng

ROVINJ	Globerate, Horizon, Interhome, Martin Rooks, Phoenix, Pilgrim, Thomas Cook, Thomsons, Yugotours, Voyages Jules Verne
PULA	Cosmos, Globerate, Horizon, Inatours, Interhome, National Holidays, Phoenix, Pilgrim, Smiths-Shearings, Sunquest, Thomas Cook, Thomsons, Wallace Arnold, Wings OSL, Yugotours
MEDULIN	Balkan Tours, Enterprise, Intasun, Martin Rooks, Phoenix, Schoolplan, Thomsons, Yugotours
RABAC	Cosmos, Flair, Holiday Club International, Independent Coach Travel, Martin Rooks, Phoenix, Pilgrim, Success, Wings OSL, Yugotours
LOVRAN	Angela Holidays, Independent Coach Travel, Sovereign, Smiths-Shearings, Thomsons, Wallace Arnold, Yugotours
OPATIJA	Inatours, Inghams, Interhome, Martin Rooks, National Holidays, Phoenix, Pilgrim, Roman City, Saga, Smiths-Shearings, Sovereign, Thomsons, Wallace Arnold, Whites Tours, Yugotours
CRIKVENICA	Consort, Interhome, Freedom Travel, Inatours, Siesta International, Yugotours
NOVI VINODOLSKI	Yugotours
SELCE	Consort, Inatours

ZADAR	Interhome, Phoenix, Yugotours
PUNTA SKALA	Peng, Yugotours
BIOGRAD	Yugotours
PETRČANE	Yugotours
VODICE	Yugotours
ŠIBENIK	Phoenix, Yugotours
PRIMOŠTEN	Phoenix, Yugotours
KASTEL STARI	Phoenix
TROGIR	Phoenix, Yugotours
SPLIT	Phoenix, Yugotours
PODGORA	Saga, Yugotours
BRELA	Inatours, Phoenix, Yugotours, Thomas Cook
BAŠKA VODA	Yugotours, Inatours
MAKARSKA	Best Travel, Globerate, Inatours, Phoenix, Saga, Sincerely Yugoslavia, Thomsons, Yugotours
ZIVOGOŠĆE	Intasun
TUČEPI	Inatours, Phoenix, Saga, Sincerely Yugoslavia, Thomsons, Yugotours
OREBIĆ	Phoenix, Pilgrim, Yugotours
SLANO	Phoenix

DUBROVNIK	Club Adriatica, Enterprise, Fred Olsen Lines, Globerate, HF Holidays, Inatours UK, Intasun, Island Sailing, Martin Rooks, Page & Moy, P&O Cruises, Palmair, Phoenix, Pilgrim, Saga, Sovereign Yacht Cruising Assoc., Sunquest, Thomas Cook, Thomsons, Yugotours
SREBRENO	Martin Rooks, Palmair, Phoenix, Yugotours
MLINI	Phoenix, Pilgrim, Thomsons, Yugotours
PLAT	Phoenix, Pilgrim
CAVTAT	Globerate, Inatours, Palmair, Phoenix, Sincerely Yugoslavia, Thomsons, Yugotours
HERCEG NOVI	Balkan Tours, Enterprise, Phoenix, Pilgrim, Saga, Sunquest
BUDVA	Phoenix, Thomas Cook, Thomsons, Yugotours
KOTOR	Phoenix, Yugotours
BEČIĆI	Paradise, Phoenix, Tjaereborg, Yugotours
MILOČER	Pan Adriatic, Phoenix, Yugotours
SVETI STEFAN	Pan Adriatic, Phoenix, Sovereign, Yugotours, Thomas Cook, Thomsons
PETROVAC	Phoenix

SUTEMORE	Martin Rooks Holidays, Yugotours
ULCINJ	Yugotours

Islands

KRK	Freedom, Interhome, Yugotours
MALINSKA	Nat Holidays, National Holidays, Smiths-Shearings, Yugotours
NJIVICE	Yugotours
MALI LOSINJ	Interhome, Thomsons, Yugotours
VELI LOSINJ	Yugotours, Thomsons
OMISALJ	Success Tours, Yugotours
BAŠKA	Yugotours
RAB	Page & Moy, Yugotours
LOPAR	Yugotours
BOL	Yugotours
BRIONI	Pan Adriatic, Yugotours
HVAR	Phoenix, Saga, Yugotours
JELSA	Yugotours
STARIGRAD	Yugotours
VRBOSKA	Yugotours
KORČULA	Club Adriatica, Interhome, Page & Moy, Phoenix, Pilgrim, Yugotours
VELA LUKA	Interhome, Phoenix, Yugotours
LUMBARDA	Phoenix

KOLOČEP   Phoenix

LOPUD   Yugotours

Lakes and Mountains
BLED   Applegates Supreme Coaches,
                                  Cosmos, Enterprise, Freedom
                                  Travel, Global Continental, Inghams,
                                  Pan Adriatic, Panorama, Phoenix,
                                  Pilgrim, Raymond Cook, Saga,
                                  Sovereign, Thomsons, Travelsphere,
                                  Wallace Arnold, Yugotours

BOHINJ   Cotsworld, HF Holidays, Phoenix,
                                  Yugotours

KRANJSKA GORA   Enterprise, Freedom, Horizon,
                                  Inghams, Martin Rooks, Phoenix,
                                  Ramblers, Siesta, Wallace Arnold,
                                  Yugotours

BOVEC   HF Holidays, Page & Moy,
                                  Yugotours

PLITVICE   Phoenix, Yugotours

ŽABLJAK   Phoenix

KOPAONIK   Yugotours

CETINJE   Yugotours

OHRID   Phoenix

Coach Tours   Angela, Applegates, Club
                                  Cantabrica, Consort, Contiki,
                                  Cosmos, Cotsworld, Cotter,
                                  Crusader, Explore, Freedom, Global
                                  Continental, Happydays,
                                  Independent Coach Travel, Intasun,

Nat Holidays, National Holidays,
Pan Adriatic, Phoenix, Pilgrim, W.
Robinson, Saga, Shearings, Siesta,
Success, Sunquest, Swan Hellenic,
Tappins, Thomsons, Topdeck,
Trafalgar, Travelsphere, Trend
Tours, Wallace Arnold, Whites,
Yugotours

2 Centre Holidays

Cosmos, Horizon, Inatours,
Inghams, Intasun, Martin Rooks,
Page & Moy, Phoenix, Pilgrim, Saga,
Sovereign, Thomas Cook,
Thomsons, Wallace Arnold,
Yugotours

2 Centre 2 Country Holidays

Continental, Cosmos, Global,
Horizon, Intasun, Page & Moy,
Thomsons

Bare Boat Charter

Adriatic Cruising Club, Club
Adriatica, Island Sailing, Yugotours

Hunting, Shooting Holidays

Balkan Shoot

Fly-Drive Holidays

Enterprise, Pan Adriatic, Pilgrim,
Sincerely Yugoslavia, Thomsons,
Yugotours

Car Hire

Best Travel, Horizon, Phoenix,
Thomsons, Yugotours

Camping

Club Cantabrica, Eurocamp,
Intasun, Nat Holidays, National
Holidays, Top Deck, Wallace
Arnold, Yugotours

Motoring

Inghams, Nat Holidays, Pan
Adriatic, Phoenix

Pensions and Farmhouses

Pan Adriatic, Phoenix, Sincerely
Yugoslavia, Yugotours

Self-Catering	Club Adriatica, Holiday Club International, Interhome, Pan Adriatic, Phoenix, Pilgrim, Sincerely Yugoslavia, Yugotours
Cruises	P&O Cruises, Peng Travel, Pilgrim, Sincerely Yugoslavia, Swan Hellenic, Yugotours
City Holidays	Pan Adriatic, Yugotours
Flotilla Holidays	Island Sailing, Phoenix, Yacht Cruising Assoc.
Naturist Holidays	Inatours UK, Phoenix, Yugotours, Balkan Tours, Peng Travel
Budget Holidays	Cosmos, Phoenix, Yugotours
Horse Riding	Phoenix
Walking Holidays	HF Holidays, Ramblers, Waymark

We acknowledge the help of the Yugoslav Tourist Authority in the publication of this list.

Who Specializes in What

SELF-CATERING

Interhome offers self-catering accommodation but not package holidays (i.e. your travelling arrangements are your own responsibility). **Yugotours** and **Thomas Cook** do a good range of self-catering packages with a dozen different destinations and good facilities: and **Phoenix** offer accommodation of an equally high standard. **Pan Adriatic**, who specialize in independent holidays, enable you to put together your own individual package, and self-catering villas is one of the options they give.

As far as self-catering goes there are a few developments, mainly in Istria, but their standards are low and they are more suitable for large families or groups than couples. For further details ask the Yugoslavian National Tourist Office in London for their leaflet.

COST-CONSCIOUSNESS

Some of the cheapest holidays on offer are through **Pilgrim Holidays**. What makes their prices seem so reasonable is the fact that they offer full board on all their holidays, therefore once you've paid the cost of the holiday your only other expenses will be incidentals such as drinks and daytrips. Other budgetary alternatives are of the type offered by **Yugotours**, whereby you choose your destination but leave the final choice of hotel up to the tour operator's rep. If all you really want is two weeks of sun and rest, this is one way of saving a considerable amount of money. It is pot luck, though – you may be very fortunate and end up in a cancelled class B hotel or you may end up somewhere you would never have chosen yourself.

Among the other cost-conscious deals available are the packages offered by **Global Overland** and **Cosmos**. The former is a coach tour from the UK which takes in a stay of several days at a Yugoslav resort, while the latter is a tour based on a flight to Yugoslavia followed by a coach tour of the country.

For a basic two-week beach-based holiday, the advice is to shop around and remember that at the end of the day you basically get what you pay for. The extra £30 or so which companies like **Thomson** or **Horizon** charge generally results in a higher quality hotel. For a holiday with a difference consider the well-priced offer made by **Pan Adriatic** to fix you up an individual package based on private accommodation in a resort of your choice. They use guest houses inspected by the local tourist authorities and their prices reflect the bed and breakfast basis on which you stay.

Another way to reduce costs is to book at the last minute, taking pot luck on where you land. The Air Travel Advisory Bureau on 01-636 5000 or 061-832 2000 provides information on the best last-minute flight deals plus villas, apartments and hotels, and their service is free.

Finally, the direct-sell **Martin Rooks** (i.e. you won't find their brochure in a travel agent's, you'll have to phone them for it) offer extremely good value for money. Their holidays use very acceptable hotels and their prices are virtually unbeatable.

CAMPING

Yugotours offer reasonably priced air-package camping and caravan holidays. The only word of caution is to have a good read of the details of the sites, which they will send to you on request. Yugoslavian camp sites aren't all bad, but you could be disappointed if this is your first experience of a camping holiday. On-site conditions can be claustrophobic in peak season, but if you're a family it's one way of avoiding hefty hotel bills.

PRIVATE ACCOMMODATION

This can be a good compromise for someone who started out by wanting to go to Yugoslavia independently but was put off by the considerable hassles involved. By staying as a paying guest in someone's home you will get the authentic feel of living in the country with the benefits of your flight and accommodation being booked for you.

On request, **Pan Adriatic** can fix you up with this type of accommodation in numerous locations, and **Club Adriatica** offer apartments where you can do your own thing. This represents very good value and is an excellent compromise between a package and a completely independent type of holiday.

TWO-CENTRE HOLIDAYS

These are becoming increasingly popular in the travel industry, and in the case of Yugoslavia a two-centre holiday can mean several things: one week in the mountains with a second at the coast; or a week on an island with the second week at the coast or in a busy town such as Dubrovnik; or a week in one of the Holiday Club centres run by some of the larger tour operators with a second week independently at the coast.

The mountains/coast combination makes for a very varied and enjoyable holiday and is an excellent way of experiencing the diversity of the country. Two-centre holidays always cost a bit more than 'static' holidays, but the cost is rarely more than is necessary for the amount of travelling and the extra administration involved. As such these holidays represent very good value and are ideal as a compromise for those who like an active week (i.e. walking in the mountains) followed by a week of beach-bumming.

Many tour operators offer two-centre holidays: **Cosmos, Horizon, Inghams, Martin Rooks, Page & Moy Holidays, Phoenix Holidays, Pilgrim Holidays, Saga Holidays, Sovereign, Thomas Cook, Thomsons, Thomson Tours** and **Yugotours**.

COACH TOURS

These divide between coach tours which originate in Britain and travel by coach to, among other places, Yugoslavia; tours which start with a flight, then take in Yugoslavia by coach along with other countries, and tours of Yugoslavia only which begin after a flight from the UK. Coach tour holidays tend to have an OAP image and to a large degree that's deserved: the average age on a coach party is rarely less than fifty. But in Yugoslavia where car hire is so expensive and train travel is a non-starter, it does actually make a lot of sense, as it's an effective way of seeing a lot of the country (though having said that, coach holidays in fact are still relatively expensive). Tour operators offering internal Yugoslavian coach tours following a flight from the UK are: **Cosmos, Pan Adriatic, Phoenix Holidays, Thomas Cook, Thomson Tours** and **Yugotours**, while those who offer coach tours which include Yugoslavia among other countries and begin with a flight are: **Pan Adriatic, Thomson Tours**, and **Yugotours** (note Pan Adriatic do not include the flight in the tour).

Tour operators who run holidays travelling from Britain by coach which spend time in Yugoslavia, based at resorts, include: **Bebb Travel, Contiki, Cosmos, Cotters, Fairmont Travel, Freedom Travel, National Holidays, Smiths-Shearings, Success Tours** and **Top Deck Europe**.

'Grand tours', with exhaustive itineraries covering all the highlights of the country are still among the most popular coach tours, though the prices that these trips have to charge ensure a market of predominantly older, more affluent members of society. These tours, however, tend to be better fun than the cheaper ones which restrict themselves to the highlights of one particular region, where you get the feeling that the 'highlights' have been put into the itinerary more to fill in time than because they actually merit seeing.

At the opposite end of the market to the expensive, middle-aged coach tour holiday are the deals offered by the company **Trek Europa**.

They advertise themselves as offering 'tours for non-tourists': adventure tours for the twenties to thirty-eights. Included in the numerous holidays they offer are tours such as: 'The Explorer' which takes in the Dalmatian coast on its way to Bulgaria and Turkey; and 'Grand Tour Europa' which takes in eighteen countries in all, including Yugoslavia. It must be pointed out, though, that these touring holidays last seven and ten weeks, not two, and therefore they cannot be thought of in the same light as a 'normal' coach holiday. They are, however, well worth thinking about if you're a student or have the summer off and want to see a chunk of Europe in a reasonably organized way. Certainly, pricewise, you'd have a job doing it for less. Accommodation is under canvas and transport is a minibus, but if you're the hardy type this could be the holiday for you. **Contiki**, who are very highly regarded, and **Top Deck** are also aiming their holidays at this young market, so check out their brochures, too, if this is the type of trip you're interested in.

DRIVING HOLIDAYS

For those who cannot see themselves fitting into a stereotyped coach tour yet, and do not relish the prospect of flying, consider driving to your destination in Yugoslavia. **Inghams** have packaged driving holidays to various destinations, but, unless you really have a fear of flying, the cost of these packages decidedly outweighs the advantages, for they do not include en-route accommodation, what they term 'long sea crossings' (e.g., Portsmouth to Le Havre/Cherbourg, or Hull to Zeebrugge/Rotterdam), or Hoverspeed Services. Neither do they include the cost of petrol, personal insurance, motor insurance or meals en route. In short, all you do get for your two or three hundred pounds is your accommodation at the other end and your channel crossing, assuming it's one of the short ones. A more sensible option is to take a FLY/DRIVE package, such as one of those offered by Yugotours. This combines the advantages of a cheap flight with the freedom of a self-drive car at the other end.

HOLIDAY CLUBS

The past few years have seen the introduction of holiday clubs in the travel market and Yugoslavia is increasingly being chosen by tour operators as a club destination. The idea behind a holiday club is that all the facilities you're likely to need for your holiday – accommodation, entertainment, sporting facilities, childminder services etc. – are all offered in one large package by the tour operator, and everyone staying 'in the club' gets the chance of using these facilities free as part of the deal. What this in fact means is that many people never leave the confines of the club – which are usually hotel complexes or 'holiday villages'. Everything is laid on for you, making it really the ultimate packaged package holiday. If you're after a quiet time, away from the crowds, this type of holiday is definitely *not* for you (club holidays are notoriously sociable occasions as you're with the same group of holidaymakers for your entire holiday). If, however, you're travelling alone, or as a family with young children, this could be ideal.

Some tour operators specialize in the singles side of things, e.g. **Club 18–30**, while others concentrate more on the family holiday angle: **Phoenix** and **Yugotours**. The Phoenix facilities, particularly in the Argosy in Dubrovnik, are particularly good.

Holiday Club International, which specialize in holiday clubs in several countries, offer a choice of holidays in Yugoslavia which could suit either the young set or the family.

If you plump for a young, good-time holiday club, expect a good many discos, parties, boozy evenings and silly games. These holidays are strictly for the gregarious. They can be great fun if you're in the mood but you must like that sort of thing or there'll be a holiday disaster.

Bear in mind that Club Med and Club 18–30 are aiming at two entirely different markets. **Club Med** is decidedly upmarket; the facilities in their holiday villages far outstrip any other holiday club's, and this is reflected in their prices. The Club Med experience is a most enjoyable one, with every possible thing you can think of, apart from drinks at the bar, included in the overall price. In Yugoslavia they offer two international villages (originally Club Med was a purely French outfit, catering for the French market, with French as the main language etc.). These clubs are at Pakoštane, on the Dalmatian coast, and at Sveti Marko, near the southern coast. In both these villages English is spoken and the clientèle is of no dominant ethnic group. You will most likely find British, French, Germans and

Italians sitting at your dinner table, and the exercise is a shining example of good international relations.

Sporting activities are at their best, and among the range you can choose from are, at Sveti Marko: waterskiing, boating, sailing, windsurfing, kayak, tennis, petanque, volleyball, table tennis, gymnastics, archery, aerobics, boat trips and snorkelling. At Pakoštane there is: sailing, waterskiing, pontoons, snorkelling, swimming, kayak, boat trips, gymnastics, judo and aerobics. All sports are free and qualified instruction is available.

Excursions to local places of interest are offered from both clubs. From Pakoštane this includes the lakes of Plivice, and accommodation in both villages is in straw huts. The food is of very high quality, and wine is provided, free, with every meal. Entertainments are laid on nightly, and within the villages are all the facilities that one could want for the full holiday experience.

Club 18–30, on the other hand, make no pretences – they offer fun holidays for young people and in order to keep their prices within the range of most young people's budgets they don't go in for terribly exotic locations or accommodations. They have clubs just outside Dubrovnik, at Srebreno and at neighbouring Mlini.

At the other end of the scale, **Yugotours** offer holidays under their 'Golden Age' section for those over fifty-five. These holidays aren't so much in the organized 'club' mould, but concentrate more on hotels where you won't be confronted with discos and midnight frolics in the pool at every turn. **Saga** also run holidays for this age group.

CRUISES

Yugotours offer various cruises from luxury trips taking in Yugoslavia, Turkey and Greece to island hopping off the Adriatic coast in a beautiful sailing schooner. The cruises are competitively priced and have the added attraction of combining a week's beach holiday with a week's cruising. **Horizon** offer a brief stay in Yugoslavia (Dubrovnik) as part of their 'La Palma' cruise; and **Club Adriatica** offer skippered cruises on several stretches of the Adriatic. **P&O** are the big name to watch out for. They offer fly/cruises and plain cruises which include Yugoslavia in their itineraries. The brochures to get hold of are Swan

Hellenic Cruises, Canberra and Sea Princess. P&O offer quality but are not cheap. **Peng Travel** offer naturist cruises.

SAILING

The following tour operators all operate sailing holidays in Yugoslavia.

(1) Flotilla holidays – **Island Sailing, Phoenix Holidays, Seven Seas Sailing** and **Yacht Cruising Association**.

(2) Boats for charter – **Adriatic Cruising Club, Club Adriatica, Phoenix Holidays, Seven Seas Sailing, Falcon** and **Yacht Cruising Association**.

(3) Sailing courses – **Phoenix Holidays** and **Seven Seas Sailing. Club Adriatica** offer aqualung diving, a children's snorkelling course and windsurfing courses.

NATURIST HOLIDAYS

Holidays at completely naturist centres and beaches are offered by **Eden Holidays, Peng Travel, Phoenix Holidays, Yugotours** and **Balkan Tours**. (For further information on naturism in Yugoslavia see 'The Naturist' section on page 25.)

SPECIAL INTEREST/ACTIVITY HOLIDAYS

HF Holidays Ltd organize walking holidays in Yugoslavia, as do **Ramblers Holidays** and **Waymark Holidays**. **Pan Adriatic** offer riding holidays; **Balkan Shoot Ltd** offer shooting holidays. **Ornitholidays** run bird-watching holidays based at Petrovac in Montenegro. **Club Adriatica** are the main tour operators to consider for a water sports holiday in Yugoslavia (aqualung diving, snorkelling, etc.). **Pan Adriatic** will organize tailor-made packages for you on request. **Panorama Holidays** run rail holiday packages in the Slovenian Mountains. **Threshold Travel** organize holidays in Yugoslavia suitable for the physically handicapped.

SUMMING UP

To sum up, then, on the Yugoslavia package holiday scene: almost without exception, the packages are good value; however it is still definitely worth your while to shop around and get hold of as many brochures as possible before finally making up your mind. Some tour operators undoubtedly are aiming their holidays at the higher price range (**Thomson's à la Carte** and Coach tours, **P&O**, **Inghams**, **Ornitholidays**), while some concentrate on the young, good-time set (**Club 18–30, Club Med, Trek Europa, Contiki**). **Yugotours** are the undisputed market leader so it is worth getting their brochure and checking their prices first. They cater for all markets and offer the best holidays. They, **Phoenix** and **Pilgrim**, are the main specialist companies for general holidays to Yugoslavia. **Club Adriatica** specialize in sailing holidays specifically in Yugoslavia and **Pan Adriatic** are the main operators for independent-style holidays in Yugoslavia.

With the decline of Spain and the relative expense of Greece as holiday destinations, it is likely that Yugoslavia's rise in popularity will continue and result in more tour operators entering the Yugoslav packaged holiday market. The extra competition should ensure good prices for the tourist for the next few years, and the favourable position of the pound over the dinar should act as a further safeguard to ensure Yugoslavia remains a reasonably priced holiday destination.

As far as the different types of holidays available are concerned: for a naturist holiday you'll be hard pushed to find a better destination than Yugoslavia, primarily because it's been specializing in naturism longer than any other country and therefore the facilities and correct attitude towards naturism exist there. For a two-centre holiday Yugoslavia is also an ideal choice because of the diversity of the mountain resorts and the beaches. The prices for two-centre holidays are particularly good in Yugoslavia when you compare them with other countries.

Camping and coach tour holidays require a little more thought. Peak-season camping in Yugoslavia can be a bit fraught and the facilities are rarely up to Northern European standards. As for coach tours – unless it's the Grand Tour of the country you're going for, they do tend to be quite expensive and tiring. Also roads in Yugoslavia – particularly in the south – leave much to be desired.

Sailing holidays are as good in Yugoslavia as anywhere else and are often more reasonably priced because of the favourable rate of exchange; and activity holidays, such as walking in the mountains and National Parks, are all better in Yugoslavia because, as yet, few people have discovered the joys of this type of holiday in this scenic area of Europe. Virtually all beach holidays, whether they be on islands or the mainland, self-catering hotel or holiday-club-based, offer exceptional value for money at present. The main thing to watch out for is the description in the brochure of the beach, many of which are shingle or man-made. (For further information read 'The Sun Worshipper' section on page 23.)

Checklist

As a final reminder to anyone taking a package holiday anywhere, check the following points before booking:

(1) Is your travel agent competent? Unfortunately many are not, and all too often it's the large chains of High Street agents who give the worst advice and service. Try to avoid the obvious trainees when you go into the shop, and have a list of questions prepared so that you don't end up having to make several trips when one would do.

(2) Is your travel agent a member of ABTA? If not, think seriously about finding one who is. There are plenty of them who are, and membership could make a big difference to you if things start to go wrong.

(3) Having chosen your country of destination, do you really know about all the packages available on the market? Many of the smaller tour operators do not get their brochures into the High Street travel agents but that does not mean their holidays aren't reliable or worth checking out. Check against the list on page 68 and phone for a brochure from any likely looking company.

(4) If the travel agent can't book the holiday you finally selected, don't necessarily accept his/her substitute recommendation. Have your own second and third options sorted out beforehand; or if there really

is no substitute, leave the whole idea and consider something completely different. Remember that travel agents are in the business of selling holidays for commissions – unscrupulous agents often don't much care what they sell, but they do like to clinch a sale before you leave the shop.

(5) As for the holiday itself, check the following before paying your deposit:

(i) Does the holiday price include all airport or port taxes and security charges (for both the UK and abroad)?

(ii) Does it include meals on the journey?

(iii) Is it extra for a weekend flight or a daytime departure?

(iv) Is transfer between the point of arrival and your hotel included?

(v) Be sure you know on what basis you are booked in at the hotel, i.e. full/half board/b & b.

(vi) Are you clear about supplementary charges made for single rooms/balcony/sea view/private bathroom etc.?

(vii) Is the insurance sufficient for you? Does it cover pregnant women/disabled people/people going on sports holidays? Is the limit on personal baggage high enough to cover all you are taking? Does it include a clause on delayed departure for your return journey? What provisions does it make for cancellations? Finally, check you're clear about the procedure in case a theft or loss does occur – often these matters have to be reported within a specified time limit and a police report procured.

(6) And finally, before handing over your money, ask:

(i) What is the position on cancellations (from both parties' point of view).

(ii) What happens if your holiday needs to be altered significantly – under the ABTA code you must be told and given the choice of accepting either the new hotel/resort/flight, etc., or a full refund. (Alterations caused by bad weather or industrial disputes will only be covered by your insurance.)

(iii) What's the score on overbooking? Is there a 'disturbance' compensation to be paid (there should be under the ABTA code); will the alternative accommodation be of an equally high standard (it must be under the ABTA code).

Once you have gone through all these points you should have a clear understanding of the contract you are signing, and your travel agent will undoubtedly be in such awe of your intimate knowledge of the travel industry that you will receive preferential treatment all the way!

If, despite all this good groundwork, you still have cause for complaint, ABTA's address is 55–57 Newman Street, London W1N 4AH. Write to them with full details of your complaint and enclose copies of all your correspondence with the travel agent or tour operator.

Independent Means

The Options

If you are determined to go it alone to Yugoslavia there are several options open to you. Getting there need not be too harrowing if you take advantage of the cheap flights coming on to the market thanks to the tour operators' increasing penetration of the charter air market, but you'll have to do a lot of homework and hard thinking about accommodation. Hotels are expensive. They range from around 19,350D to 184,900D for a double room, with an average one costing 28,000D. Hotels in the north (Istria) tend to be slightly cheaper than in the south. Add up the cost of a 14-night stay, taking into account your travelling costs and you'll see why packages make sense. The reason why hotels are expensive is that hotel prices are fixed in US dollars or in Deutsche Marks, rather than in dinars.

The alternatives to hotels: independent, self-catering, hostels, camping and private accommodation don't offer much more hope. Certainly they are far cheaper alternatives, but the standards fluctuate dramatically. Of the three, private accommodation (called 'sobe') is the best option. Rooms are officially inspected and graded into three categories. There are three ways you can get yourself into a private room in a house: (1) you can book it this end through some tour operators (see the 'Private Accommodation' section on page 104) or by writing yourself to one of the places that do it (address from Yugoslavian National Tourist Office in London); (2) you can accept the offer of a local guesthouse-owner once you get to the other end – if you want to be approached, hang around the nearest main station when one of the main trains are due and you'll see the people with rooms to let touting for business (though often these rooms have not been officially inspected by the tourist authorities); or (3) if that sounds too much of a risk, once you're over there go to one of the travel agencies such as Atlas, Generalturist, Kompas and Kvarner Express and ask them to book you into a *sobe*. They will charge a small commission, but it saves wrestling with sign language and bartering. The local tourist office will also find a bed for you for a small fee, but often they are keener to fill their hotels than private guest houses, so be insistent. The average cost of a room in a private house should be around 15,000D without any meals.

As for camping and hostelling, campsites are numerous, particularly on the coast, but they can be very busy in high season and facilities vary widely. An average cost is 4500D-5000D per person and 3000D per tent. Youth hostels cost approximately 2500D per night and also vary dramatically in their standards. Student hostels (*Studentskidom*) are often to be found in university towns. They tend to be better than youth hostels, cost around 3000D and are rarely busy. They have less regulations to spoil your fun and don't insist on you being a student to stay.

The final alternative for accommodation on a freelance basis is to check out the Sunday papers for private villas and apartments coming up for let. Check you get all the details before accepting, and insist on a recent photo of the place and full inventory before making your final commitment.

So much for the independent accommodation scene. Now let's turn our attentions to the methods of travelling to Yugoslavia.

By Air

If you're travelling by air, your first move should be to visit a good travel agent and gather as much information as possible on the different types of flight available. Unless money is no object, you'll realize there's no way you want to splash out the full £650 plus cost of a JAT (Yugoslav Airlines) scheduled flight, so it'll be down to scouring the charter deals and Sunday papers. An APEX ticket requires 14 days minimum advance booking and gives you no flexibility on your dates, flights, etc. (i.e. once booked it can't be changed). The fare from London to Dubrovnik will cost approximately £180. PEX fares have similar conditions but do not require advance purchase. A charter flight from one of the companies operating packages will be about half that. The sort of companies who offer cheap air fares to Yugoslavia are the big tour operators – **Horizon**, **Thomson**, **Cosmos** and **Intasun** – but generally they only offer flights to the larger airports such as Pula, Split or Dubrovnik. Often the flights are on weekdays and include a minimal basic accommodation (i.e. dormitory beds in a hostel) to get round the law on the sale of Inclusive Air Holidays to Europe. What this actually means is that on paper included in the price of your flight is some form of very basic accommodation (so the company can legally claim that they are selling you a package holiday consisting of travel and accommodation). In reality though, in the case of Yugoslavia, you usually have to let the accommodation back to the tour operator by signing a Property Letting Agreement (which will appear as a small box on your booking form). So basically, what this means is that you have no accommodation but you still manage to benefit from the cheap flights enjoyed by those going on a proper package holiday.

Undoubtedly this is one of the cheapest and easiest ways of getting to Yugoslavia (particularly if you don't have to let the accommodation back to the tour operator and you choose to use it basic or not), and as more tour operators begin to expand their interests in the country the number of operators offering cheap charter tickets should increase. It is only good, of course, for those who want to base their independent holiday at the coast or near to where package holidaymakers will be located for no such discounts will apply on flights to Belgrade, Zagreb or Ljubljana, or parts of the country where the package-tour operators don't go.

Bucket shops and Sunday newspaper advertisements offer other alternate ways of finding out about cheap flights to Yugoslavia, but read the small print carefully. You're unlikely to come up with any cheaper way of going than the tour operator charter flight anyway.

Note – on charter flights run by tour operators flight delays are not uncommon, and if you're a non-smoker it's advisable to book in early as there are fewer non-smoker seats than smokers.

By Rail

As author of the guide *Europe by Train* and one who has spent many months travelling Yugoslavia by train, I feel suitably qualified to pass on the advice not to attempt the journey to the depths of Yugoslavia from the UK by train before giving it a good deal of thought. Not only is it likely to work out expensive (unless you're under 26 and are therefore entitled to an Inter Rail card – available from British Rail – or a BIJ ticket – available from Transalpino or Eurotrain), but it will be a long and exhausting journey which will leave you tired and disillusioned with humanity for a while to come. (Actually it needn't be the horror story I'm making out, but unless you're travelling first class on a straight-through journey with sleepers, and not in peak season, it's likely to be.)

The direct route from London to Split is on the Tauern Express train, which runs from Ostend to Stuttgart, Munich, Klagenfurt, Ljubljana, Zagreb and Split on the coast. There is no direct rail link to Yugoslavia from the British channel ports. To get to Ostend as quickly as possible leave Victoria Station in London at 15.58 and take the Dover–Ostend Jetfoil which will connect with the Tauern Express which leaves Ostend at 21.10. (Try to get a couchette or sleeper for the overnight journey to Germany.) You arrive in Ljubljana at 17.45 the next afternoon, Zagreb at 22.30 and, after another overnight haul, you finally make it to Split at 06.25 the following morning. There is a restaurant car from Munich to Villach and light snacks are available throughout the Belgian, German and Austrian parts of the journey. Once you enter Yugoslavia, however, the catering service becomes more sporadic.

If your destination within Yugoslavia is Belgrade or if you have to travel via the capital, your best option is the Simplon Express, which goes from London via Paris and Milan to Belgrade. The only snag with the Simplon Express is the change of station required in Paris – you arrive at Paris Nord and have to leave from Paris Gare du Lyon (take line B on the metro to Chatelet les Halles, then line A to Lyon). Getting from London to Paris is no problem: the quickest link is the rail/hovercraft one leaving Charing Cross Station at 11.00 and arriving at Paris (Nord) at 17.41. Alternatively there's the 09.58 from Victoria which takes you to Dover for the Calais ferry and connects on to the Paris train which gets you to the French capital by 18.25. For those on a tight budget there is the option of the Hoverspeed coach service from Russell Square, London – leaves 08.45 – to Paris in time for the 18.55 departure of the Simplon Express from Gare du Lyon. Your route is overnight to Venice (try for a couchette or sleeper), then Trieste, Ljubljana, Zagreb and on to Belgrade, where you arrive 23.10 that night. The restaurant car runs from Paris to Dole and from Ljubljana to Belgrade. This service operates all year.

An alternative which runs in the summer is the 13.58 direct service from London Victoria to Calais Maritime which carries straight on to Venice, where it arrives around 3 p.m. the next afternoon. You then board the Venezia Express which gets you into Ljubljana at midnight or carries on to Belgrade for 08.40 the next morning.

There are still other international expresses to Belgrade but they originate in countries which are complicated to connect up with from London.

To get to Dubrovnik from Britain by rail is an even more complicated affair as it requires a two-hour bus transfer from Kardeljevo, the nearest station to Dubrovnik.

Whichever route you opt for, reservations are strongly advised, as are sleeping arrangements and prepacked food for the journey.

The 1988 price for a second-class return from London to Split is £230.10 (£328.10 first class), and £187.90 return in second class from London to Belgrade (£268.70 first class).

As these prices are on a par with most air excursion tickets (and are actually more than most charter options), think carefully about the amount of time and effort you're expending just for the journey. Really, unless you come in for the under-26 cheap tickets or are looking on the train trip as part of your holiday, you ought to drop the idea of travelling by train to your destination in Yugoslavia.

By Bus

If the train journey to Yugoslavia is bad, you can be sure the bus/coach journey on an independent basis is even worse. Because the main market for this is the young, backpacking brigade and they are usually also eligible for Inter Rail and cheap train tickets, the choice of bus services from the UK to Yugoslavia is virtually nil. It's slightly better once you actually get over the channel and further into Europe (i.e. from France, Germany) but even then the discomfort and length of journey make this a trip to be undertaken only by the stalwart. Most of the bus companies running from Britain go to Greece via Yugoslavia.

Europabus have a couple of routes which take in Yugoslavia: one originates in Ostend, the other in Munich.

By Car/Campervan

Again, the motorist faces a long and tiring journey, particularly in mid-summer. Motoring to Yugoslavia can, however, be a relatively cheap way of getting there, especially if three or four of you are sharing the driving and petrol costs (an average 30-hour journey to Dubrovnik from London will cost roughly £200 one way in petrol in a medium-sized car). Your route obviously depends on your location within Yugoslavia, but as a general guide, if you're heading for the Dalmatia coast your best route is to drive across France to Basel in Switzerland, then take the St Gotthard road tunnel, into Italy, and you head for Trieste, where you cross into Yugoslavia (two to three days). If, however, you're travelling south or inland to Belgrade or Zagreb, you're best to head for Belgium, Germany and Austria and enter Yugoslavia from an Austrian frontier. One of the nicest and quickest routes is to enter over the Wurzen Pass which leads on to Kranjska Gora. Alternatively the Ljubelj tunnel, which connects Klagenfurt to Trzickranj, is a good run; or from Graz to Maribor is also a major point of entry. Entry to Yugoslavia via the Wurzen Pass is not recommended for caravanners due to the hairpin bends and steep gradients involved. Travel instead briefly into Italy by taking the road around the mountain, follow the signs from Tarvisio to the less frequented border crossing of Rateče where the scenery is spectacular, then you immediately enter the Triglav National Park. Alternatively, at Tarvisio take the route which joins up the autostrada to Trieste. The signs for the Trieste bypass are not terribly clear, but follow the Pula signs and you won't go far wrong.

There are several other alternatives – all of which are detailed in the leaflet 'Comfortably and Safely by Car and Coach in Yugoslavia', available from the Yugoslavian National Tourist Office. (Also ask for the Jugoslavija Travel Info. booklet.)

To enter Yugoslavia by car you'll need the following documentation and equipment:

a valid driving licence (an international driving licence is not required)
car registration papers
the Green Card (international insurance certificate)
red reflector warning triangle in case of breakdown
first aid kit
spare set of light bulbs

Drive and give way on the right. The major roads in Yugoslavia are asphalt, but there are still many secondary roads of poor quality. Be careful about overtaking on narrow, winding roads in rural areas: donkeys and carts are still quite commonplace, and many older people often wander in the middle of the road in their village.

Speed limits are 60km in town, 120km on motorways, 100km on major roads and 80km on all other roads. Caravans must not exceed 80km per hour. Speeding offences may be dealt with by on-the-spot fines by the traffic police.

Petrol can be bought in two grades: premium (86 octane) and superior (98 octane). Diesel is also available. Petrol for tourists can be bought with coupons which offer you a reduced rate. You buy the coupons from your national automobile association or a travel agency. Alternatively, you can purchase them at the Yugoslav frontier on entry to the country. Unused coupons can be traded back when you leave. It is also possible now to buy petrol for cash, but you'd be unwise to do this as you lose your 10 per cent tourists' reduction.

Everyone has their own preference when it comes to a driving holiday, but speaking as someone who has driven on the Continent in everything from a Daimler limousine to a battered old Mini, I feel it's worth putting in a word here about what to look for when choosing a car to drive abroad in. Obviously luggage capacity is an important consideration. Fuel economy, spare parts and comfort are the other major considerations. Don't try to squeeze too many people into a car, and remember, you'll return with more than you set out with. When we were researching this section of the guide we used our Vauxhall Carlton 2LGL Saloon, which over any other car we'd tried gave us the best in terms of comfort, room and efficiency. It's worth bearing in mind if you intend doing a lot of holiday motoring, or if you're in a position to hire one. A car with a bit of extra power is well worth having on long journeys – and safer.

Hitch-Hiking

This option is only for the hardy. It's impossible to say how long it would take to get from Britain to Yugoslavia, but don't count on taking less than five days to get to the Yugoslavian coast from Britain.

Within Yugoslavia hitch-hiking is not illegal except on parts of the main 'autoput', but it isn't easy. Most of the locals' cars are loaded whenever they travel and the competition with other hitch-hikers is fierce. The route down the Adriatic coast is easier to hitch than the autoput (for obvious reasons), but even that can be difficult in peak season. It's easier travelling from south to north than vice versa. In the 'outback' you can be stuck for days, and as it's technically illegal to camp except in officially approved campsites, you'll find the going pretty tough.

By Sea

There's no direct route from the UK to Yugoslavia by sea. If you wish to travel by sea you'll have to consider the cruise options available –

see 'Cruises' on page 108. Alternatively, you can make your way to Trieste or Venice in Italy and sail from there across the Adriatic to Dubrovnik and other ports in Yugoslavia. From Ancona on the Italian Adriatic coast there are three- or four-day cruises to Yugoslav ports and in the summer months car ferries go from Ancona, Bari, Pescara and Venice to Pula, Zadar, Split, Dubrovnik and Bar. Details of all these services can be found in the *Thomas Cook Continental Timetable*.

As a direct way of getting to Yugoslavia, however, this must come low down on the list. It's neither cheap nor convenient, but if you really want to include sea travel in your journey, drive to Italy and use one of the ferry services from there to Yugoslavia.

Generally Useful Information

TIME DIFFERENCES

Yugoslavia keeps to Central European Time (GMT + 1), therefore in summer there is no time difference between Yugoslavia and Great Britain. (New York is five hours behind.) In winter Yugoslavia stays on Central European Time, while British (and US) clocks are turned back one hour, therefore Yugoslavia is one hour ahead.

ELECTRICITY

The voltage in Yugoslavia is 220 volt, 50 cycle AC (American appliances need transformers and plug adaptors).

WATER

The water is safe to drink but if you've a delicate stomach stick to bottled mineral water (*mineralna voda*) as the change in mineral content from your own water could upset your stomach.

Part Three

WHEN YOU'RE THERE

Tourist Information

There are tourist offices (called Drusno or Turisticko) in all major cities, towns and resorts. While they are helpful on the region or resort you are in, they are often unable to give out information on other areas of the country, so collect all this from the Yugoslav National Tourist Office in London, or from one of the larger tourist offices, i.e. in Dubrovnik/Belgrade/Split. The sort of tourist literature available once you're over there is fairly good and adequate for the average tourist but if you're undertaking a specific type of holiday (like mountaineering, sailing, touring by car), you'd be well advised to write ahead of your trip to the National Office in London asking for specific leaflets about your type of holiday. Often the offices in Yugoslavia run out of certain leaflets in peak season, and you end up with the German or French version of the pamphlet, which can be somewhat frustrating. English is quite widely spoken and you'd be very unlucky not to find one person in a Tourist Office with a degree of fluency in it.

As far as publications go, the Yugoslav Tourist Office is very good at producing maps, but their literature on the main sights of the regions leaves a bit to be desired.

Most of the tourist offices in Yugoslavia will arrange, for a small commission, accommodation in local hostels and guest houses within their area. Their opening hours fluctuate, but the larger offices are open long hours: 8 a.m. to 8 p.m. in peak season is not uncommon.

If you want to indulge in some particular type of tour or excursion once you're in Yugoslavia it's often better to go to one of the larger Yugoslav travel agents, as opposed to the Tourist Office. The best advice is to visit an agent whose head office is located in the region you wish to visit. Some of the larger travel agents are:

Atlas, Pile 1, 5000 Dubrovnik	Tel: 27-333
Centroturist, Bulevar Revolucije 70, 11000 Belgrade	Tel: 451-142
Dalmacijaturist, Titova Obala 5, 58000 Split	Tel: 44-666
Generalturist, Praska 5, 41000 Zagreb	Tel: 446-222
Globtur, Smartinska 130, 61000 Ljubljana	Tel: 213-832
Interimpev, Ivo Ribar Lola 10, 91000 Skopje	Tel: 228-644
Intours, Mitra Brkica 1, 81000 Titograd	Tel: 33-010
Kvarner Express, Maršala Tita 186, 51410 Opatija	Tel: 711-111
Montenegroturist, 81310 Budra	Tel: 41-697
Srbija-Turist, Vozclova 12, 18000 Nis	Tel: 22-077
Unis Turist, Moricahan, Saraci 77, 71000 Sarajevo	Tel: 534-200

Sightseeing

Away from the historic picturesque towns of the Dalmatian coast, Yugoslavia is not really on a par with Britain, France or Italy in the sightseeing stakes. The natural scenery of the mountainous regions is undeniably attractive, but as far as man-made sights go, you won't get anywhere better than the old walled city of Dubrovnik (see 'The Sightseer' section on page 27). Because of this, Yugoslavia is not the ideal destination for a car-based sightseeing tour of the country, though if you know where to look there are many little-known sights of interest which are all the better for their lack of commercialism and overexposure. The specific sights of each area of the country are highlighted in the relevant chapter later in the book.

Museums, galleries and recognized 'sights' usually make a small nominal charge, have no uniform opening hours (where known they will be listed with details of the sights in the text) and often close as a matter of routine one day per week. A 1–4 p.m. siesta is not unusual, and some 'sights' keep to these hours. Invariably in the case of towns and cities all the sights are grouped together in the old quarter of the city, which makes getting around them on foot easy.

One entertaining form of sightseeing is to attend the summer festivals which occur in numerous parts of the country in the summer months. Many events are held out of doors and are free. For timings and locations see 'The Socialite' on page 29.

Shopping

Shops are open, on average, 8 a.m.–12 noon and 4–7 p.m. Monday to Friday, and 8 a.m.–2 p.m. Saturday. Increasingly, self-service stores and the larger department stores are not closing at lunchtime, and some are even opening on Sunday mornings. Food shops open even earlier, many opening in two shifts, 5.30–9.30 a.m. and 4–7 p.m. Some are opening Sunday mornings.

Good buys in Yugoslavia include leather, wooden items and woollens in Slovenia, wool carpets and rugs from Serbia and filigree work: these are among the best bargains and most popular souvenirs on offer. Prices are fixed except in markets. Some shops give a 10 per cent discount if you pay by foreign currency or with dinar or travellers' cheques.

Don't expect too much in the way of grand department stores. Even in Dubrovnik or Belgrade there's no equivalent of Harrods, and the choice of goods can be a bit limited.

Food and Drink

Much of what you're offered will depend upon which part of the country you're in. In Slovenia food has an Austrian influence, around the Adriatic the Italian flavour is strong, while in Bosnia and Macedonia Turkish cuisine dominates the local offerings. In Northern Croatia and Serbia tasty Hungarian influences can be detected and it's generally thought that Serbian cuisine offers the most scope in the way of regional dishes. Standards vary dramatically, as they do in any country, but in general, though Yugoslavia can hardly be said to rival French or Italian cuisine, you will still be offered tasty and filling fare. The secret is to hunt out a good local family-run restaurant – preferably not too much of a tourist trap – and stick to it.

Looking then in more detail at what you can expect, starting with breakfast: most hostels will offer a standard continental breakfast of tea/coffee (stick to the coffee unless you're fond of insipid, brown water) with bread and jam. You can also get eggs (usually hard-boiled unless you state otherwise). Their bread is generally very tasty and will come crusty and warm from the oven if you're in a small resort with a local baker. British breakfasts (bacon and eggs, etc.), however, are not usually found. If you're based in the centre or south of the country, check whether the coffee on offer is Turkish, which is extremely strong and sweet. If it is, and this isn't to your taste, invest in some instant coffee (preferably brought from home) and simply ask for boiling water (*topla voda*). As an alternative the hot chocolate on offer is generally good (though you may feel a little odd drinking this at breakfast time) or try their lemon tea, which for some reason tastes just like the British version. Your own teabags to strengthen the local brew are another alternative.

Lunch and dinner are the main meals of the day and you can choose from a variety of establishments to eat them in: a '*bife*' is a cafeteria/snack bar which serves mainly sandwiches, salads and drinks. Not really recommended unless you're counting the pennies. An *expres restoran* is a larger version of the 'bife'. It offers a limited number of dishes (hot and cold) on a self-service arrangement. They can be a bit rough and ready, though undoubtedly they are cheap. A *mlecni restoran* is basically a dairy which sells pastries, yoghurts and some bakery which can usually be consumed with a drink of milk or drinking yoghurt on the premises. A *kafana* is basically a café serving alcoholic drinks as well as snacks, meals and beverages. A *slasticarna* is like an ice-cream parlour which will also sell cakes, pastries and coffee. A *kenoba* is a wine cellar which will usually also serve a snack, and a *restoran* is any form of restaurant (it includes the word 'riblji' in its title if it is a fish restaurant).

The chances are that you'll spend most of your time in a *restoran* of some form, or in a *gostiona* which is a family-run inn. These really are your best bet for wholesome, authentically prepared cuisine combined with atmosphere and a favourable bill at the end.

In hotels breakfast is usually served between 7 and 9 a.m., lunch is from noon to 2 p.m. and dinner from 7 to 9 p.m. As a rule the more developed the resort, the later dinner will be available in the restaurants. By law prices must be on the menu or posted outside. There should not be a service charge added to your bill, but a tip of 5–10 per cent is customary. Tourist menus (*turisticki meni*) are available in tourist resorts and usually represent very good value. If you're on half board, check if the meal is flexible or if it must be taken as the evening meal.

As for the food itself, the Yugoslavs eat a lot of meat. Dishes with generous portions of lamb, veal and mutton are common and much is made of vegetables. The meat is usually well cooked but good beef is very difficult to find. On the coast fish and seafood are good, and salads are invariably excellent. Stuffed tomatoes, marrows and paprikas are widely eaten, and about the only difference between lunch and dinner (both of which are pretty massive three-course meals) is that soup is served as the first course to lunch but rarely to dinner. Soups are particularly tasty, especially in Serbia where delicious Hungarian recipes are used. On the Istrian coast pasta dishes can be found and meat is often charcoal-grilled. Some of the most widely available specialities to look out for are:

Cevapčiči – spiced meatballs
Ražnjiči – souvlaki/kebab-type offerings
Sarma – mince and rice in vine leaves or sauerkraut
Bureks – meat or cheese pasties
Bosanski Ionac – Bosnian stew

Cheeses are a bit disappointing by British or French standards but most regions produce their own local cheese. In Yugoslavia they are usually eaten as a first course rather than to finish the meal.

Dessert is usually either fresh fruit or cake. Pancakes are popular in the north and Turkish sweet flaky pastry concoctions can be found in Bosnia and Macedonia. Often ice-cream and pastries are best bought in specialist shops rather than taken as your dessert in a restaurant, where the quality and freshness can be less good.

Of course, if you've chosen to stay in an international-type hotel, in theory you need never eat any of the local specialities and can stay on a diet unchanged from home for the duration of your holiday. If you do, though, you'll miss out on a very important and enjoyable aspect of your trip to Yugoslavia.

As far as drinks are concerned, Yugoslav wines are excellent – far better than those you may have bought at home, for the Yugoslavs rarely export their best – they keep it in the country, so now's your chance. Wines are very reasonably priced in restaurants and are often cheaper when bought in shops or wine cellars.

Local wines (house wines) are ordered simply by their colour:

'*crno*' is the red, '*belo*' is the white, and '*ruzica*' is rosé. Often they are served in jugs of various sizes. The more widely known wines are Riesling, Traminer, Pinot and Teran from Slovenia; Refosk from Istria; Omis and Opal in Split and Bakarska Vodica, a sparkling wine found on the Croatian coast. Zilavka is a dry white from Herzegovina, and Kavadarka is a rich heavy red from Macedonia. Grk from the island of Korčula is a strong white. You'll find that most of the islands produce their own wines. The list of Yugoslav wines is endless, but rest assured you're bound to find one to suit your tastebuds and pocket before you've been there too long.

The news on beer is not so good. The local stuff (which resembles lager) is a bit of an acquired taste, though it's not all bad and the imported brew is relatively inexpensive. Fruit juices are very good value – Fructol is a particularly good brand and represents excellent value (and much better for you than carbonated drinks).

As for liquors, Istra Bitter is a mild herbal aperitif which is quite acceptable and far cheaper than the imported spirits and aperitifs. Rakija is the generic name for all brandies – Sljivovica Rakija is plum brandy and Yugoslavia's most famous liquor, while Maraskino is a liquor made from morello cherries. All Yugoslav spirits are very strong and tend to be drunk at any time of the day, not just after meals. Three other well known liquors are Vinjak – a type of cognac – and the spiced spirits Mastika and Pelinkovac.

Food and drink are very competitively priced in Yugoslavia. It's possible to eat a snack-type lunch for around 6000D and to have a fully cooked meal for around 10,000D. A three-course meal with wine will cost around 14,000D a head, with wine at about 4000D for a decent bottle. Local beer and spirits cost around 2000–4000D, as do fruit juices. Coffee is around 2000D.

For those on a self-catering holiday food prices are very reasonable, but the variety is not so staggering. There are very few good food supermarkets and cold meats, cheeses and savouries can be hard to find. Invariably the cafés serve only drinks, so get your picnic together first if you feel like a snack. The open-air markets will provide you with all the fruit and vegetables you need, and if you can find a good bakery you'll be all set for picnics. Corner shops abound, so picnicking is easy.

It would be misrepresentation, however, to pretend that Yugoslavia is in the same league as somewhere like France or Germany for food shopping. Self-catering is perfectly possible, but it's not the most ideal country in which to do it.

Nightlife

As yet, even in the most developed Yugoslavian resorts, the nightlife scene is still fairly basic. This can be regarded as both good and bad. Good in that the crass commercialism of Torremolinos-type resorts is noticeable by its absence but bad in that many holidaymakers actually enjoy the disco and nightclub scene and it's not really there for those who want it. What exists is usually a poor imitation of Western-style nightlife with tepid discos and predictable entertainment acts, but, to be fair, this is beginning to change, especially in the Holiday Clubs and Villages. The nightlife is becoming of a more acceptable standard. Among some of the liveliest resorts in Yugoslavia where the nightlife is at its best are: Portoroz, Dubrovnik, Poreč, Rovinj, Opatija and Split.

Apart from the summer festivals (see 'The Socialite', page ??, for details) there are more specific festivals throughout the summer which add their own form of entertainment to the host town. Some of the best are: the Ljubljana International Jazz Festival, which takes place in mid-June; the International Review of Original Yugoslav Folklore in Zagreb in late July; the Yugoslav Children's Festival at Šibenik from mid-June to early July; and an assortment of musical and folklore entertainments held in the Skadarlijska Veceri district of Belgrade from May through the rest of the year.

One particularly enjoyable and photogenic event held at varying times all over Yugoslavia is the Peasant Wedding fête, when couples of the town and surroundings (and even a few tourists) get married *en masse*, followed by a rowdy celebration throughout the whole town. Plitvice has its *Kmecka Ohcet*, as it is called, in late May; Galicnik in early to mid-July; Bohinj in mid-July; and Bled in early August. Check for a local one with the Tourist Office of the resort you're in.

One final spectacle worth seeing is in Korčula. It's the Moreška sword dance and mime, danced by the locals, which takes place every Thursday in summer.

The *korzo* (see 'The Socialite' on page 29) is always another cheap and entertaining way of working up an appetite for your evening meal.

In general there is less nightlife available on the islands, so if you're a keen night owl, choose your destination carefully.

Communications

Keeping in touch with home from Yugoslavia is not particularly easy. While it is perfectly possible to phone, telex or write to Britain, the speed of the postal service and ease with which you can get a clear line are not always in evidence. As for sending money on, the amount of hassle involved and the time it takes in transit make it far easier to bring an emergency fund with you in the first place.

POST OFFICES

Post Offices are open 8 a.m.–7 p.m. Monday to Friday, and 8 a.m.–12 noon on Saturday in major centres and are identified by a yellow PTT sign hanging outside. Post boxes are also yellow. You can send telegrams and post from Yugoslav Post Offices, and international telephone booths are also located in the main Post Offices. Often the telephones are open 24 hours, but facilities depend on the size of the town you're in. Stamps can also be bought from tobacconists' and news stands. The postal service is slow, and even airmail will take twice as long as you'd expect. If you're sending a parcel or registered letter you must present it to the counter clerk unsealed. Airmail costs relatively little and is well worth the extra few dinars.

POSTE RESTANTE

Only possible in larger cities. American Express (who hold mail for card holders) are called 'Atlas' in Yugoslavia and will be found in all major cities.

TELEPHONES

To telephone home you'll have to use an international telephone (not those on the streets) in the Post Office. In all but the most remote areas of the country you can dial direct to Western Europe. To phone through a telegram message, the number is 96, enquiries is 988, police is 92, fire 93 and ambulance 94. The international dialling code from Yugoslavia to Great Britain is '9944' followed by the British area code, omitting the initial 0 (e.g., London would be 99441 . . .).

Don't phone from your hotel as they add on a surplus charge. Finally, allow yourself plenty of time to make an operator-controlled call, as between waiting for the operator to answer your call and finally connecting you, you can be left hanging on for around fifteen minutes or more. There are no cheap rates for phoning.

Moving Around the Country

This is about the worst bit of a holiday in Yugoslavia. Transport once you're there is both very expensive and haphazardly run. Of all the options open to you the simplest and one of the cheapest (if you pay in hard currency) is to take the organized excursions offered by the larger tour operators. This will save you a lot of hassle and leave the treacherous business of driving on often tortuous roads to someone used to it. If, however, this does not appeal, and you really don't go for the wide-eyed-tourists-on-a-bus bit, the alternatives are these: car hire, trains, buses or taxis.

CAR HIRE

A car in Yugoslavia is still something of a luxury. That's why when you see the locals out in cars they're generally packed full with no room to spare (which is why hitch-hiking in Yugoslavia is such a dead loss). Cars are generally imported and therefore not cheap, and petrol is expensive and rationed for the locals. Because of all this, car hire prices are over the top by any standard, and in fact a week's rental in Yugoslavia will set you back almost as much as the price of your entire two-week package holiday (around £300 for one week's hire of a small/medium-sized car excluding petrol; inclusive of insurances). You are wise to do your research and booking of the car from home before you get to Yugoslavia. Prices are very rarely cheaper once you're over there and if you're travelling in high season you could find prices even higher than normal due to increased competition. The disadvantage of booking this end is that, unless you're travelling with friends, you don't get an opportunity to share the car and costs with other holidaymakers. However, if you wouldn't be doing this anyway, there's no advantage waiting until you're there.

Avis, the largest car hire company in Europe, is also, in our experience, the best. They operate in 93 countries, their prices are among the most competitive, and their service is hard to beat. It's best to hire your car *in the UK*, before you go. This way you get a guaranteed price in sterling which cannot be altered whatever happens to exchange rates, and you also have much more of a comeback if things go wrong. You can book either through your travel agent or through an Avis office.

For those of you who do not want to commit yourself to car hire until you see the resort, or more importantly find out what the weather is doing once you're there, Avis operate a scheme called 'Driveaway Cheques', whereby you buy cheques in the UK, on a no-commission basis, which allow you to choose car rental on the days you want and pay for them with these cheques. All the paperwork and hanging around is done in the UK, so no time is wasted when abroad, and you are entitled to all the same conditions of rental as if you had hired the car in advance: guaranteed price, unlimited mileage etc.

If you choose not to hire a car after all, the vouchers can simply be traded back in the UK at face value, so no money is lost. For flexibility and value this scheme makes a lot of sense, though obviously if you are going to a busy resort in peak season you would still be better advised to make a definite booking in advance, as there can be no guarantee that the car you want will be there on the day you want it.

In Yugoslavia Avis operate in 19 towns and cities, including all the major resorts, with more than one office in several towns.

As regards documentation and the small print – you only need your normal British driver's licence (an international one is not necessary). Third-party insurance is compulsory, and a refundable deposit must be paid to the car rental firm unless you hold an internationally recognized credit card. Some companies charge a local tax on top of the standard rate. The minimum age is generally 21 and you must have been driving for two years.

Obviously the rates and cars vary with the car rental companies. Petrol and traffic fines are the driver's responsibility. Help can be summoned in case of breakdown by phoning 987, and yellow patrol cars provide free help for motorists.

Tourists must buy petrol with vouchers which are obtainable from agencies throughout the country. You shouldn't have any problem with rationing as long as you have the vouchers. There is a 10 per cent discount on petrol vouchers bought abroad or at border points with hard currency. Two grades of petrol are available: Premium (86 octane) and Superior (98 octane).

There is no charge for returning a hired car to a different town as long as the car hire company has an office there, but a charge is made if the car has to be returned to a town which has no office.

(For further information on driving in Yugoslavia see the 'By Car' section of 'Independent Means' on page 118.)

TRAINS

In the summer trains are usually very crowded. The rail network around the coast is not at all comprehensive, therefore using the train for excursions is a bit of a non-starter. To get between major towns and cities, though, it's a useful means of transport, though seat reservations are necessary. Go for an express or rapide train (which require a supplement) if you want to travel at any reasonable sort of speed.

The Belgrade–Bar line is worth taking for the spectacular scenery it offers as it winds its way through the mountainous centre of the country.

BUSES

There is an impressive network of regional bus transport – primarily because for much of the country it is still the main mode of transport for the majority of people. It is not an expensive way to get about the country, but unless you can book your seats ahead of time (which you can in major towns with proper bus stations) you could find conditions cramped and uncomfortable. If you can, always buy your tickets ahead of travel, particularly in the south of Yugoslavia where the buses are more chaotic.

The timetables are anything but clear so you're probably best advised to enquire from the local Tourist Office or at your hotel. There are several bus companies operating the same routes, so make sure you know the name of the company you are travelling with.

In comparison with organized excursion coach trips the buses will work out far cheaper, but take into consideration that excursions often take in more than one place of interest and you'll be lucky to find a bus route which conveniently takes in all local places of interest.

TAXIS

Taxis, like cars, are regarded as luxuries and therefore are quite expensive (at least as much as at home). There are taxi ranks in the main towns and tourist centres. Most taxis have meters; if they don't, enquire the price of the fare before getting in, and hold the driver to it. Prices go up at night and if you're carrying luggage. Tipping around 10 per cent is customary. There are no 'communal' taxis.

Problems/Emergencies

MEDICAL

Chemists (*apoteka*) should have a sign in their window with the name and address of the nearest all-night chemist. If it's a minor medical problem you'll be as well going to the chemist. If it's serious, get to a hospital (telephone 94 for an ambulance), and remember British citizens are entitled to free treatment against payment of a nominal fee.

POLICE (MILICIJA)

The Yugoslav National Police wear a grey-blue uniform and are armed. Contact them in case of theft and insist on a copy of your statement for insurance purposes (also inform your travel rep). Telephone 92 in emergencies. (As yet the crime rate in Yugoslavia among tourists is refreshingly low.)

EMBASSIES AND CONSULATES

The British Embassy is at Generala Zdanova 46, Belgrade (Tel: 1645055). The British Consulate in Zagreb is at Ilica 12 (Tel: 445-522) and in Split at Titova Obala 10 (Tel: 414164) – next to the tourist office. Contact them in case of loss of passport and papers.

WORK

It is not possible to gain employment in Yugoslavia other than through British firms with bases in the country.

WOMEN

Women travelling alone will still find the going tough in the more remote inland areas of Yugoslavia. Take your lead from the local women – they never travel alone, or if they have to they cover themselves up well. Remember, parts of Yugoslavia are Muslim so if you insist on wandering about in shorts and T-shirts expect hassles and pawings as you'll be considered fair game. If things get nasty, see the police and make as much noise as you can.

Potted History of Yugoslavia

The present-day country of Yugoslavia, an amalgam of differing peoples, languages, religions and customs, is one of the most heterogeneous states of the world. Within its 256,000 square miles lie three main mountain ranges, extensive plains, major rivers, remote forests and wild places with such rare European creatures as the wolf and brown bear, and many miles of magnificent, dramatic coastline.

Yet the achievements of the people of Yugoslavia both past and present in fine cities and buildings and in historical events stand in comparison with those of the Western and Eastern European culture. Paradox abounds in the country. From modern and cultivated Slovenians to peasant farmers in Macedonia, the meeting of East and West has been crucial in the history and making of the nation.

Yugoslavia means 'land of the south Slavs', taking its name from the Slavic peoples who first came to the area in the sixth and seventh centuries AD, migrating southward from their northern homelands. However, other peoples had already lived and made their mark on the region. Several caves in Yugoslavia indicate man's presence during the Palaeolithic Age. The oldest known artefacts date from 5000 BC from the houses of the prehistoric settlement on the Danube near Darji, Milanov. Man at this time was discovering crops which could be harvested annually, and thus changing from a hunter-gatherer to an agricultural society with an ordered social system.

Towards the end of the Bronze Age the people living in the Balkans first came into contact with ancient Greece. From the ancient Greeks comes the first historical evidence of the peoples of Yugoslavia. By 1200 BC the Illyrians in the west and Thracians in the east of the country had established their own aristocracy.

Later, in the fifth century BC, Greeks founded colonies on several Adriatic islands and on the Dalmatian coast part of a great flux of peoples on the move. Celts moved into the area coinciding with the rise of the Roman Empire which inevitably came to rule this part of the world following a series of campaigns in the second and first centuries BC. Indeed the 'Pax Romana' in Illyria was the only time prior to the twentieth century that the territory of Yugoslavia was under one common rule such was the subsequent upheaval and historical cross-play of competing states and powers. The Roman influence penetrated across the country and even today there is much evidence of the grandeur that was Rome – the Emperor Diocletian's palace at Split and the amphitheatre at Pula being but two examples. Following the division in the Roman Empire in the late fourth century AD, the Illyrian provinces (as Yugoslavia was then known) were divided also, with Serbia, Macedonia, Montenegro and Bosnia-Herzegovina being ruled from Constantinople, and Slovenia, Croatia and Dalmatia remaining under Roman rule.

The grip of Rome was at this time gradually slackening. A great outburst of 'Barbarians' was assailing the Empire on all sides. Slavic tribes from north of the Carpathians first raided and then settled in the region from the sixth century onwards, either driving out the Romanized inhabitants or assimilating them into their own Slavic culture. It was not, however, a one-way traffic. Christianity was first introduced to the Slavic peoples through these contacts, and they rapidly came under the influence of the Church.

From the eighth century on, the territory of Yugoslavia became embroiled in the countless wars and upheavals that have beset the region up until the twentieth century. Initially a number of independent Slavic states arose. Serbia, Macedonia, Croatia and Dalmatia all enjoyed a measure of independence based on the support of Byzantium. External forces were nevertheless always a threat to Slavic independence, either from the west from Venice, or from the east – the Hungarians and Turks – or from the north – the Austrians. In 1409 Venice gained control of Dalmatia and the Adriatic islands, a territory held by the republic until 1797. Only the city state of Dubrovnik retained its independence by means of careful diplomacy and the influence of its trading prosperity. The Turkish threat had by now also become a reality, for in 1371 the Turks had advanced into and controlled southern Macedonia. Eighteen years later at the Battle of Kosovo the Serbs lost not only the battle but also, ultimately, control of their own homeland to the Turkish conquerors. By the early sixteenth century Yugoslavia was split between three empires – the Turks, who controlled Serbia, Bosnia-Herzegovina, Macedonia, Montenegro, part of Croatia and Slovenia; the Austrian Habsburgs, who ruled the remainder of Croatia and Slovenia; and the Venetians, who were the overlords of Dalmatia and the Gulf of Kotor.

This pattern of foreign domination, which lasted until the creation of the state of Yugoslavia in 1918, was to have a profound effect on the development of the subjugated Slav peoples. The Turkish influence in particular introduced a peculiarly oriental feel into central Europe. Turkish rulers introduced Islam, now still with some million adherents, and snuffed out the flourishing western-orientated culture of Serbia. Daily life gradually took on an oriental pattern, a pattern which still exists in many areas especially in Bosnia-Herzegovina and the south.

After the Turkish threat to western Europe had finally subsided in the seventeenth century there followed a long period of decline, though it was to take a further 300 years for the Turks finally to relinquish control. During the seventeenth and eighteenth centuries there was an almost continuous state of unrest on the Turkish frontiers with Venice and Austria and within the conquered lands as the Slavs agitated to throw off their overlords.

The nineteenth century in Yugoslavia opened with more unrest. However in 1806 Napoleon, continuing his sweep through Europe, captured Dubrovnik and annexed it to the newly created Illyrian provinces which lasted only until 1815 when the territory including those areas formerly controlled by Venice reverted to Austrian control.

By the mid-nineteenth century Turkish power had waned sufficiently to encourage Slav independence movements to flourish. The kingdom of Serbia came into being in 1882, following the Congress of Berlin, while Montenegro, which had never fully been subjugated by the Turks, gained full independence in 1878 following several successful uprisings. The Habsburg Empire, however, was also flexing its muscles as the absence of Turkish control created a power vacuum in the area. Croatia, Slovenia and Dalmatia all remained under Austrian-Hungarian control. Bosnia-Herzegovina was annexed by Austria in 1908 – a reaction against the Pro-Slavic movement and one which created much international tension. Nevertheless the Turks were finally driven out of the region following the first and second Balkan Wars in 1912 and 1913, whereupon Macedonia came under Serbian control.

Of course the Balkan area had been a continuous area of unrest and a source of conflict with the major powers throughout the nineteenth century as the Slav peoples, helped and encouraged by Russia, had sought to free themselves from the Turks. Britain, France and Austria had all been involved in an intricate game of bluff, threat, diplomacy and subterfuge to further their own interests, wary of the Russian motives in the region. In 1914, however, the whole area blew up in Europe's face with the assassination of the Austrian Archduke Franz Ferdinand in Sarajevo. The resultant conflict led to the mass slaughter of the First World War and the end of the *ancien régime* in Europe. Out of the eventual peace rose the new kingdom of Serbs, Croats and Slovenes, the basis of the union of the southern Slavs.

Although the new kingdom of Yugoslavia was a constitutional parliamentary monarchy, continual internal conflict within the new state resulted in the King declaring a dictatorship in 1929. The rise of fascism in Europe ultimately caught Yugoslavia in its maelstrom. The monarchy and government surged further and further to the right throughout the 1930s as the European crisis deepened. After the outbreak of the Second World War the regent, Prince Paul, met with Hitler and signed a Tripartite Pact with Germany and Italy pledging Yugoslavia to the Axis cause. However it was soon found out that the Chetniks were assisting the Germans against the Partisans. The bitter struggle of the Partisans in defeating enemy troops and liberating Yugoslavia forms a proud chapter in Yugoslav history, but the cost was great – 1,700,000 Yugoslavs lost their lives.

Tito was declared Marshal of Yugoslavia in 1943 and the country was declared a Socialist Federal Republic on 29 November 1945. However after the Second World War Tito was not prepared to give up the hard-won Yugoslavian freedom to Stalin's idea of a Soviet-controlled communist Europe. Tito resisted this and by 1948 Yugoslavia had broken free from Stalin. The country adopted the non-aligned status it maintains today, even after Tito's death in 1980.

Part Four

GUIDE TO THE COUNTRY

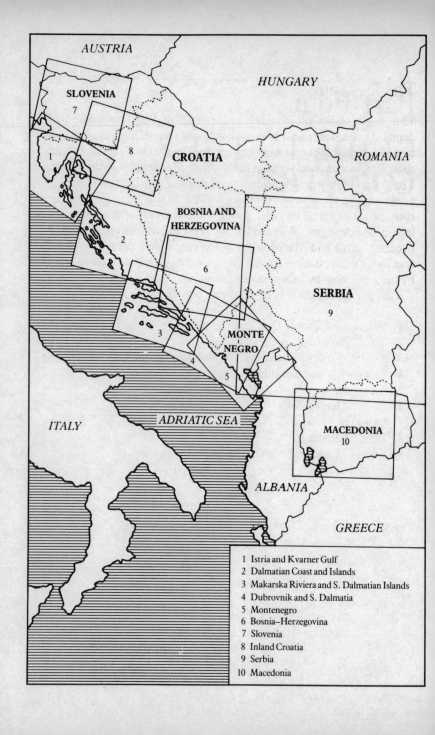

AUSTRIA

HUNGARY

SLOVENIA

7

8

CROATIA

ROMANIA

1

BOSNIA AND
HERZEGOVINA

2

6

SERBIA

9

3

MONTE
NEGRO

4

5

ITALY

ADRIATIC SEA

MACEDONIA

10

ALBANIA

GREECE

1 Istria and Kvarner Gulf
2 Dalmatian Coast and Islands
3 Makarska Riviera and S. Dalmatian Islands
4 Dubrovnik and S. Dalmatia
5 Montenegro
6 Bosnia–Herzegovina
7 Slovenia
8 Inland Croatia
9 Serbia
10 Macedonia

The Structure

This guide makes no pretence to cover all of Yugoslavia in equal depth. As it is written for holidaymakers, not travelling academics, it concentrates on the areas where tourists go. In the main this means the coast and islands from Istria in the north to Montenegro in the south. The only other area where holidaymakers are to be found in any numbers is in the alps of Slovenia. Because of this these parts of the country are covered in great detail while the rest of Yugoslavia – inland Montenegro, Bosnia-Herzegovina, inland Slovenia, inland Croatia, Serbia and Macedonia – is less extensively covered and the text about these places is geared more towards people who are touring by car and living by independent means.

This part of the book is divided into ten sections:

(1) Istria, the Kvarner Gulf and the Northern Adriatic Islands
(2) The Dalmatian Coast and Islands
(3) The Makarska Riviera and the Southern Dalmatian Islands
(4) Dubrovnik and Southern Dalmatia
(5) Montenegro
(6) Bosnia-Herzegovina
(7) Slovenia
(8) Inland Croatia
(9) Serbia – including Vojvodrna and Kosovo
(10) Macedonia

Istria, the Kvarner Gulf and the Northern Adriatic Islands

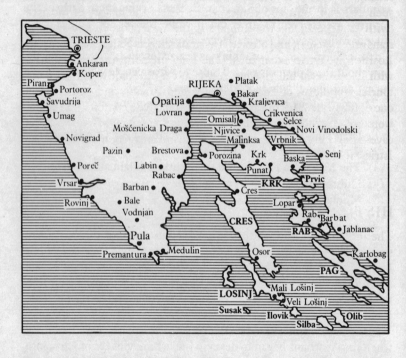

The heart-shaped region of Istria lies just over the border from Italy and because of its proximity to this country, Austria, and even Germany it is the region of Yugoslavia which attracts more holiday-makers than any other. We Northern Europeans may have to fly to Yugoslavia, but it's only a few hours' drive away for all those Germans and Austrians you see on the beaches. This does not mean, however, that Istria is the Blackpool of Yugoslavia (though undoubtedly it is the cheapest area of the country for package holidays), and there are still plenty of secluded bays, peaceful olive groves and wooded hills to enjoy; and just inland from the coast you'll find a land where the meaning of mass tourism is still unknown. The limestone hills slope down to the deep blue sea; there are still the sort of picturesque fishing villages that Spain's southern coast could boast thirty years ago, and the mild Mediterranean climate is considered the best in Yugoslavia. It all sounds perfect, doesn't it? Well, it is a pretty good holiday setting. There's everything you could really want: interesting towns such as Piran, Pula and Koper which reflect the history of the area (with influences from the Romans to the Venetians, Austro-Hungarians and Italians); and attractive islands such as Rab, Cres, Krk and Losinj for daytrip excursions. The hilly unspoilt interior of Istria, with its medieval hill villages, seems like a different world from the tourist complexes of Poreč, Portoroz and Rovinj, and makes Istria one of the best places to base yourself if you have a combination of sun worshippers and keen sightseers in your company. The Postojna caves and Plitvice lake are further inland attractions close to the Istrian resorts.

HISTORY

The influence of four centuries of Venetian rule can still be clearly seen in Istria. The gracious buildings, the campaniles, the lions of St Mark – the emblem of Venice – the ornate piazzas all remind one strongly of Venice, yet the differences are strong too, largely created by the following occupation by the Austrians and the rule from Vienna.

Many of the resorts of today date back to the late nineteenth century when the Austrians began to develop the fishing villages of Istria into sophisticated holiday resorts. Places such as Opatija, Split, Hvar and Dubrovnik came in for this treatment, so Istria is no newcomer to the tourist industry.

It took until 1918 to shake off Austrian rule when Istria was handed over to Italy as reward for joining the Allies, and it was 1944 before all the coast and islands became Yugoslav.

For a more detailed account of this region's history turn to the Dalmatian section or to the history of Yugoslavia on page 137.

COMMUNICATIONS

The airport used by the majority of tour operators for resorts in Istria is Pula, about two hours' flying time from London. There is also a smaller international airport on the island of Krk which is connected to the mainland by a bridge. Railway stations are to be found in Pula, Rijeka and Koper; and buses run between all the major coastal towns.

All the major tour operators run excursions through Yugoslav travel agencies to the local places of interest, including a bus trip to Venice. Travel between the Istrian mainland and the islands is possible. Car and passenger ferries, the motorized excursion boats, run between Rijeka and Brestova to Porozina on Cres; Crikvenica to Silo on Krk, and Senj to Baska on Krk, Baska on Krk to Lopar on Rab; Pula to Mali Losinj on Losinj; Senj to Lopar on Rab; Jablanac to Stara Novalja on Pag; Karlobag to Pag and Jablanac to Misnjak.

TOURIST INFORMATION

The main travel agent in Istria is Kvarner Express. Their head office is at Maršala Tita 186, Opatija.

THE CLIMATE

Spring is a particularly attractive time of year to visit this region, when the cherry trees, almonds and hazels are out and the climate is wonderfully mild. Istria has a mild winter and a long pleasant summer with plenty of sunshine but not the oppressive heat of inland Yugoslavia. Evenings tend to be slightly cooler than the Mediterranean.

CULINARY SPECIALITIES

Food reveals an Italian influence, seafood, fish and pasta being the mainstay of many menus (though unfortunately the sea is producing less seafood these days, so it is pricier than it used to be). Tasty spit-roasted meat can be found, and among the desserts are delicious pastries in the Viennese fashion.

As for Istrian wines, you could try the strong red known as Refosko and the even stronger red – Teran. The white wines of the region include Malvazija, which is strong and can be sweet or dry, and Pinot. The Kvarner islands also produce some good wines. Grk from the island of Korčula is a strong white worth buying.

WHERE TO GO FOR WHAT

Sightseers will enjoy Pula, Rovinj and Poreč on the coast and inland Motovun, the Postojna caves and Plitvice lakes. *Swimmers* and *sun worshippers* should look out for Medulin, Lovran and Opatija, while *families* will enjoy the larger resorts such as Poreč, Umag and Rovinj. Portoroz will suit the older tourist while Poreč is the liveliest place for nightlife.

As regards festivals and nightlife in Istria: Opatija has something in the way of music or folklore entertainment virtually every night, usually held in the open-air theatre. In June the Istrian Song Festival takes place, with performances in all the larger resorts. The Yugoslav Folklore Festival happens in mid-July, also with performances in several places. The Yugoslav Cinema Festival takes place in Pula in late July. There are entertainments and sporting events at Portoroz all summer long, and folklore evenings are held six nights a week in the beautiful inland hill village of Motovun around seventeen miles from Poreč.

It has to be said that the beaches in Istria are not spectacular. In fact many of them are pebble not sand. They are however generally safe for children as they are shallow and gently sloping, and most hotels have sun terraces and pools as compensation. Some of the best natural beaches are at Medulin, Lovran, Losinj, Savudrija and Opatija. Bear in mind that Istria is perhaps not the most attractive region of Yugoslavia, but it gives the best value for money, and has all the ingredients for those just wanting a relaxing time in the sun.

The Istrian Coast

We are covering each resort and town from north to south as they lie on the coast. We start therefore with Ankaran, in the bay of Koper, just over the border from Italy, and work our way down through Koper, Portoroz, Piran, Savudrija, Umag, Novigrad, Poreč, Vrsar and Rovinj to Pula and Medulin in the south of the gulf, then along the eastern side of the coast to Rabac.

The 'Kvarner Riviera', as it is called by some tour operators, takes in the next stretch of coast, and the resorts highlighted here are Plomin, Mošćenice, Mošćenička Draga, Medveja, Lovran, Opatija, Rijeka, Bakar, Bakarac, Kraljevica, Crikvenica, Senj and Jablanac.

ANKARAN is the preferred beach for people based in or near the town of Koper. It lies about twenty minutes by motorboat away from the town, and has one of the best beaches of the area. There is a very good campsite worth considering if you are freelancing, or other accommodation options include a converted Benedictine monastery. The beach lies in what is known as the Bay of Koper, and is approximately half a mile long with a sandy, not rocky base, making it suitable for children.

KOPER is the first major Yugoslavian town you reach, once over the border from Italy. The largest town of the Slovenian part of Istria, it was originally an island but is now joined to the mainland. The new port of Koper with its skyscrapers and concrete boxes can be happily ignored as, despite appearances from a distance, it lies on the outskirts of an attractive fifteenth-century town, not in the middle of it. The Venetians took over the town in 1275 (hence the lion of St Mark – the symbol of Venice – found on many of Koper's buildings), and until the terrible plague of 1551 the town was one of the most important centres of the region. Many Italians still regard the town and surrounding coastal area as Italian as it only became part of Yugoslavia in 1954.

The main places of interest to see in the town are found in the **town square** – Titov Trg, with its fifteenth-century **loggia** and impressive **cathedral**, begun in 1450 and not finished until the end of the sixteenth century. The **belfry** goes back as far as the thirteenth century and is worth the effort of climbing for the view of Koper's old centre, with all the narrow streets leading off the main square. Opposite the loggia is the **Praetorian House** – once the residence of the Venetian governor and now the town's law courts. This was originally two buildings but they merged into one in the fifteenth century and were added to until the ornate example you see today emerged.

The Baroque **Belgramoni-Tacco Palace** houses the civic museum, with its fine art treasures (including works by Bellini and Carpaccio), and an interesting collection of Roman remains of the region. Keen art lovers should also take the trouble to find the Church of St Ana where further works of Carpaccio can be seen.

There are few places to stay in Koper, but most people in this area stay at the resort of Portoroz, which is less than ten miles from Koper and has much more in the way of nightlife and tourist-related facilities.

PORTOROZ – Port of Roses – is the resort more or less attached to the town of Piran. Portoroz is one of Yugoslavia's most sophisticated and well established resorts with a year-round tourist industry and many very good hotels. The man-made sandy beach is remarkably good for Istria and the whole resort has a well cared for appearance, probably due to the fact that the well sheltered bay and good climate has been attracting tourists for a lot longer than the last two or three decades. Portoroz's popularity dates back to the beginning of this century, and this is reflected in the variety and quality of nightlife on offer: smart restaurants, casino, nightclubs, etc. The **Bernadin holiday complex**, a mile from the centre, is particularly good and offers as good a nightlife as you will find in Yugoslavia.

Subtropical plants and flowers can be seen in the parks as proof of the mild weather, and also on show in the park on Seca Point is a collection of modern stone sculpture – the exhibits being the works of the annual international 'Forma Viva' Symposium held there every summer.

PIRAN: because Portoroz is such a popular resort and most of the major tour operators run holidays there, hotels now stretch virtually into the town of Piran, the small medieval city a mile or so north from the centre of Portoroz. This is one of the most attractive Venetian towns on the whole of the Yugoslav coast, and is reason enough for wanting to base yourself at Portoroz.

Piran's history is varied – in the Middle Ages it was a buccaneers'

outpost; by the thirteenth century it was under Venetian influence –
the way it remained until the late eighteenth century, hence the
Venetian architecture and replica of St Mark's campanile which
dominates the red-roofed skyline of the centre of Piran.

The town centre is Tartinijev Trg, named after the famous Italian
composer and violinist Tartini who was born here, and the **Tourist
Office** is in the impressive fifteenth-century red building which bears
the motto '*Lassa pur dir*' ('Let Them Talk') – apparently so inscribed
as the house was erected by a rich Venetian for his mistress; though
ironically their love did not endure the talk of the townsfolk. The
street behind leads to the **Cathedral of St George** from where you can
take an impressive photograph of the whole of the Gulf of Trieste.

You can walk for hours in the narrow winding streets of the old
town and you will always come across something new – it's that sort of
place: remnants of medieval walls, decaying Baroque mansion
houses, the old city's water supply . . . As for specific sights – there is
an **art gallery**, a **theatre**, an **aquarium**, and a **town museum**. All are
moderately interesting if you have a particular passion for paintings,
history or that sort of thing, but none are 'musts' on an itinerary. The
most interesting thing to do in Piran is to stroll around and soak up the
atmosphere.

Tourist-type restaurants and nightlife are probably better in
Portoroz but a night out in Piran will show you more authentic
Yugoslavian entertainment. The **Ljubljana Fish Restaurant** on the
seafront in Portoroz is worth trying.

SAVUDRIJA: if you are keen to spend some time on a relatively quiet
and good beach, consider an excursion of fifteen miles or so to the
small resort of Savudrija. This now-developed fishing village is set
among pine woods and has a very good beach. Even better is to stop
off en route between Portoroz and Savudrija (assuming you are
travelling by car) and, armed with a picnic, spend the day on one of
the still secluded beaches which are found nestling between the pine
woods on this attractive stretch of coast.

UMAG is the next town and holiday centre to be found on the west
coast of Istria. It lies about five miles south of Savudrija positioned on
a promontory, and has only fairly recently been developed for

tourism. The old part of the town still has some charm, and the commercialized areas where the hotels and restaurants are to be found are outside Umag proper – at Punta and Katoro, a few miles north of the town. It must be said, that the industry just outside Umag does detract from the atmosphere of the place; however the safe sandy beach, and the fact that the tourist area is sheltered by vineyards and pine woods makes this only a small consideration.

The hotels and 'tourist villages' here tend to be on a large scale – the type where it is possible not to leave the confines of the resort unless you really want to. Bathing is not the strong point of this resort – most of the bathing areas are rocky. Entertainment for tourists is laid on, and because this is such a popular resort for family holidays 'holiday clubs' tend to predominate with entertainment centres and multiple bars and restaurants. The main 'Za-Za' entertainment centre includes a casino and nightclub. The new resort of Umag has been designed specifically with the Northern European tourist market in mind, so you'll find all the facilities and activities you could want are laid on here (including the naturist beach of Katoro, near to the town).

As for Umag itself – it's a moderately busy port, with a few interesting buildings reflecting its past. The most noteworthy is the eighteenth-century church on the main square. More interesting is BUJE, a medieval hill town about eight miles east of Umag. It has a mixture of Baroque and Venetian buildings including an attractive old church and bell tower. The September Wine Festival held here is worth remembering, as is the international gathering of young musicians held in the summer months in the nearby village of GROZNJAN. Their outdoor performances make a refreshing change for an evening's entertainment.

NOVIGRAD is the town on a small promontory on the north bank of the River Mirna, about ten miles south of Umag and sixteen miles north of Poreč. It means literally 'New Town', though considering it's been called this since the Byzantines claimed it from the Romans in the fifth century, it's all relative. The Turks and then the Venetians added their touch to Novigrad which in its day was an important port, making its money from the transporting of timber down the River Mirna.

Today the resort of Novigrad lies about a mile from the town centre. It is an attractive holiday complex though there is a rocky shoreline and no sandy beach (in fact the beaches in the town itself are better). Sports facilities are on offer in the Laguna complex, and the proximity of the pine woods makes for pleasant surroundings. The nightlife is pretty ordinary. There is not terribly much going on in Novigrad except a few dances in the hotels or the prospect of eating out in the harbour-side restaurants and cafés. In short Novigrad, as a resort, is best suited to families, not the young set.

The town itself has an attractive harbour and a pleasant atmosphere in the old winding streets. The 'sights' are the Baroque church of **Sveti Pelagije** where the body of the third-century child martyr St Pelagius is buried; and the **Urizzi Mansion** which houses the museum where locally-found Roman remains can be seen.

POREČ is Yugoslavia's largest resort, occupying almost ten miles of Istrian coastline. The town of Poreč nestles in the centre of all this activity but remains remarkably unscathed by the high level of package tourism based all around it. Virtually every major tour operator running to Yugoslavia offers a holiday to Poreč, and as a result the hotel complexes on offer provide the holidaymaker with every type of facility; and, of course, the nightlife is good.

There are sports facilities, tavernas, shops, cafés, restaurants, pools, naturist beaches (at Lanterna, Cervar and Funtana) and numerous holiday clubs on offer, making a holiday based here one on which you needn't leave the resort if you don't want to. It would be a shame if you didn't, though, because Poreč itself has some very fine sights.

The main complex is The Green Lagoon – **Zelena Laguna** – and it's here that the nightlife and sporting facilities are at their best. More attractive though, is the **Plava Laguna** – Blue Lagoon – one of the most tranquil complexes in a pinewood setting. The lagoon complexes are south of Poreč town, while to the north, worth noting, is the very attractive **Pical tourist village** and the **Materada beach complex**. Of the hotels the best are the Galijot, Kristal, Diamant, Lotos-Plavi, Luna, Parentium, Pical, Riviera, Rubin, Turist and Zagreb.

In general the beaches are nothing to write home about, with the usual Istrian complaint of too much rock and not enough sand, but the number of swimming pools, sunbathing terraces and water sports on offer make up for it for all but the most dedicated beach lovers.

Naturists have access to the Kuversada beach. There are regular bus services linking the lagoon holiday complexes with Poreč and with the Pical tourist village and Materada complex. Those travelling independently should aim for private rooms which can be arranged through Meterava Tourist.

And to Poreč itself: this is one of Istria's most interesting towns with a colourful history and just enough sights to keep you interested. It dates back to the first century AD and you can still see the remains of the Roman temples of Mars and Neptune to this day. The main town square – Trg Slobode – is in fact modern, but as you walk on you come to a five-sided tower which is a thirteenth-century remnant of the old city's walls. The winding streets show a mixture of Gothic, Romanesque and Renaissance buildings, some of which are ex-palaces, hence the elaborate carvings and intricately worked balconies and windows.

The sight of Poreč, however, is undoubtedly the **Basilica of Euphrasius**, built on top of previous churches as far back as 550 AD by Euphrasius, the Bishop of Poreč. Today the basilica is kept as a museum. Roman remains, glittering gold mosaics (every bit as impressive as those in Istanbul or Venice) can be seen: note particularly those on the triumphal arch and in the apse. The bell tower which adjoins the basilica is worth the climb for the glorious panoramic view from the top. The harbour is the location for most of Poreč's seafood restaurants and cafés.

The **Regional Museum** is housed in the Baroque **Sinčič Mansionhouse**, and in the newer part of the town stands the eighteenth-century **Church of St Mary**. Older buildings of interest cluster round the Euphrasian basilica: the **Canon's House** stands south of the basilica and dates back to 1251; the **Romanesque House** with balcony is near Marafor Square; and the **House of the Two Saints**, also dating from this period, takes its name from the relief of two saints on the upper storey of the building.

As for excursions – the little island of ST NICHOLAS is a five-minute boat trip away, or there's the chance to visit an inland hill town, such as MOTOVUN, sample some local food and entertainment in a rather beautiful setting. While there, take in the **castle**, the **loggia**, the **town hall**, and the **Baroque church** with its Romanesque campanile.

It's still possible with most tour operators to make excursions from Poreč to VENICE and to LAKE BLED in the Slovenian Alps, though neither of these worthwhile trips is cheap. If you go all out and hire a car, consider the following places for daytrips: PAZIN – about a twenty-mile drive from Poreč; see the castle built on the very edge of the chasm into which the River Fojba disappears, and if you're keen to learn a bit more about the way the locals live, a visit to the **Ethnographica Museum** in the castle where you can see the typical costumes and traditional tools and household articles used by Istrian peasants.

A mile or two from Pazin is BERAM, a typical Istrian village worth going to for the Gothic frescoes in the **Church of St Mary**. These show the 'Life of Mary' and the 'Life of Christ' and are very fine examples, thought to have been painted by a local man known as Vincent of Kastav in the late fifteenth century. Among the better hotels available here is the **Hotel Galijot**, which has bags of character and is a lovely place.

VRSAR, about five miles south of Poreč, is the next resort you come to on the Istrian coast. This was originally the summer home of the bishops of Poreč and you can still see the remains of their **castle** today, along with the other main sight of the town – a thirteenth-century basilica called the **Church of St Mary**. The actual resort of Vrsar is, as usual, a bit away from the old town – around half a mile in this instance. As a resort, Vrsar is more suitable for those who prefer a fairly quiet time. It has also become a popular destination for naturists.

The main tourist complex is the **Panorama Hotel complex**, which has the usual nightlife and sporting facilities and offers concreted sunbathing areas to compensate for the rather narrow rocky beaches. The omnipresent pine trees and attractive harbour add character to the place, and, in all, the ingredients of an enjoyable hotel-based holiday are here to be found. A good alternative is the adjacent **Hotel Belvedere**.

Most people heading for Vrsar, however, come for the naturist facilities. The island of KUVERSADA just off the shore is one of Europe's largest naturist centres, and the modern **Pentalon Naturist Village**, about one mile south of Vrsar, acts more or less as an extension of the Kuversada camp. The Kuversada camp is considered by many to be one of the leading naturist resorts in the country, though the absence of long sandy beaches does, I think, detract from its overall appeal, and makes somewhere such as the naturist centre at Ulcinj in Montenegro more enticing. Kuversada dates back to the 1960s and consists of an autocamp and bungalow-type accommodation on the mainland, with camping on the island itself.

While on the subject of naturist centres (and note this implies an enclosed area where *only* naturists are allowed), there is another one in this area – the **Monsena Centre**, just a couple of miles from the next large resort down the coast – Rovinj. The road between the two naturist centres (the main road from Vrsar to Pula) is worth taking in as an excursion, naturist or not. It runs across the tip of a six-mile fjord called the **Limski Kanal** and affords a spectacular view from the top of the sheer cliffs. The Monsena Naturist Centre is based on self-catering bungalow accommodation and offers a good base for a family holiday in an attractively landscaped setting amid pine and olive trees. This centre, in common with all naturist centres in Yugoslavia, has all the facilities on site that you'll need, i.e. sports, restaurants, cafés, supermarket, children's playground, etc. Again, though, the beaches leave a bit to be desired. Naturist beaches near Rovinj also include those at **Valalt**, **Rubin** and **Crveni otok**.

ROVINJ itself is a very attractive old town and an ideal holiday location for those who wish to combine a bit of sightseeing and sunbathing with active nightlife. This is probably the most charming of Istria's holiday towns. It remains unspoilt, despite its popularity with holidaymakers, because all the tourist areas have been developed away from the town.

The old town is built on a hill, overshadowed by its Baroque cathedral – the church of **St Euphemia**. Originally Rovinj was an island, but today it stands as a promontory on the mainland. It is surrounded by fourteen little islands which make perfect settings for sunbathing picnics (naturist or otherwise), and there are frequent ferries from the town to the main ones.

In Rovinj the other sights are the seventeenth-century **bell tower**, next to the **cathedral**, and down by the harbour, in the Trg Maršala Tita, the **town hall** (also seventeenth-century), which houses the town museum, and the **clock tower**. But just wandering through the narrow streets of the Venetian quarter down by the harbour is a pleasant enough experience, and will make you understand why Rovinj is often considered as Italian in character as it is Yugoslavian. A good walk can be enjoyed in the park on the **Muntrav promontory**, south of Rovinj. It's worth a visit to see some of the rare Mediterranean flowers.

The resort of Rovinj is situated along the south shore of the town. The **Monvi Complex** is the main centre of action, and where you'll find most of the nightlife. There are also hotels on the two largest off-shore islands: **Katarina** and **Crveni otok** (Red Island). Crveni otok actually consists of twin islands which are linked by a causeway. One is uninhabited and acts as a naturist reserve; the other is the setting for a luxury hotel complex.

Most of the hotels at Rovinj are well equipped and have better than average facilities. Among the best is the **Hotel Eden**. The **city beach** bordering on to Ulica Jugoslavenske Menarice is okay but crowded. For peace and quiet, head for the naturist **campsite** at Valatla (also a cheap place to stay if you're travelling independently and are short of cash), or for the **best sandy beach** in this region (and another campsite) take the ferry from Obala Pino Budicin to Crveni otok.

Excursions on offer normally include a daytrip to the Roman amphitheatre and sights of nearby PULA; a tour of the hillside villages; and some companies do daytrips to VENICE and to the POSTOJNA CAVES. The stud farm at LIPICA is another favourite from this part of Istria. Given how difficult these trips are to make on an independent basis, you're probably as well to take the organized excursions. If, however, you do get hold of a car you won't be disappointed by making the twelve-mile or so journey to DVOGRAD in the Lim valley. This medieval town was abandoned in the seventeenth century and just before the locals fled to escape the plague, apparently they buried their valuables. Today those who believe this tale – plus a few tourists – come to look around the place to see if they're in luck.

Other places of interest on the road to Pula are the village of BALE, with its medieval buildings, and the ancient town of VODNJAN – a typical Istrian hilltown.

PULA is the Istrian destination for history lovers. Today it is a busy town and port with a healthy tourist industry thanks to the well-preserved remains dating back to the first century which draw visitors in their thousands every summer. A book could be written on the history of Pula alone, from its early days in the fifth century BC through its Roman occupation, and finally, to its Austrian occupation. Suffice to say, though, that these were the major influences on the city, and that there are numerous leaflets and guides available in Pula to fill you in on all the details should you be interested.

As for the city's sights: the landmark of Pula is the **Roman amphitheatre** which is in an unbelievable state of preservation considering it was built back in the first century. This remarkable arena could seat 23,000 spectators at a go to watch spectacles such as gladiator fights. The benches were carted off by the Venetians, who in fact tried hard to carry off the whole thing – and would have, too, if it hadn't been for the intervention of the Venetian conservationist, Senator Gabriele Emo (hence the plaque on the west tower thanking him). Today's amphitheatre plays host to more peaceful happenings than the feeding of Christians to the lions, and the only strains you're likely to hear coming from the arena are those of an orchestra or operatic singer. You can see round the amphitheatre and all its underground passages and chambers from 8 a.m. to 8 p.m. in summer and 9 a.m. to 9 p.m. out of season. Don't miss the underground gladiators' chambers which today house Roman artefacts.

Modern Pula (not the most attractive of cities, it must be said) lives side by side with ancient Pula in much the same way that old and new juxtapose in Rome. Other sights that date back to the year dot are the **Temple of Augustus** (again, first century) which stands in Republic Square, next to the medieval **town hall**, which now incorporates what is left of the **Temple of Diana**. If you've got this far without getting lost you've done very well, but the best advice now is to head for the **Tourist Office** and arm yourself with a map before attempting to get any further. They're at Trg Bratstva i Jedinstva 4. The **Porta Gemina** is the second-century double arch that acts as the entrance to the **Archaeological Museum**, where you can see many artefacts and objects which date back to prehistoric times and have been found locally (open 10 a.m.–2 p.m. daily). Behind the museum on the hill you see what remains of a second-century Roman theatre.

The **Triumphal Arch** at the beginning of Prvomajska Ulica dates back to the first century BC and was built in memory of the Sergi family who played a large part in Pula's life for many centuries until their descendants were banished from the city by the Venetians in the 1330s. Further down this street you come to a steep road on the right which leads to **Sveti Franjo**, the Franciscan monastery church of the fourteenth century. Note the use of shells in the decorating of the west portal, and the fifteenth-century wooden altarpiece.

There are Roman-dating bits and pieces scattered all over Pula (pillars, mosaics and the remains of buildings) and the best way to ensure that you see them all is to take an organized tour of Roman Pula.

The fifteenth-century **cathedral**, just off the main quay, Obala Maršala Tita, is worth a look for its Roman and Byzantine mosaics and its early Christian architecture. From here it's only a short walk to the **Kastel** – the castle on a hill in the heart of the old town which was rebuilt by the Venetians in the seventeenth century, and today is used as the museum devoted to the history of the 'National Revolution'.

As for Pula as a holiday base – the beaches in the town are not ideal for sunbathing as they're rocky and pebbly, not sandy. (They're not actually in the town, either – they're at Stoja and Zelenika, half an hour away by bus.)

The holiday resort of Pula lies quite a bit out of the town and consists of several holiday complexes. The main one is **Verudela**, about three miles from the centre of Pula. It is very attractive, situated on a woody promontory, and offers good sheltered swimming and water sports facilities. Again, though, there's a lack of sand on the beaches, and the nightlife is based solely in the hotels – Pula itself has surprisingly little. The other main holiday complex is the **Zlatna Stijene**, and for campers the Riburska Koliba site just south of Pula is good. For those seeking independent accommodation, try **Arenaturist** at Trg Bratstva Jedinstva 4 (tel: 23276). They'll fix you up with private rooms. Alternatively there are five campsites near to Pula.

As for daytrips: some of the small villages which have now become resorts are worth a visit. To the south (about eight miles) is PREMANTURA, on Istria's southernmost point, which is famed for its seafood. Heading back a few miles, BANJOLE has about the best beach in the area, and if you cut over the Pomer road you'll come to the resort of MEDULIN.

MEDULIN, a favourite summer holiday resort of the Romans, is a smallish village set in flat countryside about six miles from Pula. It's a good family holiday base as there are lots of children's facilities and the water sports are good. Although it's really quite a small place it does get busy in peak season, particularly on the beach which is about two miles long and consists of greyish sand interspersed with rocks. The hotels are set on the shore starting about half a mile from the village, and there's a well-located naturist beach at the **Kazela naturist resort**.

Camping Medulin is situated on a small peninsula about ten miles from Pula. It's a very large site but as it's split into various sections and landscaped with pine trees you don't get the impression of being one of a crowd. In peak season it can get very busy so book ahead if you can. There are numerous facilities – shops, restaurants, bars, etc., and a summer club for the nightclubbers. Camping Medulin offers a 10 per cent discount to International Camping Card holders.

Most of the major tour operators offer holidays at this resort, using the beach as their main selling point. It is one of the best in Istria, but because of this it can become crowded in July and August. Excursions to VENICE, the POSTOJNA CAVES and the LIPICA STUDFARM (where the famous Lipizaner horses of the Spanish riding school in Vienna are bred), are among the daytrips on offer. The average quality **Hotel Belvedere** is one favoured by many tour operators so check between the brochures for the best price. The **Mutila** is a reasonable alternative.

RABAC is one of the resorts on Istria's eastern coast. The last few years have seen this quiet fishing village transform itself into one of the region's busiest resorts. It is not a bustling small port town but still retains something of its original village atmosphere, and the scenery in this area is unspoilt and attractive. Because Rabac is on its own as a resort in an otherwise uncommercialized area, it is not the place for those keen on sampling the alternative nightlife of neighbouring resorts, but between the two main hotel areas there is just about enough to do, certainly during the day in the way of sports and daytrips, and at night there's organized nightlife for tourists. The beaches (sand and pebble mixed) are of a comparable standard to other Istrian resorts. The water sports are good, but as yet it's bring your own equipment because what's for hire is minimal.

The approach to Rabac is really quiet dramatic as you descend the three miles of sheer twisting road which has brought you from the hilltop mining town of LABIN – one of the places you can visit as an excursion. The views of the Kvarner Gulf, once you're south of Labin, with the humps of Cres and Krk islands, make this a particularly rugged and attractive area.

The **Mimosa Hotel Complex** is where most of the larger tour operators offer accommodation, though some of the nicer, more atmospheric hotels are positioned above the harbour. These include the new **Marina** and the **Lantena**.

As for daytrips – in addition to the ones laid on by the major tour operators from all the Istrian resorts (Venice, Postojna Caves, Lipica Studfarm), there's the chance to visit the island of CRES, or to explore the vicinity. There's an hourly bus to LABIN, the medieval hill town which looks destined to disintegrate any day now due to the network of coal mines in the hill on which the town stands. Subsidence is such a problem that houses have been known to fall down literally overnight. (Don't worry, most of the town's inhabitants have been rehoused in the modern mining settlement of Podlabin.) See it whilst you can, and admire its buildings, some of which date back to the fourteenth century. There's also a **museum of mining**, and a fine view over the Kvarner Gulf and Cres can be enjoyed from the battlements of the **medieval castle**.

PULA is thirty-eight miles from Rabac and as such is another perfectly feasible daytrip (see page 159). En route to Pula the road winds into the Rasa valley from where the River Rasa flows into the bay named after it which was regarded as the ancient boundary between Istria and Dalmatia. Not far from here is the town of BARBAN which can act as a watering hole en route to Pula, while you look round its old churches and see its medieval city gates and fortifications.

PLOMIN lies north of Rabac on the way to the resorts of LOVRAN and OPATIJA. It is a town gradually declining into ruin, situated at the point of a sea inlet called Plomin Bay. The only reason to stop off here would be if you were keen on history and architecture, for its Romanesque church is about the only sight of the town. The next town of note on the road north is BRESTOVA, which is where the car ferry for the islands of Cres and Losinj leaves from. After this you enter the Kvarner Riviera proper, and feel the charm of small resorts wedged between the Ucka Mountains and the Kvarner Gulf which culminates in the established holiday base of OPATIJA.

MOŚĆENICE and **MOŚĆENIČKA DRAGA** are particularly pretty. Mošćenice is a small walled town of great charm, surrounded by woods, while Mošćenička Draga is a small resort with a long pebble beach and a few good hotels, such as the **Mediteran** or the **Marina**. It can be quite lively in season, particularly down by the harbour, and it's a good place to base yourself if you're travelling independently and want some of the perks of the nightlife and entertainment that the nearby package resorts can bring, without all the crowds. A few tour operators have recently introduced packages in Mošćenička Draga, but it's still comparatively unspoilt. From here it's quite feasible to walk the mile or so to Mošćenice, perched high on the hill. Sights here include the Baroque **Church of St Andrew** and the **old town walls** and gate.

MADREJA is another small resort, close to Lovran and north of Mošćenička Draga. Its pebble beach is often thought to be the best on the Kvarner Gulf. The camp site here is a good base for touring visitors keen for a few days' relaxation.

LOVRAN

Is the next major resort up the coast. This is becoming increasingly popular, with more and more tour operators running holidays here. The name Lovran means 'laurel' and refers, no doubt, to the fact that this old town, dating back to the sixth century, is surrounded by groves of laurel, pine, oak, cherry and chestnut trees. Lovran has been a popular holiday base for almost a full century now, its potential first being realized by the Austro-Hungarians. The gardens of the attractive hotels add to the charm and elegance of the place, and the proximity of Opatija is a plus for those seeking an active nightlife.

Most of the hotels along the seafront date back to the nineteenth century, and are of a higher standard than those in other resorts. The **Beograd** and **Lovran** are particularly good, with more character than normal. The old town is entered through the one remaining **city gate**, and the main sight there is the **Gothic Church of St George** which contains fifteenth-century frescoes. The main drawback is the busy main road which passes through the centre of the town. If you are a light sleeper make sure you're not booked into one of the hotels situated on the main road as in peak season the traffic is very heavy.

Again, beaches are not the strong point of this resort – basically you're restricted to pebble and shingle areas where you can lie and sunbathe. There's a good footpath along the whole shoreline to Opatija and Volosko which passes by the little villages of IKA and ICICI where the wealthy have their villas.

Lovran has some nightlife and a few attractive restaurants and cafes, and with the addition of Opatija only a few miles away the keen night owl has plenty of scope. There's also good walking potential in Lovran: Mount Ucka beckons the very fit and dedicated, while marked paths lead the less keen to several local villages for a meander. All in all it is an attractive town with a lot to offer, but like most of the Istrian-Kvarner resorts, not suitable for the *real* sun worshippers.

OPATIJA is the largest and oldest of the resorts on Istria's east coast. It is a charming, lively, very attractive 'traditional' resort, and is a good place for nightlife and excursions. Its popularity dates back to its days as a health resort for the wealthy of the Austro-Hungarian empire. Among its sights are the medieval Benedictine **Abbey of St James** and the **Prvi Maj Park**, which contains the first of the holidays villas – **Villa Angiolina**. When Opatija was linked up to the main railway network of central Europe in the nineteenth century it led the way for the town to become a major holiday resort.

The mild climate, lush vegetation and well laid out gardens make Opatija a firm favourite for starring on holiday posters, and with the islands of Cres and Krk, and the 4580 foot Mount Ucka as backdrops, it's not surprising.

Tito Avenue is the main street and here you'll find the luxury, Edwardian-period hotels, the good shops and the Côte d'Azur atmosphere. Entertainments from opera and folk dancing (in the open air theatre every week in summer) to a night at the casino or a day at the motorcycle racing (in Preluk) are on offer, and there are no shortages of restaurants, bars and cafés.

There is a manmade sandy beach (the most popular is the Kvarner Lido), and most hotels have their own rocky areas for sunbathing, so Opatija comes off better than most resorts in this part of Yugoslavia. Water sports are also widely available.

Given a choice of hotels, the nineteenth century ones are invariably those to pick if you're looking for character and atmosphere, though often the more modern ones, further out of the town, will have more in the way of facilities and organized entertainment. The **Kvarner Hotel**, now over 100 years old, is one of the nicest places to stay in Opatija and boasts a swimming pool into the bargain. Good, cheaper alternatives are the **Atlantic** or the **Slavija**. An excursion to VOLOSKO via the seaside promenade is worthwhile, to see the eighteenth-century houses and the type of fishing village Opatija used to be before tourism arrived. So is a trip to one of the Kvarner islands: CRES, KRK, LOSINJ and RAB (see relevant pages for details of islands). If you have the energy, a walk up the old road to Mount Ucka will afford you some superb photos of the Gulf of Kvarner, complete with the islands rising out of the sea.

RIJEKA: you're unlikely to stay in the city of Rijeka, but if you're based at Opatija or Crikvenica you may well spend a day here, or pass through it while touring. It is not Yugoslavia's most attractive city, it must be said, but as the country's most important port and a place which has been at the centre of much of this region's history, it is worth a mention. Though it dates back to Roman times there is little in the way of historic remains to be seen as the earthquakes of 1750 and the bombs of the Second World War left a trail of destruction in their wake. A potted history of the city reads thus: under the Habsburgs in the fifteenth century it developed into an influential port. By the eighteenth century the town had become Hungarian, as it remained more or less until September 1919, when the Italian fascist

Gabriele D'Annunzio and his troops occupied the city and claimed it for Italy. It remained in Italian hands until 1945 despite the fact that the Susak district of the town on the other side of the river was actually Yugoslav. Since 1945 the whole city has been recognized as Yugoslav, and its name changed from Fiume to Rijeka (both names mean 'river').

From the tourist's point of view Rijeka's main importance is as the port from which to explore the islands or coast, or as the main point of departure for a trip to Venice. If you find yourself with time to spare in the city the following places are worth a look. From Tito Square, climb the 412 steps to the medieval castle and **church of Trsat**. The steps date back to 1531; the little fortress was built by the Frankopan Counts, as was the **Church of Our Lady**, which they erected to commemorate the miracle of Trsat (the church is built on the spot where the angels are meant to have put down the house of the Virgin Mary in May 1291 after carrying it from Nazareth, and before moving it again in February or December 1294 to Recanati in Italy). This church on the hill above Rijeka remains a place of pilgrimage, even today.

Other sights are the **clock tower** on the main square (Narodni Trg), which is thought to be originally thirteenth century, though was later embellished by the Austrians; and taking the archway in the clock tower you enter the **old town**. Here you find the **old gate** – the oldest monument left in Rijeka, dating back to Roman times.

The Baroque **Cathedral of Sveta Marija** with its leaning bell tower is off Uzarska Street, to the right. The Church of **St Jerome**, and the Church of **St Vitus** are the two other buildings of note in the old town. In St Vitus see the Gothic wooden crucifix with a bronze hand and stone attached to it. This dates back to 1296 when a local notorious gambler was playing cards outside the church, and losing, he took out his revenge on God for deserting him by throwing a stone at the crucifix. The story goes that no sooner had he thrown the stone than the figure on the cross began to bleed, and as he exited the ground just outside the church opened and swallowed him up, leaving only the offending hand which was then ordered to be cut off and burnt. The hand on the crucifix today is there as a reminder.

These are the main places of interest to the tourist. If you wish to base yourself in Rijeka there are a few hotels: the **Bonavia** is undoubtedly the best, though it's not cheap, or try the **Neboder** or **Park**. There's *camping* nearby at Preluk and Zurkovo.

The road from Rijeka right down to the Albanian border is the Jadranska Magistrala – the Adriatic Highway – which in its first sixty or so miles takes you through the Croatian Littoral and to the resorts of Bakar, Bakarac, Kraljevica, Crikvenica and Novi Vinodolski.

BAKAR and **BAKARAC**, situated on rocks at either end of a wide bay, are the first towns of any size after Rijeka. In recent years the hoteliers have crept into both towns, though the level of development is still quite low-key. The ruined sixteenth-century **castle** at the top end of Bakar is worth a call in, and there are a couple of interesting old churches in the old quarter: **St Andrija** and **St Margareta**.

KRALJEVICA, more interesting than Bakarac, has two castles on its shore. **Stari Grad** (Old Castle) and **Novi Grad** (New Castle) were built by the two main influential families in the town's history: the Frankopans and the Zrinjskis. Most tourists stay outside the town at **Ostio Point** and **Uvala Scott** holiday villages (the towns along this stretch are somewhat spoilt, by the industry located here because of the convenience of Rijeka). There's a bridge linking Kraljevica to the island of Krk and Rijeka airport.

CRIKVENICA is the largest resort on this part of the Croatian coast and an ideal base from which to tour the Kvarner Riviera. It is a lively, attractive town which became a popular resort back in the 1920s. There are imposing buildings, parks, tree-lined promenades and a partly sandy beach, which in conjunction with the particularly mild climate makes Crikvenica a busy place in summer. Most of the hotels used by package tour operators are located in the little fishing port of SELCE or in the holiday village of KACJAK. The **Therapia** and **Omorika** hotels in Crikvenica are particularly good. There's a fairly active nightlife and several very good restaurants in the town. The **Jadran Restaurant** is thought to be one of the best for seafood. A pleasant walk from the town takes you to the fifteenth-century Frankopan family **castle** which stands on a hill overlooking the Vinodos Valley, beside the River Dubracina.

Alternatively you could take a daytrip to the islands of KRK (see page 169) or VRBNIK or MALINSKA using one of the regular ferries from Crikvenica. The next resort on the coast – NOVI VINODOLSKI – is also worth a trip. Only about five miles from Crikvenica, its main attraction is yet another castle which belonged to the dominant Frankopan family. It stands on the hill in the old town and dates back to the thirteenth century. The view from the **Church of St Philip and St James** here, over the Velebit Channel and on to Krk, is quite spectacular. The ruin on the hill above the harbour is the remains of a fifteenth-century monastery; in fact there are medieval remains dotted along the entire valley on this part of the coast.

SENJ is fourteen miles on from Novi (as it's usually abbreviated). This town is steeped in history and is best known by the Slavs for its association with the Uskoks – a band of Serbs who, in the late fifteenth century, rose against the Turks who were occupying most of the surrounding territory. In fact the Uskoks turned into a bloodthirsty, avaricious band of pirates who preyed on all the ships in the Adriatic, but this did not detract from their hero-like status in the eyes of the south Slavs. Eventually they took on too much, though, when they dragged Austria – whose control they were technically under – into a war with Venice. The Austrians disbanded the thousand strong Uskoks and made Senj into a peaceful Austrian base. The Slavs make much of the Uskoks' independent spirit and heroic deeds, and many stories and songs in their honour still exist today.

Today's Senj has a few buildings and monuments to remind the visitor of its past. Take a look at the beautifully positioned **Nehay Fort**, sited on a hill just outside the town. This sixteenth-century fortress is now a museum but it was originally used as a defence tower against the Turks. The other sights are located in the old quarter of Senj: the Frankopan family *castle*, the **Great Gate**, the old Baroque square of **Velika Placa** and the fourth-century **cathedral** on Stari Trg. There are also the remnants of the *old city walls* and towers, but as a whole Senj is a rather peculiar looking place as it still has not really recovered from the bombing it took in the Second World War.

Ferries to Rab and Krk run from Senj but services for car ferries to Rab are far better from Jablanac, twenty-four miles further down the Adriatic Highway. From Senj you can travel the fifty or so miles inland to the **PLITVICE LAKES** (see page 280) through the **Vratnik Pass**, where the scenery is wonderful, but the road is not. You take the road to the east at Zuta Lokva and head for the Plitvice National Park. This trip to the heart of Croatia could well turn out to be the highlight of your holiday, so if you've got the chance, take it.

JABLANAC is a quiet, pretty town at the foot of the Velebit Mountains in Zavratnica Bay. There's nothing much to see except for the ubiquitous Frankopan family castle in a suitably dominant position within the town. Ferries to Rab and Pag operate from Jablanac, and this is the main reason for most tourists finding themselves here.

If you are based here, consider a visit to nearby **KARLOBAG** to see its Capuchin convent or a trip to the island of **PAG** where the main sights are the fifteenth-century **cathedral** and the **Princes' Palace**. The coast south of Karlobag is pretty bare and as yet undeveloped, so if you're looking for an away-from-it-all location for rough camping, carry on. Going inland near Starigrad-Paklenica, you'll come across the Paklenica National Park – an area of great unspoiled natural beauty. Carrying on down the Adriatic Highway, the road veers west and crosses the Maslenica Channel to Zadar.

The Northern Adriatic Islands

KRK

Krk is the largest and northernmost of the Kvarner Islands. It's linked to the mainland by a road bridge, numerous car ferries and hydrofoil, and there's now an international airport on the island too. Its main town bears the same name as the island, and this is pronounced in a similar way to the Scots word 'Kirk'. The island's population numbers around 15,000, making it the most densely populated of the Adriatic islands.

PRIVATE. Keep Out   The scenery is rugged and majestic: the south of the island is the most attractive, while the east is desolate and bare. It has an attractive coastline of indented bays and a green unspoilt interior for those who want to avoid crowds.

Tourism moved in comparatively recently; the main settlements are in PUNAT, BAŠKA, VRBNIK, MALINSKA, NJIVICE and OMIŠALJ. The north-west coast of the island is the area where most development will be seen as fishing villages turn into resorts within the space of one season. It's not a vastly developed island yet, though, so don't worry. Fishing and farming remain the main occupations for the locals and there's none of the crass commercialism that you'll find on some of the larger Greek islands, as yet anyway.

The island's history can be traced back to Roman times, though the evidence of Stone Age settlers found in the caves near Baška and Vrbnik would indicate it has been inhabited longer still. Its zenith was in the Middle Ages when the Frankopans – the Princes of Krk who ruled the Croatian Littoral – used Krk as their main base before they lost the island to Venice.

KRK TOWN sits at the head of Punat Bay and its buildings bear witness to its past importance. Today's Krk has only about 1250 inhabitants, but in the days of the Frankopans ten times as many lived there. The narrow streets and old fortified constructions make this a town of considerable character. Among the buildings you should seek out are: the **Bishop's Palace**, with its collection of sixteenth- and seventeenth-century paintings; beside it the **Frankopan castle**, and to the left the **cathedral**, built in the twelfth century on top of a sixth-century basilica, which in turn had been built with the stones of the original Roman baths. (Note the capitals on the Roman pillars and the Roman mosaic floor, seen from a trap-door in one of the side altars.)

Linked to the Cathedral by an arched passage is the tenth-century **Basilica of St Quirinus**, and above it is an eleventh-century Romanesque church which is entered via the bell tower. If you're staying in Krk town, the **Drazica Hotel** can be considered a good choice.

On the other side of the bay from Krk is the town and now resort of PUNAT. There's a sandy beach here, good sea bathing, a naturist camp and evidence of the past in the shape of some elegant eighteenth-century houses. The little island of KOSLJUN is a five-minute boat ride away and is a trip worth taking to see the sixteenth-century **Franciscan monastery**, which houses a museum of local interest and a fortified Romanesque chapel.

BAŠKA is the village on the southern tip of the island, which because of its long beach (though it is mainly pebble), medieval town and churches which date back over a thousand years, is considered one of the most beautiful spots on the island. Two hotels worth considering are the **Velebit** and the **Corinthia**. There's a pebble beach for naturists at Baška.

VRBNIK is the resort of the east coast. It is picturesquely situated on the summit of a rocky outcrop and is a conglomeration of medieval streets and buildings built on the hillside overlooking the pebbly beach. The view from the cliffs right over to the Dinaric Alps is magnificent.

 MALINSKA on the south-west coast is the main resort on Krk. The hotels and developments are mainly located in the adjoining holiday village of Haludovo as Malinska village as such is quite small with only a few shops and cafes surrounding the harbour. The hotels at Haludovo are of a high standard and offer pebbly beaches, rocky bays and special concreted areas for sunbathing. The water sports here are particularly good, and the hotels put on a fairly comprehensive programme of nightlife – the **Marina Bar and Restaurant** is particularly attractive – and many tour operators run packages to this resort.

From Malinska it's possible to walk the shoreline to **NJIVICE**, two and a half miles to the north. This resort is situated in the bay of Beli Kamik and is a good place for family beach-based holidays, being quieter and more relaxed than Malinska. The beaches, again, are shingle not sand, but there are concreted sunbathing terraces and the hotels aim to provide most facilities needed by holidaymakers.

OMIŠALJ is the northernmost resort on Krk. Perched above the sea, this hilltop medieval village still has some of the buildings that were standing in the days when it was a Frankopan stronghold, like, for instance, the Romanesque **Church of St Mary**. New developments that have taken place are down by the sea, but there are paths from the hotels up to the old town. There's not much here in the way of nightlife, so it's a good base only for those who want a quiet time.

RAB

Rab is undoubtedly one of Yugoslavia's loveliest islands. One of the best views of it is seen from the boat as you approach the island. The four campsites tower over the old medieval town of Rab, the island's capital, which sits from the boat as you approach the island. The four campsites tower over the old medieval town of Rab, the island's capital, which sits on a narrow finger of land stuck out into the sea, and the Romanesque cathedral and old Venetian houses stand as reminders to the island's colourful past. Rab does better than most with its share of beaches – **Lopar**, the main resort in the north of the island, has a particularly fine beach, and the **San Marino holiday complex**, much favoured by tour operators, offers as good a setting for a beach holiday as you'll find in Northern Yugoslavia. The climate on the island is very agreeable – it's on the same latitude as the French Riviera, so a fine array of sub-tropical plants and flowers can be found on all parts of the island, with the exception of the north-east coast which is barren and arid in comparison. There are ferries from KRK, SENJ and JABLANAC to Rab, or it can be reached by ship from the port of RIJEKA.

RAB TOWN is often compared in appearance to Dubrovnik because of its pantiled old buildings, narrow winding streets and colourful harbour. The old part of town is, as usual, where to head for to see the sights: the **Prince's Palace** in Tito Square should be your first port of call – not only to admire this thirteenth-century building, but because here you'll find the **Tourist Office** where you should be able to collect a map and some useful leaflets. Thus armed, set off through the passage next to the office which leads to Oreskovic Street, known as Bottom Street (the town's other two main streets which run parallel are Middle Street and Upper Street), to see the old Venetian houses. In Ivo Lola Ribar Street (Middle Street) the buildings of note include the **Dominis-Nemir** palace where the archbishop of Senj and Split was born. This remarkable man did not meet with Vatican approval, however, due to his liberal ideas and scientific studies, so he ended up changing camp, becoming a Protestant, and taking up the posts of Dean of Windsor, Master of the Savoy, and eventually Vicar of West Isley in Berkshire, England. (For further details see J. Cuddon, *The Companion Guide to Yugoslavia*, pages 27 and 28.) He is also meant to have discovered the solar spectrum several decades before Newton was on the scene. All this did him no good, however, and he ended his days in the Castel San Angelo prison in Rome, where he was imprisoned by the Pope (he returned to discuss religious matters with the Pope, his friend, but unfortunately for Dominis that Pope died and his successor wasted no time in imprisoning him).

In the upper town stands the **Cathedral of St Mary Major**: a twelfth-century building with a pink and white facade. The pieces to note here are the Gothic Pietà over the doorway, the six-sided stone canopy with ninth-century carvings, and the fifteenth-century choir stalls. Close to the cathedral is the most attractive of the four bell towers which dates back to the twelfth century and is a fine example of its type. The view from the top is worth the effort.

The **Benedictine Monastery and Church of St Andrija**, founded in the eleventh century, is the next church along this street. You can get the key for the church by ringing the bell – it will be put in the hatch. Other sights worth tracing are the **town loggia** and the Franciscan **Monastery of St Euphemia** with its thirteenth-century Madonna by Vivarini and its impressive library. By this time you'll probably have had your fill of old buildings, so cool off with a stroll through the giant pine trees of **Komrcar Park** set above St Euphemia Bay.

The hotels in Rab town tend to be concentrated in the district called **Varos** or on the **Suha Punta peninsula** in a wooded setting three miles from Rab. Those down by the harbour in the town have most character – the **Istra**, **Imperial** or **International** are all good, or out at Suha Punta try the **Carolina** or **Eva**. For private rooms **Kvarner Express** or the **Tourist Office**, near the waterfront, will fix you up. Alternatively try **Macolic Franica**, 27, 8 Marte b.b. (behind the waterfront supermarket) which is a cheap hotel. There's a naturist beach at Rab town – **English Bay** – which consists mainly of pebble, but is still suitable for children. Others nearby are at SUHA PUNTA and DRAGA-LOPAR.

Rab town offers a good variety of nightlife with lots of restaurants and cafes (try the Prošek local wine), an open-air theatre and laid-on entertainments in the hotels at Suha Punta.

For those seeking privacy away from the main town, take a daytrip to the KALIFRONT PENINSULA. There are paths through the beautiful woods here which will take you out in secluded bays where you can find a quiet corner even in peak season. South of Rab is BANJOL, with good beaches and a few hotels, and on the road to Pudarica (where the car ferry leaves for the mainland) is BARRAT which is noted for its lobsters. The road from Rab to KAMPOR goes via the old **Monastery of St Euphemia** and passes the **Slav Cemetery** which commemorates the 4500 Slav victims of the Italian-run concentration camp which operated on the island in the Second World War.

LOPAR, eight miles from Rab, is a fishing village now making its money from tourism. This resort offers the best beach on the whole coast, so don't expect it to be deserted. The **San Marino holiday complex** is the main development here, situated next to the mile-long sandy 'Paradise Beach'. This is an ideal location for sun worshippers and families.

CRES

Cres (pronounced Tsress) is the second largest of the Yugoslav Adriatic islands. Once adjoined to Losinj by a strip of land, later separated by a canal, today they are again united, this time by a bridge, but despite their close proximity and shared history the islands appear most disparate to the eye. Cres is an island of barren, windswept, limestone hills and has a total population under 4000; Losinj, on the other hand, has more than double that population and though much smaller than Cres (less than one-fifth of the size) its lush vegetation and mild climate come as a stark contrast to the conditions on neighbouring Cres. In fact it's only one side of Cres that deserves the reputation of being barren – the east – for the western coast is covered with pine woods and vines.

The main tourist area is the hotel complex built on a hill, west of the little town of Cres. The beach is not particularly good, but most people here come for the large naturist beach on the other side of the bay – Nedomislja beach. Whilst on the subject of naturism, there is a large naturist centre on Cres – the **Baldwin campsite** – in the south of the island.

Apart from the town of Cres, the other main area for tourist accommodation is the village of **PUNTA KRIZA**, in the south of the island on the road to Osor. Here you can find private houses offering bed-and-breakfast-type facilities. The regular ferries from Losinj to Pag and Hvar stop off here. There's also a sheltered pebble naturist beach here.

A road runs the length of Cres, from POROZINA in the north, where the ferries to the mainland RIJEKA and BRESTOVA leave, down to OSOR in the south (and right on to VELI LOSINJ in the south of Losinj). This road offers one of the most spectacular (and terrifying) drives in Yugoslavia – passing along, among other things, the top of a ridge with a 1000 foot sheer drop to the sea.

CRES TOWN is an attractive fishing port whose past links with Venice can be seen through its buildings and monuments, twisting, narrow lanes, courtyards, churches, city gateways and defensive walls. The main sights are located in the area around the harbour. In the main square (Narodini Trg) is the fifteenth-century **municipal loggia**, where the citizens used to assemble; also here you'll find the sixteenth-century **clock tower** which goes on to the **Cathedral Church of St Mary of the Snows**. Close by is **St Isidore's Church**, the oldest church on Cres, with its fourteenth-century bell. Other sights worth a look are the renovated **Bishop's Palace** and the **Gothic Franciscan Friary Church**, found in the monastery just outside the limits of the old town which are marked by the defensive city walls and two city gates. These gates are the **Bragadina Gate** (1581) and the **Marcella Gate** (1588). A popular excursion from Cres town is to take the boat trip to the **Blue Grotto** on the west coast of the island.

LOSINJ

A bridge spans the 40-foot wide channel between Cres and Losinj, and this is how most people approach this attractive wooded island, with its popular resorts of Mali and Veli Losinj. Known for its exceptional climate (an average of 300 cloudless days per annum) and beautiful coastline, this is one of the best places for water sports enthusiasts to base themselves, and tourism is now the island's main industry. Both Cres and Losinj only became Yugoslavian in 1945, having since 1920 been Italian, and before that the Austrians had a century's rule.

MALI LOSINJ is the largest town and the island's main resort. It is a most attractive place with a busy harbour and lots of cafes, shops and restaurants. There's a fair amount of life in high season, so nightlife is no problem, and the conditions in the bay here are ideal for water skiing and windsurfing. The hotels are dotted around in the pine woods near the shore of Cikat, a ten-minute walk from the town. The beaches here are not terrific, but look good (rocky bays, backed by pine woods). Of the modern hotels the **Vespera** and **Aurora** are equally well equipped, while the **Alhambra** and **Bellevue** have more character.

OSOR is situated at the south end of the island, on the straits between Cres and Losinj. Today this little village is home to only around 100 inhabitants, yet in Roman times there is evidence that this was a flourishing town of 35,000. When the Venetians moved their base to the town of Cres in the fifteenth century, the process of degeneration accelerated, and the result is seen today. What is left as proof of this once important town is the early Romanesque **cathedral** at the centre of the village, the **Bishop's Palace** and the old **Burghers' houses**. The city walls also give an indication of the previous dimensions of this town.

From Cres there are regular boat services to the little village of VALUN, across the bay, and from here there's a track running inland to the island's freshwater supply – Lake Vrana.

On the east of the island the only place worth a visit is the village of BELI. In Roman times this was the base from where the shipping between Cres and Krk was controlled. Today what there is in the way of sights are the parish church and the old market square, but the entire little village is rather quaint and picturesque, and the sort of place worth a visit as it is completely untouched by tourism.

There are naturist beaches at Mali Losinj, near Cikat Bay, and at the **Aurora** and **Vespera hotels**. There is also a naturist camp on the little island of VELI ORJUL, reached by fishing boat from Mali Losinj harbour, though it is pretty basic. The beach (non-naturist) at Cikat Bay, near the hotel complex, is the most popular, so to escape the crowds keep walking south: the further you go, the quieter the coves, until right at the southern tip of the island there are small sandy beaches which are often virtually deserted.

As for sights in MALI: the **Venetian tower** and the adjoining **Church of St Mary** (1676) are worth seeing, and from there the view over the islands and sea is magnificent. From the church take the path which leads up to the **castle**, which dates back to the fifteenth century. In Cikat Bay there's the **Church of the Annunciation**, used by sailors as a place of pilgrimage in the days when shipbuilding and seafaring were the main industries of Losinj.

About three miles south of Mali Losinj, at the opposite side of the island (for Losinj is twenty miles long but only two and a half wide), is

VELI LOSINJ, a beautiful old town with a pretty harbour and painted houses that date back to the Venetians. A new tourist complex has been built here, though this hasn't completely spoiled the atmosphere because, as usual, it's somewhat outside the town and in an attractive woodland setting. The beaches are pebbly, and the one at the entrance to the town harbour gets crowded in summer, so head north to those at NEREZINE, or to the one in the next cove at the village of ROVENSKA. In general the beaches on the east side of the island are not as good.

The old buildings in Veli Losinj to look out for are the **Uskok tower**, built in the fifteenth century by the Venetians to fend off buccaneers, the **Church of St Anthony**, the **Church of St Mary** – another pilgrimage church built on the promontory – and the **Church of Our Lady of the Angels**, which dates back to 1510.

The third main settlement on Losinj which is becoming an increasingly popular resort, though as yet there are no hotels and accommodation is still based on private houses, is NEREZINE. You could do an independent holiday here or in neighbouring SVETI JAKOB.

Boat trips from Mali to the small islands of OLIB, SILBA or ILOVIK make a pleasant excursion and this would be the thing to do if you fancied a day away from it all, on a deserted beach – just you and your picnic. On all three you'll find a beach, a tiny village and a few inhabitants, and that's about it. Alternatively, a half-day excursion could be made to the island of SUSAK, which is said to be the only sandy island in the Adriatic. Private accommodation could be arranged here; and while on the island try some of the local wines, especially the pink sweet one called Prošek.

For car ferries to the mainland you have to go via Cres, but there's a passenger service taking in Pula – Ilovik – Unije – Mali Losinj – Silba – Olib – Rab.

The Dalmatian Coast and Islands

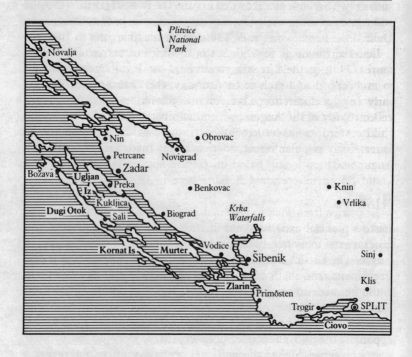

This next section covers the area on the coast from Zadar to Split, including the islands of Kornat archipelago. The main resorts are Zadar, Petrčne, Biograd, Vodice, Šibenik, Primošten, Trogir and Split. We divide what is often generally referred to as 'Dalmatia' into two sections, so if you're looking for a resort which lies south of Split, or for one of the larger islands such as Brač, Hvar or Korčula, turn to the next part of this chapter.

This part of Yugoslavia, south of Istria and north of Dubrovnik, offers scenery on a grand scale, and interesting historic towns with remains stretching from the Romans to the

Venetians. To be frank, it's not the best area for beach-based holidays as the beaches are little improvement on those in Istria, and some of the hotel complexes do lack charm and sophistication, but if it's a sightseeing holiday you're after, with good weather guaranteed, this region is well worth considering. The daytrip potential is excellent, with visits to the medieval city of Trogir, the Roman remains at Split and some fascinating islands; and the climate is hard to beat, with Dalmatia enjoying an average 12 hours of sunshine daily in July.

Local summer folk festivals act as an added incentive to draw the tourists. The one held in Split steals the show. It runs from mid-July to mid-August and includes concerts, opera, drama and ballet. In early July 'Melodies from the Adriatic Shores' is the name for the collective festival of light music; and in Šibenik there is a festival for children in late June–early July. If you're in Zadar, head for St Donat's Church for the series of concerts held there in July and August.

HISTORY

Historically Dalmatia has been influenced to a large degree by the geographical mountain barrier separating the region from the rest of Yugoslavia. Greeks, Romans, Hungarians, Venetians, Austrians, the French and then the Austrians again all successively ruled this area. Although the inhabitants are Croatian Slavs, a greater Western European influence (compared to the more central and southern parts, where the Turks held sway for 500 years) is immediately apparent. Slav people first came to this area, bursting out of their northern homelands, in the sixth and seventh centuries AD. After a period during which several medieval Slav states sprang up in the area, Venice secured control in 1409. The long period of Venetian rule and influence, from 1409 to 1797, is marked by the many buildings in the Venetian style still standing. Only Dubrovnik retained its city-state status by strengthening its citadel and relying on wealth and trade with the competing powers in the region. Except for a brief interlude, from 1809 to 1815, during the Napoleonic Wars when the French Emperor created his 'Illyrian Province' out of this coastal region, Dalmatia was under Austrian and Habsburg rule from the late 18th century until the First World War. (Indeed, reaction to Austrian rule by the Southern Slavs was one of the strongest unifying forces in the ultimate creation of Yugoslavia after the First World War.) Dalmatia, having been united with the remainder of Croatia under Austrian rule, became part of the new kingdom of Yugoslavia after the war and henceforth was bound up with the history and development of the new state.

COMMUNICATIONS

The airports for this part of Yugoslavia are Zadar and Split. The rail base is Split, and buses run the length of the coast. Regular car and passenger ferries from Rijeka call at Zadar and Split, and there's a ferry from Zadar to Ancona in Italy.

The main Yugoslavian travel agency in Dalmatia is Dalmacijaturist, whose head office is Titova obala 5, Split. They have branches in most resorts and organize excursions.

THE CLIMATE

Dalmatia enjoys a mild winter and warm summer. Rain, even in peak season, is always a possibility so be prepared with a waterproof. The sea breeze of the maestral keeps the temperature always comfortable, making it an ideal climate for the very young or old.

CULINARY SPECIALITIES

Fish and seafood are the specialities. Smoked ham in the form of 'dalmatinski pršut' is a delicious hors d'oeuvres, or try the mouth-watering assortment of mixed fish grill known as 'pržene na ulju'. 'Paški sir' is a good after-dinner cheese, and the pastries and home-baked bread are surprisingly good. Ice cream is another pleasant surprise as more cream and less preservatives are still the order of the day here.

Postup and Dingač are good red wines, while Grk from the island of Korčula is the best white. Rosé is also available, as is dessert wine. Prošek is the one generally proffered.

WHERE TO GO FOR WHAT

Dalmatia is a good area for water sports enthusiasts, and most resorts offer water skiing and windsurfing. The beaches are not sandy, but you'll find cemented sunbathing areas and the sea is good for swimming (but watch the sea urchins!).

Fishing excursions are offered and are particularly good in the Kornat archipelago. Duck shooting is offered near Lake Vrana, south of Zadar (contact a local travel agent in Dalmatia, or the tourist office, for further details).

Regional specialities for keen shoppers are lace from the island of Pag (available in most tourist centres), leather goods, copperware and pottery. Zadar produces a wide variety of liqueurs, sold in decorative bottles.

ZADAR

The ancient peninsula town of Zadar was the capital of Dalmatia in times past, and today is a popular holiday destination, ideal for those looking for a fairly lively time with plenty to see and do. Had the town not been flattened in the Second World War there would be many more beautiful old buildings left to see, but the Roman remains, the churches which date back to the ninth century, and the busy shopping centre provide the visitor with a greater than average number of things to see and do.

The main hotel complex is at BORIK, about two miles north of the town. The beaches are sandy (though it is fairly grey sand), and get busy in high season. The nightlife and sports facilities are good and the best hotels are the **Barbara**, **Novi Park** and **Slavija**. The complex has open-air and indoor pools, several restaurants, a night club and a campsite and offers various sports.

There are two naturist centres within reach of Zadar: **Punta Skala**, about eight miles from Zadar, and **Starigrad**, about thirty miles. Both are complete naturist centres with holidays based in hotels there, and catering specifically for naturists.

Independent travellers seeking private rooms should try **Croatiaturist**, 17 Tomislavov Trg (tel. 441436) near the station, or **Generalturist** at Zrinjevac 18 (tel. 445229), along from the Tourist Office. Both will fix you up at a reasonable cost, but both close on Sundays.

One of the cheapest hotels is the **Moša Pijade Centrotel** at Trg Zrtava Fasizma. Or if you're really cutting corners, you can camp at **Camping Mladost** on the Sava River. Take tram 14 towards Savski Most to its terminus. This very good campsite opens May to September.

Two restaurants worth checking out are **Zagrebacki Plavi**, just north of Ulica Socialisticke Revolucje and Heinzelova Ulica; and in the old city near St Mark's – **Gornji Grad** at Meldoska 2.

If you're in Zagreb the last week of July you'll fall into the International Folklore Festival which has free performances at Trg Katerina at 8 p.m. and at Trg Republike at 9 p.m.

Head for the old town of ZADAR to sightsee. Here you'll find plenty to keep you interested, particularly if you're keen on history. Much of the town is closed to traffic so sightseeing is a joy. Make **Tourist Information** your first stop. It's at Zrinjevac 14 and hands out maps and lots of useful leaflets. Two other useful addresses are: American Express (ATLAS) at Zrinjevac 17, open 8 a.m.–8 p.m. Monday to Friday, 8 a.m.–1 p.m. Saturday; and the main Post Office, which is at Branimicova 4, open Monday to Saturday 7.30 a.m.–7.30 p.m.

The main sights are situated around the remains of the Roman forum. The circular structure is the early ninth-century **Church of St Donat**, one of the oldest buildings in the country. Its foundations are the paving stones of the forum, and many of the columns and stones you see incorporated into the structure date back to these Roman origins. The building is no longer used as a church but serves as the venue for occasional summer concerts. Walking round the foundations to the front of the church, you'll come across several box-shaped walls which are the remains of the shops of the Roman forum. The Roman column situated nearby was used as a pillory from medieval times until 1840.

Next to St Donat's on the north side of the square is the **Archbishop's Palace** – Zadar has been the seat of an Archbishop since the mid-twelfth century. Behind this is the **Cathedral of Sv. Stošija** (St Anastasia), the biggest church in Dalmatia and, many think, the most impressive. It is considered to be a perfect example of Romanesque architecture. The structure dates back to the twelfth and thirteenth centuries and is worth seeing for its fine façade and the two exceptionally attractive rose windows. The ninth-century sarcophagus of St Anastasia lies in the left apse inside the church, and while inside note also the Gothic choir stalls in front of the main altar and the fourteenth-century canopy above it. The frescoes on the wall show Christ and St Thomas à Becket. From the top of the campanile behind the cathedral there are fine views over the old town and environs.

Other churches worth a visit are: **St Chrysogonus'**, a twelfth-century building with a beautiful west front and Baroque altar, behind which is a fourteenth-century relief of the Madonna and Child; the **Franciscan Monastery**, worth a look for its art treasures; and two interconnected old churches – **St Andrew's** and **St Peter the Old's** – located on Sarajevska Street and containing Roman columns and altars lifted from the forum.

The **Archaeological Museum** houses its sizeable collection in the building adjoining the Benedictine convent – **Sv. Marija** – and here you will find a collection of religious art relics, finely worked gold paintings, which the nuns will show to interested individuals. In the Archaeological Museum you can see among the remains from Zadar's long past an interesting collection of something rarely seen – Roman glass.

The market place – **Narodni Trg**, or National Square – is the main meeting place in Zadar and where the evening stroll invariably leads you. Here you'll find the sixteenth-century **Guard House** and clock tower. This now serves as the Ethnographic Museum. Across the square is the old law court and today the town loggia. Taking Omladinska Street you come to the Church of St Simeon (Sveti Šimium) where the most sacred treasure of Zadar is kept – the fourteenth-century silver sarcophagus in which the remains of St Simeon are found. This relic attracted many pilgrims over the centuries, including King Henry IV of England. If you've a taste for the gory you can actually ask one of the nuns or priests to lift the lid and show you the remains of the saint's body. Beyond the church is the **Square of the Five Wells**, called today Liberation Square (Oslobodjenja Trg). Here you see the five wells built by the Venetians, and leading off this square (via Meduliceva) you come to the **land gate**. (On the way take a quick look at the Captain's Palace on the right-hand side.) The land gate dates back to 1543 and shows the emblem of its builders – the winged lion of Venice. Beyond the gates lies the small harbour of Foša and from there modern Zadar stretches ahead.

As for excursions – the small coastal town of NIN is the most popular daytrip. It lies 10 miles north of Zadar and dates back to Roman times, hence the remains of the small forum. The tiny ninth-century **Church of the Holy Cross** is hailed as a fine example of pre-medieval Croat architecture, and is definitely worth a visit. Nin was the capital of medieval Croatia and one of the places the early Croatian kings favoured, but, to be frank, there is little of splendour or great interest left to see today.

Another excursion is to the SEA OF NOVIGRAD or Novigradsko More. Take the main road east around 19 miles to get to this wide bay which is linked with the Adriatic through a narrow channel. Novigrad town is well worth a look (see page 153) and from here you can take one of the boat excursions to the ancient village of OBROVAC (while here, take in the vista from the old Turkish fort over the Zrmanja canyon). If you're game to go further, head inland from Obrovac to reach the amazing PLITVICE NATIONAL PARK, which has splendid forests and excellent walking potential. Alternatively you can head north for the island of PAG (go left at Posedarije and cross the bridge from the mainland).

PAG is often described as having a lunar-type landscape – rocky, windswept and prohibitive. It is well worth visiting. The island is famed for its cheese (made from sheep's milk) and for handmade lace. The salt pans lie close to the town of Pag, where all the main sights are located: the **parish church**, the unfinished **Bishop's Palace** and the **Prince's Palace**. The sandy beach here is quite good, and long enough to accommodate all the visitors as it stretches the length of the bay.

The other main settlement and tourist centre on the island is at NOVALJA, formerly a fishing village. The main things of interest here are the Roman aqueduct and the remains of early Christian churches. There are several good beaches, and tourist facilities are increasing each year as this island becomes more popular. To escape any crowds, head to the outer extremity of the island – the fishing village of LUN.

The other main excursion from Zadar is to the island of UGLJAN – located directly opposite the town a half-hour boat trip away. The main tourist facilities are at the villages of PREKO and KUKLJICA. Preko has a good beach and a small picturesque harbour with promenade.

Climb up to the fortress here for an excellent view over to Zadar. The main holiday complex on the island is near to Kukljica – the Zelena Punta. The sports facilities here are good, and among the other beaches there's a naturist one, reached by boat.

Ugljan town has a few places of interest, the main one being the fifteenth-century Franciscan Friary with its Gothic church. Elsewhere on the island there are the remains of a Roman villa near the cove of Bataláža, and at Mulin you can see the ruins of a mausoleum and cemetery basilica, dating back to the fourth to sixth centuries. As an excursion it offers an interesting day's outing and a pleasant escape from the crowds of Zadar. The island is attractive and, away from the developed areas of Preko and Kukljica, remarkably quiet and unspoilt. The side facing Zadar is forested and lush, and the more attractive.

Eight miles north-west of Zadar is **PETRČANE**, a tiny fishing village where Yugotours offer packages. The coast around here is attractively wooded and the hotel provided – the Pinija – is very acceptable, though the village has too few facilities to merit a classification as a proper holiday resort. Also the beaches are shingly. For a real away-from-it-all beach holiday you're better advised to head for one of the islands of the Kornat archipelago. Although tour operators do not operate to these islands, private accommodation is available for independent travellers.

THE KORNAT ISLANDS consist of over a hundred small islets around Zadar, mostly uninhabited and designated a National Park, and present an ideal base for a fishing or scuba-diving holiday. It is not the area to head for if you're looking for a sophisticated nightlife or luxurious hotels. There are only a few summer houses on the occupied islands and supplies of everything (including water) have to be brought in by boat, so this gives you an idea of the type of place to expect.

Most of the inhabited islets lie between Ugljan and Dugi Otok. IZ is the largest, though the most spectacular sight is to be found on **DUGI OTOK** (literally 'Long Island') – that is the huge cliffs at its south-western end. At the north-eastern end of Dugi Otok is **BOZAVA**, where Yugotours now base holidays, ideal for those seeking a quiet time. Trips to these islands can be arranged from the larger mainland centres such as Zadar, Biograd, Murter, Sibenik, Sali and Vodice.

Sixteen miles south of Zadar the coastal road takes you on to **BIOGRAD** or Biograd na Moru (the 'White Town on the Sea'), passing en route the beacon of Filip Jakov. Biograd today is a busy resort with a popular beach, set attractively in pine woods. It's not an ideal resort for sightseers or nightclubbers, though, as there's not much going on. The few hotels are located near the ferry to the island of Pašman which Biograd directly faces.

Sadly there is little left today to remind one of Biograd's colourful past when it was the capital of this region and home to the medieval Croatian kings. The blame for this lies with the Venetians and the Turks who in the twelfth and seventeenth centuries respectively flattened the town. Its revival since the Second World War has been almost entirely due to tourism.

The land around Biograd is extremely flat and abundant in vineyards and gardens, but unless you're content to take repeated walks here, or simply lie on the beach, a holiday in Biograd will not suit you. If you're mobile, however, a daytrip to the village of VRANA (about five miles) may interest you, for here is one of the very few examples of Turkish architecture left in Dalmatia – the **Maškovića Han**. Another trip is on the tenth of each month to the fair at BENKOVAC, fifteen miles inland from Biograd. Local handicrafts can be bought at the market and tourists flock here for that purpose, but remember to bargain.

Apart from the hotels in Biograd, and the large, well equipped holiday centre at nearby Crvena Luka, there's a Club Med holiday camp situated near to the village of Pakoštane. There's also camping at Crvena Luka, three miles from Biograd (take the side road off the Zadar–Šibenik coast road). Naturists can strip off on the bay at Crvena Luka or on the little island of St Katarina, off Biograd, or at the coastal resort of Pirovac. If you're keen on sporting activities or nightlife you'd be better basing yourself at CRVENA LUKA, rather than in Biograd itself.

Alternatively there's the resort of **VODICE**, which is slightly larger and busier than Biograd. This harbour town has large, modern hotel complexes on either side of its bay, with the Olympia complex stealing the show for facilities. The beaches are mainly concreted sunbathing areas and they can become crowded in high season, though it's possible to escape to smaller ones nearby if you're mobile.

Vodice is named after the freshwater springs there (over a thousand wells tap this water). As for the town itself: there's a Baroque church, the yellow limestone cottages down by the harbour and numerous bars and restaurants around the main square, and that's about it. On the 27 July is 'Fisherman's Night' and in August the donkey races liven up the town somewhat, but most of your nightlife will stem from your hotel so choose carefully.

The island of MURTER (take the inland road), connected by a bridge to the mainland, makes a good excursion from Vodice. This island is still relatively unspoilt by tourism and for those wishing to get away from it all it's a good destination. There are numerous sandy coves around Murter (the town of that name on the island) and the low hills offer healthy walking for the active.

Undoubtedly the biggest and most interesting town in this area, though, is **ŠIBENIK**. Although it is undeniably an industrial town, and, again, the beaches are not terrific, it is a fascinating place with some genuine 'sights' to see; also the hotels are well equipped and boast facilities of every kind. The main hotel complex is the **Solaris**, about three and a half miles from the town centre, set in gardens and with numerous sporting facilities. Its best hotels are the **Ivan**, the **Niko**, **June** and the **Andrija**. There are cemented sunbathing areas to compensate for the lack of sandy beaches, and although you can see the tops of the factories from the hotels it is still possible to have a really relaxing holiday here, and it's certainly one of the best places to base yourself if you're keen on sports, nightlife and the odd daytrips. There's a summer festival in June to July and a children's festival at the beginning of July which adds to the activities and nightlife on offer.

The town of Šibenik itself was founded in the eleventh century and, having reached its zenith in the Middle Ages, underwent the same fate as virtually all the towns in this region – destruction, occupation and repeated warring with the Turks, Venetians, Austrians and Italians. Fortunately many of the buildings from

Šibenik's golden age survived and these form the core of the sights. The harbour, which is almost fully enclosed, is actually a bend of the Krka River with Šibenik strategically positioned in its estuary.

The **Cathedral of St James** is undoubtedly the city's finest sight, and is one well worth seeing even if you're not a fan of old buildings, for this is considered one of the country's finest churches. It took over a century to complete (fifteenth to sixteenth) and it encompasses both Gothic and Renaissance styles. It was the work of four different architects. The statue in front of the church is by Dalmatinac (or Orsini of Zadar, as he is often known) who did much of the fine decorative work within the cathedral, such as the frieze on the outside walls of the apses and the magnificent baptistry. The body of the cathedral is of the very attractive local stone, and the construction of the roof from solid stone slabs is considered a feat of engineering. The slabs are jointed together in such a way that the roofs of the dome, apses, nave and aisles show no visible means of support. Note also the carved pulpit (1624), the sacristy, and the singers' galleries.

In the square outside the cathedral stands the **City Loggia**, the hall where the municipal town councillors would have met when it was built back in the sixteenth century. On the other side of the cathedral is the **Bishop's Palace** which was built in the fifteenth century, and beside this is the old **Sea Gate**. The Town Museum is housed in the former Rector's Palace which was the residence of the Venetian administrator, and among its collection are local artefacts dating back to Neolithic times.

A meander through the narrow alleyways of the old quarter will prove colourful and entertaining. There are several interesting old churches to visit, but the atmosphere of the place is the main thing to go for. Take the steps up the twisting streets from the cathedral to the **Fort of St Anne** and the old cemetery below the fort for a good view over the town. The other two forts of the town are **Fort Barone** (reached from Poljana Maršala Tita) and **Fort St John** – the highest of the three which is situated to the north-west of the town. The New Town is reached via the main street of Ulica 12 kolovoza 1941, passing the National Theatre en route, but as with most towns, there's little of interest to keep you in the new section long.

Day excursions are plentiful and good from Šibenik. The best one is undoubtedly to the KRKA WATERFALLS on the Krka River, about ten miles north of the town. This can be reached by bus, car or boat. (If you're driving, go up the hill from Poljana Maršala Tita and take the road to Gulin and Drniš. At Gulin take a left and go down the steep hill through the wooded Krka valley.) The water plunges down over 160 feet, cooling the air as it travels into the basins below – lovely on a hot summer's day. From here you have the option to take the boat out to the Franciscan Monastery of VISOVAC, famed for its ancient paintings and manuscripts. It is possible to make it a round trip from Šibenik – travel on to Skradin and Kistanje from the falls and return via Knin, Vrlika, Drniš and Otavice.

ZLARIN, MURTER and PRVIĆ are the three closest and most interesting of the Kornat Archipelago islands to visit. Zlarin, once the base of a coral industry, today only has one workshop, but it's worth a visit to see the women's traditional costume (though the number wearing it decreases annually). For Murter see page 187. On Prvić is the grave of the inventor Faust Vrančić who is credited with some of the earliest work on parachutes. There is, however, nothing terribly riveting for the average sightseer on any of these islands, and it might be best to head for the livelier holiday resort of PRIMOŠTEN (see below) with its beautiful fifteenth-century church and all the usual holiday facilities. Nearby Rogoznica has excellent beaches, making an ideal sunbathing and picnic spot in which to unwind after the rigours of a morning's sightseeing.

The old fishing village of **PRIMOŠTEN**, set on a hilly promontory on the coast between Šibenik and Split, is an attractive and atmospheric setting for a fairly good family holiday. Old narrow lanes, red-roofed houses, lively cafes and restaurants, and modern hotels in the nearby Marina Lučica and Adriatic complexes combine to offer a good holiday base. The village is built on an islet now connected to the mainland by a causeway and has as its main sights the **Church of St George** (rebuilt 1760), the **Church of Our Lady of Mercy** (1553) and the little **St Roch's Church** (1680). Daytrips to Split, Šibenik and the Krka Falls are offered (don't miss the Split excursion) and there are naturist facilities at the large Marina Lučica hotel complex. The beaches are not spectacular (they consist mostly of rock, pebbles and concreted sunbathing areas) but sand has recently been imported at Marina Lučica. The Adriatic complex is particularly attractive. It is on a wooded peninsula facing the village, and among its best hotels are the **Zora** and **Slava** which offer comprehensive sports facilities, an indoor swimming pool, and a floorshow every couple of weeks.

TROGIR is one of the largest resorts in the area north of Split. This extremely beautiful walled medieval town stands on an island connected by a bridge to the mainland, with a mobile bridge linking it with its neighbouring island of Čiovo. The buildings in Trogir are in a very good state of preservation and many remark that the town resembles a living medieval museum. Certainly if you're keen on historic buildings there are few places to equal Trogir in Yugoslavia. The main hotel complexes are, as usual, located outside the town; about two miles to the north. The beaches are average/poor apart from the one at Medena, but the variety of sports facilities on offer compensates, and the standards in the hotels are generally high. Among the best are the **Motel Trogir** (half a mile north on the coastal highway), the **Hotel Jadran**, and the very good **Hotel Medena** and **Medena Apartments**. There's camping at two sites: Soline and Rozac. For details, ask at **Tourist Information** – Palača Ćipiko, Rade Končara.

As to the town of Trogir: it was founded in the third century by the Greeks (see the first-century bas-relief of the Greek god of Opportunity in the Benedictine convent found on the kitchen floor of an old Trogir house in 1928), and subsequently underwent Byzantine, Croatian, Venetian, French and Austrian rule. During the Second World War the Italians and Germans added to this cosmopolitan mix of invaders. The Venetian influence, however, is the main one still seen in the architecture of the town.

As with the other ancient walled towns of Dalmatia, traffic is banned from the old town, so sightseeing is a relaxed, pleasurable pursuit. You enter the old town through the Renaissance **Gate of St Ivan** (seventeenth century); from here bear left through the narrow lanes, past the Baroque houses and palaces to reach the town square – Narodni Trg – which is dominated by the main sight of Trogir – the **Cathedral**, dedicated to St Lawrence. It took from the twelfth century to the sixteenth century to complete this magnificent structure, with its delicate campanile. The main portal is Romanesque and was built by the Croatian, Radovanus. It is a stupendous work, full of activity and different images: lions, saints, Adam and Eve, imaginary figures, hunting scenes, soldiers, peasants, shepherds – stop for five minutes and take a good look to appreciate it. Its creator certainly appreciated its worth: look at the inscription in the tympanum of the door (completed in 1240) where Radovanus refers to himself as 'the most excellent in his craft, as the statues and reliefs show'.

Other parts of the cathedral worth special attention are the baptistry (1464), but more especially the St John's Chapel with its thirteenth-century octagonal pulpit, fifteenth-century Gothic choir stalls and paintings by Bellini in the sacristy. Climb the campanile for a wonderful photo over the old town.

Opposite the cathedral is the fifteenth-century **Ćipiko Palace**, richly embellished in Venetian Gothic style. It is actually two palaces separated by a lane. Look out in the courtyard for the painted wooden head of a cockerel seized from a Turkish ship by the commander of the Trogirs, Alviz Ćipiko, during the battle of Lepanto in 1571.

On the south side of the town square is the column-fronted **Loggia**, the old centre of the city's municipal happenings, which was used as both the law court and the market hall. The City Tower lies to the east end of the loggia, and behind it stands the narrow little **Church of St Barbara's**, dating back to the eleventh century.

If you leave the square by the narrow street next to the **City Hall** (see the fifteenth-century staircase in the courtyard) you come to the waterfront. Turn right here to get to the **Abbey of St John the Baptist**, which lies south of the City Hall. This is a thirteenth-century Romanesque church containing the Ćipiko (of palace fame) family tomb, and also a few remaining original frescoes from the time it was built. If the church is closed, ask at Tourist Information in the town square.

The other main buildings of note in Trogir are the **Lučić and Fanfogna family palaces** and the **Kaštel-Kamerlengo fortress**, at the far end of the quay. This stronghold at the end of the town walls is no longer used to block entry to the harbour, but today is the venue for outdoor concerts. North of the fort, on the quay, beside the football park, stands a temple-like Gloriette built by Marmont, governor of Dalmatia and one of Napoleon's marshals.

The isle of ČIOVO, where 'new' Trogir is currently expanding, has two main sights to visit: the **Convent of the Holy Cross**, which dates back to the fifteenth century and which is worth the effort to see for its fine cloisters; and the **Church of St Jerome**. Čiovo would hardly count as a daytrip, however. For this you should look to the SEVEN CASTLES (Sedam Kaštela), a string of villages along the bay north of Split, so called because of the seven castles the nobility of Trogir erected to defend their islands from the invading Turks. To reach these villages take the narrow road which hugs the coast for around 10 miles, leaving the Adriatic Highway at Solin. The villages are Kaštel Sućurac, Kaštel Gomilica, Kaštel Kambelovac, Kaštel Lukšić, Kaštel Stari, Kaštel Novi and Kaštel Štafilic. NOVI is worth a look to see the Church of St Roch. In LUKŠIĆ see the Church of St Mary, and in SUĆURAC see the fourteenth-century fortress. A trip through the Kašteli is more to try and capture the atmosphere, however, than to see specific sights. If this is what you're after, take the most obvious daytrip from Trogir to Split.

SPLIT

The city of Split, Yugoslavia's second port and the administrative capital of Dalmatia, is today a large industrial centre and modern city with all that that entails: high rises, pollution, shopping centres, suburbia, etc. Despite this, though, it remains a thriving holiday base, and the reason can be found by looking at the number of exceptional buildings which reflect the city's colourful past – the most obvious example being the Roman Emperor Diocletian's Palace. Split therefore is a base for those keen on sightseeing and nightlife. It is not suitable for the ardent suntanner (the local beaches are poor) or for those keen on long, pollution-free walks. Having said that, though, this *is* almost possible if you stay at the attractive wooded **Marjan Hotel complex**, situated on a peninsula five miles south-east of the city. Split is also an ideal base for people interested in seeing some of the nearby islands, such as Hvar, Brač and Korčula, as island-hopping from Split is easy with regular ferries and hydrofoil connections.

Dalmacijaturist, 12 Titova Obala (tel. 42142) will fix up independent travellers in private rooms – open 7 a.m.–9 p.m. daily – as will the Tourist Office. For camping try **Camping Trstenik** on Put Trstenik, two and a half miles east of the city (tel. 521971), buses 7 or

17. This arrangement may suit those interested in seeing the islands but who still like to return to a lively centre for nightlife and a variety of restaurants after a day's sunbathing or restful sightseeing.

Some of the best hotels for nightlife are the **Marjan**, the **Bellevue** and the **Lav**. The **Hotel Central**, Narodni Trg 1 (tel. 48242), outside the west gate of the square, is a good choice for those keen to stay within the confines of the old town. Most of the hotels are relatively new and modern as they were built for the Eighth Mediterranean Games in 1979.

As for restaurants: the **Ero**, 3 Marmontovo Street, by the old town, has Slovenian specialities; the **Adriano** on Titova Obala on the waterfront specializes in Serbian dishes; the **Dva Gloluba**, beyond the Marjan hotel, is good for seafood (though not cheap), and the **Konoba Adriatik** in the old city centre is atmospheric and puts on a menu of national delicacies. For authentic Dalmatian dishes try the **Zagreb** on Lavčevica, near the old town. The choice of restaurants in Split is as good as you'll find anywhere in Yugoslavia, and far exceeds what you can expect on the islands or in the smaller resorts nearby.

One final practical point – AMEX (ATLAS) is located at 7 Trg. Preporada (tel. 43055), inside the old walls to the right. It opens for foreign exchange Monday to Saturday 7 a.m.–9 p.m. The Tourist Office is at 12 Obala Bratsva Jedinstva, open Monday to Saturday 7 a.m.–10 p.m., Sunday 7.30 a.m.–12.30 p.m. and 4 p.m.–8 p.m. in summer; Monday to Saturday 8 a.m–8 p.m. in winter.

The sights of Split are also more numerous and more exceptional than is average, and at least three days' solid sightseeing is required to get around the basics. The main sight of Split is also the most obvious: above the promenade, down on the seafront, **Diocletian's Palace**, dominating the landscape. The only other landmarks which overshadow the palace in this area are two church towers, but it is Diocletian's Palace which steals the limelight and remains the main reason for the hundreds of thousands of visitors Split attracts each year.

Detailed historical accounts are widely available from Split's tourist information literature, so we can confine ourselves here to the absolute basics required for an understanding of this city and her monuments. In 78 BC the Romans occupied the then Greek settlement at Solin, four miles from today's Split, and began the process of further developing this thriving community. In the civil war between Pompey and Caesar the city supported Caesar's victorious side and as a result it was elevated in size and importance to become the main administrative and economic centre in Dalmatia.

In AD 295, in Salona, as it became known under the Romans, work on a palace began. It was initiated by the emperor of the day – Diocletian, a native Dalmatian, who, it was said, wanted to spend his last years here. Work on the palace took ten years to complete, and when Diocletian abdicated in 305 his palace awaited him.

Ironically, Salona became an important centre for Christianity in the fourth century. Ironic because although Diocletian himself married a Christian, he continued to persecute them as to do so was still politically expedient. The demise of Salona came in 614, when the town was destroyed by the Slavs and the Avars. Diocletian's Palace came in useful then as it served as a refuge for the townsfolk. The city was not rebuilt and it wasted away until its excavation in 1884. Today the ruins of Salona can be seen at Solin, just before the exit road for Split on the Adriatic coastal highway.

Returning briefly to the palace: after Diocletian's death it became a residence for exiled Roman VIPs. With the demise of Rome the palace began to be used as housing for the locals – arcades were walled up and houses made from the divided-up structure, and so the town developed within the confines of the palace walls. When it could no longer hold all the inhabitants the town began to expand outside the walls, with fortified town walls being added in the fourteenth and seventeenth centuries to fend off the advances of the invading Turks. By the late eighteenth century, after the fall of Venice in 1797, control passed into Austrian hands, only to be passed on to the French in 1805. The Austrians regained the town in 1813 and maintained control until the end of the First World War, when it became officially Yugoslavian. In the Second World War Italian and German troops occupied Split and the town was badly hit by air raids.

To view Diocletian's Palace, enter via the Porta Aenea in Titova Obala, down by the seafront. Remember, this palace cannot be viewed, as other buildings can, from the outside. You'll probably be in the palace when you're wandering around looking for it! Shops are embedded within the palace walls; main streets cross the palace at right angles and houses nestle where imperial rooms once stood. (The Zagreb Bank is a shining example of the new being incorporated into the old.) It's best to refer to one of the plans of the palace, available from Tourist Information.

The **Bronze Gate** is found down by the waterfront, and to its left is the entrance to the basement cellars (Podrumi) which come as a welcome cool relief on a hot day. These are situated directly below the emperor's apartments (now demolished). Straight ahead of this entrance up a flight of steps is the Peristyle, or courtyard, with its six massive Corinthian columns on each side. In summer this is the venue for outdoor concerts and an open-air café. At the south end of this courtyard is the entrance to the imperial apartments, though unfortunately nothing remains of the splendid marbles and mosaics which once decorated this vestibule, nor do the imperial apartments stand today. East of the courtyard is the Cathedral of St Domnius (Sveti Dujam) converted in the seventh century from the emperor's mausoleum (unfortunately his sarcophagus no longer remains). The Egyptian sphinx guarding the entrance dates back, amazingly, to the fifteenth century BC. Some of the original decoration from Roman times remains and the outside structure has hardly changed at all, but most of the interior dates from the thirteenth to seventeenth centuries. It was restored last century. Climb up the steps of the tower, above the entrance hall, for a good view.

The mausoleum is octagonal in shape and surrounded by columns. On the interior frieze, which runs around the dome between the cornices, are portraits of the emperor and his wife, Prisca. Note the finely carved wooden doors illustrating scenes from the life of Christ. These date back to 1214 and were the work of Andrija Buvina. Other things to look out for are the hexagonal Romanesque pulpit (thirteenth century); the carved choir stalls in the seventeenth-century chancel, which are the oldest in Dalmatia; the collection of gold and silver in the Treasury, and, left off the high altar, the relief of Christ scourging himself, which is the work of the local sculptor Dalmatinac and dates back to 1448.

Across the courtyard an alley leads to a small Roman temple, thought to have been dedicated to Jupiter. This was converted into a **baptistry** in the Middle Ages.

Beyond the Cathedral, walk down the wide street with its original

Roman paving to arrive at the Silver Gate (Porta Argentea), or pass though this gate to reach the bustling open-air city market. Dioklecijanova Ulica leads to the Porta Aurea, or Golden Gate, in the north wall, and this leads out into a public garden and the bronze statue of Bishop Gregory of Nin, remembered for his work in establishing the use of the Slav language in church services in the tenth century. Off Diocletian Street is the City Museum, housed in the palace of the Papalić family.

The Iron Gate (Porta Ferrea) on the west side of the palace takes you into the **People's Square** (Narodni Trg). The triple-walled **loggia** on the north side of this square is the old town hall (fifteenth century) which today is an **Ethnographic Museum** – worth seeing for the local costumes and handicrafts. Close by is **Renaissance Square** (Trg Preporoda), dominated by the fifteenth-century **Hrvojeva Tower**, originally part of the fortifications erected by the Venetians to fend off the Turks. The statue in the middle of the square is of Mazko Marulić – an early Croatian writer. In Trg Braće Radića the Baroque **Milesi Palace** houses a **Maritime Museum**, for those interested in early ships and nautical matters.

The final 'sights' to seek out in Split are the **Franciscan Friary**, Sveti Frane (down by the seafront at the far end of Trg Republike), with its beautiful cloister, and the **Archaeological Museum** (take Ul Heroja A. Jonica off Trg Republike and continue north of the old town, going towards the City Stadium), where most of the finds from the Roman excavations at Salona are kept.

If you've time left in Split, two further museums which may interest you are the Museum of **Croat Archaeology** (open Tuesday to Saturday 9 a.m.–1 p.m., 4 p.m.–6 p.m., Sunday 10 a.m.–12 noon), and the **Meštrović Gallery** (open 10 a.m.–7 p.m. daily) which contains many of this sculptor's greatest works in the setting of his former home. These museums are close together on the shore road of the Marjan peninsula (bus 12). Near here is a small castle (Kaštelet) with an interesting chapel (the Church of St Cross) and wooden carvings depicting the life of Christ.

There are several daytrips worth making from Split: for those interested in archaeology and history there's the excursion to the ruins of the ancient city of SALONA, situated near Solin, four miles out of town on the road to the airport. Look out just before the site for the remains of the aqueduct which brought water to Diocletian's Palace. It still carries water even today, from the Judro River into the town. All that remains of the town are the foundations and some of the walls; no part of it is intact. In its day there was an arena, a theatre, Roman baths and various temples. Several churches and basilicas were added when Christianity was adopted, but many of these buildings were destroyed when the Slavs and Avars captured the town in AD 614. Most of the treasures are housed in the Archaeological Museum in the northern sections of the town, on Zrinjsko-Frankopanska Street.

Another excursion is to the hilltop fortress at KLIS, five miles from Split. From the towers of this Turkish stronghold you can see all the way from Trogir to the island of Brač. The Turks erected three sets of walls to the fortress and put up a mosque for their worship. This was later converted into a Christian church by the removal of its minaret.

Twenty miles from Klis lies the town of SINJ. This is worth a visit if you're here in August – on August the 5th to be precise – as then a spectacular tournament takes place – the Sinjska Alka. This contest of spear-throwing from horseback commemorates a successful encounter with the Turks. The descendants of the original local heroes of the mid-eighteenth century thrust their lances at a suspended ring (the 'alka'), clad in their colourful local costumes.

Also in early August, in nearby VRLIKA, there's a country fair known as the *dernek* at which the locals sport colourful costumes and sell their handicrafts.

From Split it's also perfectly feasible to take in the 'Seven Castles' (see page 192) or the ancient town of TROGIR (see page 190) for a day's trip. Even ŠIBENIK is possible if you've a car, or can give it a whole day. The options south of Split are Omiš, sixteen miles from the city, and on into the area known as the MAKARSKA RIVIERA with its attractive holiday resorts.

The Makarska Riviera and Southern Dalmatian Islands

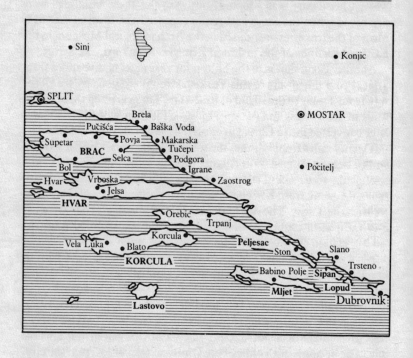

The section of land lying between Split in the north and Dubrovnik in the south is commonly known as the Makarska Riviera. It runs for thirty-four miles and is considered one of the most attractive stretches of coast in Yugoslavia. The Biokovo mountain range, the offshore islands, the white pebble beaches, pine woods and sheltered caves make this one of the most beautiful areas in Europe for a holiday. The seaside villages of this region, lying in the shadows of the massive grey mountains, come alive every summer with foreign visitors. The resorts of **BRELA**, **BAŠKA VODA**, **MAKARSKA**, **TUČEPI** and **PODGORA** are the main centres for international hotels and organized holidays. To escape the crowds, head inland – try taking the road in from the village of DUBCI, through Zadvarje, on to the waterfall at CETINA. Or, for the more energetic, you could make a stab at one of the BIOKOVO range: Sveti Jure at 5726 feet may be a bit strenuous but there are gentler alternatives. Daytrips to Split, Sarajevo, Dubrovnik and Mostar are possible from resorts in the Makarska region.

The Makarska Riviera

BRELA is a small quiet resort at the north-west end of the Makarska Riviera, ideally suited for those wanting a relaxing family holiday. An increasing number of tour operators are running to Brela, and the quality of the local hotels is constantly improving. The resort of Brela is really Donja or Lower Brela, with its superb pine forest which stretches from the Biokovo mountains to the coast. Gornja or Upper Brela is almost 1000 feet higher up, on the mountain face, and in contrast is not at all touristy. The only real 'sight' of Brela is located here: the **Bogomil Stones**, graves of a peculiar religious sect from the Balkans, active in medieval times.

The long pebble beach is attractive and the water is clean. Bathing is possible on both sides of the harbour, with shade provided by the pine trees. Water sports are available, though for scuba diving one has to travel on to Makarska. The best hotels are the **Maestral**, the **Soline** and the **Berulia**.

Excursions to the islands of Hvar and Brač are organized, and with Split only thirty miles away a daytrip to the city is feasible. For the energetic there's a hill walk up Veliki Kuk (1919 feet) where from the top you'll be rewarded with spectacular views of the islands. Alternatively take a trip into the mountains – follow the winding road up through the Vrulja Gap to Šestarovac, Zagvozd and Grabovac to reach Imotski, about thirty miles away. A different type of walk, but equally attractive, is the one and a half miles to the nearby resort of Baška Voda, reached via a wooded footpath which skirts the coast.

A good hotel is the **Maxira**, a quiet place – like most hotels in this resort – suitable for most people.

BAŠKA VODA was until the 1970s a quiet fishing village but now, like its neighbours, it earns its bread from tourism. Another good base for a family holiday, this attractive resort lacks only a beach. Despite this, Baška Voda is a very pleasant holiday destination and has as its sights two Baroque churches. There is a delightful coastal walk to Promanja, two miles away.

MAKARSKA, the 'capital' of this stretch of coast, is a highly attractive port town at the foot of the Biokovo mountain range. It lies in a broad curved bay, bordered by pine trees, and boasts one of this region's finest beaches (though to be honest beaches are not the forte of this region). Several tour operators base holidays here, and it's a good place to stay for those seeking a fairly relaxing holiday but with some sights and nightlife. It's one of the largest and busiest resorts in this area, and by comparison with other places it has a lot to see and do.

As far as sights go – the **Franciscan Monastery** on Srécko Borić Street (to the south of the town) houses an impressive seashell collection; the **Church of St Mark** in the main square is worth seeing for the sixteenth-century icons kept in its sacristy; and in the beautiful Baroque **Ivanišević Palace** you can see the Museum of National Liberation.

The **Dalmacija** and **Meteor** hotels are the town's best, with pools, access to pebble beaches and organized nightlife. For less expensive alternatives and those freelancing, try the **Motel Kuk**, north of the town, or the **Hotel Beograd**. Excursions to various places are on offer including Split, Trogir, Dubrovnik, Mostar, Hvar and Bisevo, with its lovely 'Blue Grotto'.

The resort of **TUČEPI** should really be called Kraj, which is the official name of this coastal settlement, but invariably it is referred to by the name of Tučepi which is really the old hillside village, situated some 2600 feet above the new resort. As a holiday centre it is very pleasant – the hotels are good and the long beach, though again pebbly, not sandy, is gently sloping, clean and therefore suitable for children.

Close to the hotels on the coast is the **Church of St George**, some seven hundred years old, and on the site where today the very good **Alga Hotel** stands was the medieval summer residence of an abbot.

PODGORA at the southern end of the Makarska Riviera is a lively and popular small resort in a picturesque setting at the base of Mount Biokovo. In peak season it gets incredibly crowded, to the point of the beach becoming uncomfortable. This lack of space restricts the sporting activities to water-based ones. The beach is narrow, pebbly and offers little privacy due to its proximity to the main street. Despite these drawbacks, its setting and the comprehensive facilities offered by the hotels, especially the **Minerva** and the **Mediteran**, make Podgora a good holiday resort for those wishing to unwind.

Because of its unfortunate recent history – she suffered no less than forty air raids in the Second World War and was victim of an earthquake in 1962 – many of her old historic buildings have been destroyed. What remains is the **Baroque church**, which dates back to 1764, and the seventeenth- or eighteenth-century **watch towers** in the little settlements of Marinovići and Ruščići in the upper part of Podgora, on the hillside (largely abandoned after the earthquake).

The white monument of seagull's wings on the hill commemorates the fact that it was in Podgora that, in 1942, the partisans established their first naval base – a fact which earned the village the title 'cradle of the Yugoslav navy'.

To reach quieter beaches, travel a few miles further down the coast to the little village of IGRANE. Even before you reach it you'll notice a change in the countryside. It becomes much wilder and more dramatic. Igrane and its neighbouring villages of ZAOSTROG and ZIVOGOŚĆE are realizing their tourist potential and turning rapidly from quiet fishing villages to mini-resorts. Their sheltered waters and proximity to the larger Makarskan resorts will undoubtedly prove popular in the years to come.

In Igrane look out for the eleventh- or twelfth-century **Church of St Michael** above the village, and the seventeenth-century **watch tower**; also the **parish church** (1752) in Igrane itself. Zivogośće has the ruins of a Franciscan friary.

The best beach on this stretch of coast is considered to be at **Gradac**, within easy reach of Podgora.

The Southern Dalmatian Islands
(*the Islands off Split*)

PRIVATE. Keep Out The islands off Split – Brač, Hvar, Korčula, Vis, Lastovo, Peljesac and Mljet – make wonderful bases for peaceful holidays, ideal for those who aren't too fussed about seeing a lot of the country or having a very active nightlife. The physical beauty of these islands, particularly Korčula and Hvar, is making them increasingly popular destinations for package holidays, but, in the best Yugoslavian style, the large hotels are generally located on the outskirts of the old attractive villages, and invariably the hotels, apartments and villas are constructed in the vernacular architecture with the red-tiled roofs, balconies, and in the simple Mediterranean style that enhances, not detracts from, the landscape. Ferries or hydrofoils ply the water between Split and these islands, though not with such regularity that it is simple to get to the mainland for an evening's entertainment, so bear this in mind if you're the restless type. On the plus side is the fact that you really do escape what little commercialism there is in Yugoslavia as these islands are even more friendly, relaxed and unspoilt than the mainland resorts, making them popular with older people and those with young families.

BRAČ
Brač (pronounced Brach) is the third largest of all the Adriatic Islands and becoming increasingly popular with tour operators. Away from the coastal resorts the island remains extremely undeveloped and unspoilt, and even in the main resorts of Supetar and Bol life still continues at a very relaxed pace. The little villages on Brač are surrounded by vineyards and olive trees, divided up by boulders and hills of limestone. Historically Brač was important as a quarrying area – in fact marble from Brač has ended up in Diocletian's Palace in Split, and, more surprisingly, in the White House in Washington. As it's only 45 minutes from Split by steamer, daytrippers are a common sight. The boat docks at Sutivan, but if you stay on you will get to the main town of the island – Supetar.

The curved harbour of **SUPETAR**, facing Split and Makarska on the mainland, is one of the town's most attractive sights. The colourful stone buildings date back to the rule of the Austro-Hungarians, and only a few minutes from the harbour lie the original low-storey houses with their tiny windows and their tall chimneys which are characteristic of Brač and constructed in such a way as to avoid destruction by the powerful wind – the bora. The hotels are east of the harbour, a short distance away, shaded by pine trees. Among the best and most attractive holiday bases are the **Hotel Kaktus** and the **Mirta Pavilions**. Both are constructed as hotel complexes of separate pavilions, based round shared catering and entertaining facilities. Restaurants and cafes are clustered round the harbour and are good bases for a bit of man-watching, and there's a surprisingly active nightlife in July and August: open-air cinema, fairs, discos, live entertainment, etc.

The news on the beach front is not so good: there is absolutely no sand and even the pebbly and concreted areas are packed out in high season; still, if you're really keen you can always make your way to the famous beach of **Zlatni Rat** (the 'Golden Horn') in Bol, on the south coast of the island. At the end of the long beach in Supetar is the cemetery containing the mausoleum of the Petrinović family who came from Chile to live in Brač and proceeded to make their fortune mining saltpetre.

Further down the coast from Supetar, going east, is the village of SPLISKA, and close to here is the stone relief of Hercules, said to date back to the third century. Farther east you come to PUČIŠĆA where the largest quarries were located and which was once a thriving base for the craft of stonemasonry. The **parish church** here is worth a look for its attractive wooden altar and painting of St Roch by Titian's pupil, Palma Giovane.

Heading inland you find the village of SELCA where the craft of stonemasonry was taken to its limits: virtually *everything* you can see is made out of stone. From POVJA the steamer returns to Split.

On the opposite side of the island lies **BOL**, the second largest tourist settlement after Supetar, though apart from the beach of Zlatni Rat the resort consists only of a couple of restaurants and cafes down by the harbour, and the nightlife outwith the hotels is non-existent. For those seeking a relaxing fortnight in the sun, in beautiful unspoilt surroundings with the mountains and sea close by, it is an ideal place. The **Hotel Bretanide** is one of the best on Bol, in a position close to the beach which is reached by steep steps.

In Bol itself, see the seventeenth-century **mansion house** on the sea front, the **Church of Our Lady of Mount Carmel**, the **Gallery of Modern Art** and the **Dominican Monastery**. For archaeologists and historians the **local museum** may prove of interest as it contains prehistoric remains and historic documents. The ruins up on the hill above Bol are what's left of a village after the Second World War.

The energetic can climb the 2553 feet up VIDOVA GORA, the highest mountain in the Dalmatian islands, though in the heat of the summer this is not to be recommended. A strenuous climb from the bay of Blaca takes you up to the **Hermitage** – a medieval refuge for priests which was occupied until 1973 when the last hermit died. He was an extraordinary man: a distinguished astronomer who possessed an extensive library of books. Visitors can see in the monks' cells and the observatory. It is well worth the effort to make it up there.

HVAR

The island of Hvar (pronounced 'Whar') is deservedly one of the most popular holiday destinations in Yugoslavia. The reason? Its exceptionally good climate, which has earned it the name of 'the Madeira of the Adriatic'; the charm of its old villages; the scented hillsides of lavender and rosemary which perfume the air; and the interesting sights of its capital – Hvar town. It is an island of great scenic beauty – clear blue water, steep hills of vineyards and olive groves, traditional red-roofed houses, and, away from the three main resorts of Hvar, Jelsa and Starigrad, an unspoilt rural interior, untouched by the passage of time. In short, you'd be hard pushed to find a more idyllic setting for a relaxing holiday.

The island is forty-three miles long, the longest of the Adriatic islands, with dramatic mountains in the west and a fairly flat landscape in the east. The local industry of lavender growing and pressing makes for a heady perfume accompanying excursions in the hills and interior, and, of course, results in the omnipresence of bottles of the essence sold as souvenirs (at very reasonable prices). A potted history of the island shows Hvar has had many masters, but the main forces to shape it came from the Romans, Venetians and Austrians. It is the Venetian one, however, which is strongest felt as the architecture of Hvar town so closely illustrates.

For sights and entertainment, **HVAR TOWN** is the best place to be based on the island. It is far busier and more highly developed than the other resorts but obviously this results in its being more crowded in peak season. There are several good hotels in the town, but a particularly fine one is the **Hotel Palace** – an old Venetian loggia near to the harbour. The **Amfora** and **Adriatic** are modern equivalents offering equally high standards (though the position of the Adriatic, being down by the harbour, is preferable). Unfortunately Hvar suffers from the same old Yugoslavian complaint of few beaches, and those that there are being rocky, but the atmosphere of the town and the amount of excursions on offer make up for this for all but the most ardent sun worshipper (who shouldn't head for this part of Yugoslavia anyway). There is one town beach, but you're better advised to take a boat out to one of the nearby small islands where naturist beaches are to be found. (**JEROLIM** is particularly good.) The streets are traffic-free and life centres on the harbour with its open-air restaurants and cafés. Apart from the entertainments laid on in the hotels, there is often dancing in the evenings in the livelier restaurants, though the locals seem happier taking their evening promenade in the main square and down by the port.

The **Sea Gate** leads into the main **piazza**. On the left is the **sixteenth-century loggia** with its clock tower and attractive arcades; at the end of the square, beyond the medieval well, is the sixteenth-century **Cathedral of St Stephen**, with its seventeenth-century tower. Note the 'Madonna with Saints' painting by Umberti (1692) and the thirteenth-century 'Madonna and Child'. On the south side of the square is the **Arsenal**. Galleys used to enter it from the arched entrance on the waterfront. In 1612 when a second storey was built on to the building, it became a theatre – the first indoor theatre in the Balkans. Today it is still occasionally used. The opulent interior you see dates from 1800.

Walking along the quay, left from the Arsenal is the **Franciscan Monastery** – a fifteenth-century building still in use today. In the church are some interior paintings and there is a museum of religious artefacts housed in what was the old refectory. In the garden outside the refectory stands a cypress tree, now in its fourth century.

Above the town is the **Spanish Fort** (bus from the harbour) from where there is an excellent view over the old town, and higher up still stands the **fort** erected in the days of Napoleon's rule over the island (1806–13), though this cannot be visited as it now serves as a military radar station.

One final place of note worth finding is the **municipal gardens**. Take the paths from the right-hand side of the harbour. Beyond the gardens is the modern part of Hvar where some of the large hotel complexes are situated. The ruined monastery on the hillside is the venue for occasional summertime concerts and outdoor plays.

STARIGRAD, the island's second resort, is reached via the winding road over the hills, originally built by the French when they occupied this part of Dalmatia. This was the town settled by the ancient Greeks in the fourth century, when they called it Pharos. A quiet attractive place with a beautiful waterfront of Baroque buildings, it stands on the northern shore of the island and is protected on either side by pine woods. The hotels (the **Arkada** is best for nightlife and facilities) lie one mile outside the old town, and rooms are available in private houses. Sights include the **sixteenth-century house** of the Croatian poet Petar Hektorović. This is particularly worth seeing for its attractive courtyard and the fishpond enclosed in cloisters. Its architecture belies its previous use as an old fortress against the Turks. The nearby **Dominican Monastery** has a Tintoretto painting and there are two churches worth visiting. Overall, though, Starigrad is best suited for those seeking a relaxing holiday based largely in the hotel, by the pool. There are several cafés down by the waterfront, but you'll have to rely on your hotel for nightlife.

PRIVATE. Keep Out **VRBOSKA**, at the innermost tip of a deep narrow inlet on the northern side of Hvar, is a pleasant little village for those seeking a 'get-away-from-it-all' atmosphere. The hotel **Adriatic** is particularly suited to the sporting-oriented, and provides an ideal base for those keen on improving their tennis, swimming, badminton and water sports. Its location is superb – set among pine trees and gardens – and close by there are two churches worth seeing: **Sveta Marija**, built as a fortress just in case the locals found themselves in trouble, and **Sveti Lovrinac**, which houses a painting by Paolo Veronese. Down by the harbour is a beautiful green islet, often pictured in holiday brochures featuring Hvar.

The last resort on Hvar is **JELSA**, half way along the island and in a particularly beautiful setting of pine forests and hills. This relaxing little fishing village is becoming increasingly popular and as far as tourist facilities go it ranks next to Hvar town. (That still doesn't mean that there's terribly much, and it is still a quiet, unspoilt resort.) In high season when the tourists outnumber the locals there is enough in the way of nightlife and entertainment to satisfy most holidaymakers, and it is the charming sort of town which people seem to return to year after year. The hotels are just outside the village, and of the selection the **Jadran** and **Fontana** are overall the best. Beaches are poor – it's virtually impossible to get a decent sandy beach – but there are cemented sunbathing areas and rocky coves, or there are always the hotel pools. The main square down by the harbour is a popular place to sit and manwatch, and for the more energetic a walk up through the old town (take the steps up from the square, past the church, and carry on into the winding alleyways) will reward you with a glimpse of the old way of life in Jelsa and take you up into the mountains.

Hydrofoils are the main means of transport for getting around the islands. The disadvantages of being based on Hvar are that excursions to the mainland take a long time (meaning many have to start as early as 6.30 a.m.), and they are expensive. It is just about possible to visit places as disparate as Dubrovnik, Split, Mostar and the Krka Falls, but it requires some thought beforehand. As the quality on some of these tours is questionable (guides speaking poor English, connections running late etc.), enquire locally to see if you can make these trips independently.

KORČULA

A favourite island with the British with an exceptionally charming capital town, Korčula is reputed to be the birthplace of Marco Polo. Cruise ships, today replacing the trading ships of centuries past, call in at Korčula on their way from Venice to Dubrovnik, stopping to let their passengers see the famous Moreška dance which commemorates the local battles with the Turks. The main resorts for package holidays on Korčula are Korčula town and Vela Luka, which is situated on the western tip of the island, about thirty miles from the capital. As with the other islands, a holiday on Korčula is best suited to those seeking a fairly quiet relaxing time, but, having said that, there is more going on in Korčula town than in most island resorts and the nightlife is good in high season. The villages of Čara, Smokvica and Blato are becoming popular with the independent travellers, though for scenic beauty and atmosphere there is nowhere on the island – or, many would say, on any of the Adriatic islands – to rival Korčula town. As Korčula is less than a mile from the mainland, excursions are far easier than from the other Dalmatian islands. The historic mix of rulers on the island reads slightly differently from that of the other Dalmatian islands for though Venice and Austria were still the two main influences, in the case of Korčula Britain took over control from 1813 to 1815, after the brief French rule under Napoleon. Also, looking further back still, Korčula differs in that after the Neolithic settlers it was not the mainland Greeks who occupied the islands as they had Korčula's neighbours, but the Trojans, then the Dorians who held sway in 1200 BC and the fourth century BC respectively. By 35 BC the Romans had taken control and Korčula's history was linked with the rest of Dalmatia. Many well-preserved reminders of Korčula's past can be found on the island, particularly in Korčula town.

The medieval walled town of **KORČULA** stands on a small peninsula and today is a credit to the craftsmen who rebuilt her historic buildings after they were virtually destroyed in the Second World War. The architecture that you see ranges from the fourteenth to the sixteenth centuries: Romanesque-Gothic styles. The main sight is the **Cathedral of St Mark** in the main square, begun in the early thirteenth century, though not completed until the sixteenth century. It incorporates many interesting features including a beautiful carved stone door and two paintings by Tintoretto, and is a classic example of the mix of Romanesque and Gothic styles. Next to the cathedral is the fourteenth-century **Abbot's Palace** which today is a small museum housing the treasures of the cathedral and other works of art. Across the square, the beautiful Renaissance mansion house you see is **Gabriel's Palace** which today acts as the Municipal Museum, with a collection devoted to local history.

Next to All Saints' Church is the **Guildhall** with a collection of religious paintings including some icons from the Greek island of Crete which found their way to Korčula after the Candia war in the seventeenth century.

The birthplace of Marco Polo (so the locals insist) is near to the town's oldest church, **St Peter's**, which was started back in the tenth century. (Take the small street on the right from the church to get to the house.) Today the house is part museum, though as the whole question of validity is at stake and there's little to see inside don't be too upset if you don't make it along. There are numerous more Venetian loggia and beautiful old buildings in the old town (which in its heyday had as many as 4000 inhabitants); perhaps the best plan is just to wander round the entrance to the city – the elaborately carved **Land Gate** – and soak up the atmosphere in the surrounding narrow streets. As with Venice, the best sightseeing tours in Korčula are those you make yourself, unguided, away from the treadmill of tourists, where you unexpectedly stumble across some forgotten Renaissance house abandoned in the great plague of the sixteenth century. Outside the town walls are two places worth finding: the **Dominican Friary** on the seafront heading west, and **St Nicholas's Church** with a copy of Titian's St Peter above the altar.

Most of the hotels are further round the bay from the picturesque harbour where the cafés and restaurants are to be found. The **Marco Polo** is the best of the bunch and is a particularly comfortable and well equipped hotel, though the **Park** is also good. Or, if you don't mind being further away from the sights of Korčula, the **Bon Repas** hotel and pavilions are also well kitted out. Entertainments are laid on in the hotels, but for a really different spectacle be sure you make it along to one of the performances of the ancient sword dance – the moreška (your rep or one of the tourist agencies will have details of performances: generally it's every Thursday in summer).

There's no shortage of places to eat or drink as Korčula is well used to tourists, and for the sportsmen there's a windsurfing school and an assortment of other sports based at Hotel Marco Polo (guests at the Park Hotel share these facilities). The beaches on the island are not great and you really do just as well to stay by the hotel pool, but if you're determined there are frequent boats to several of the twenty or so small islands which lie in the channel between Korčula and the mainland. The nearest one, **Badija**, has been made into an excellent sports centre, and on many of the other ones naturist sunbathing is possible.

A popular excursion is to the beautiful island of MLJET (see page 11) or to the inlet of VRNIK, about two miles away. The quarry the Romans dug there is still in use today. From it you get a view over twelve of the neighbouring islands.

LUMBARDA, at the south-east end of Korčula, about four miles from Korčula town, has the best sandy beach for miles around (some say in the whole of the Yugoslav Adriatic), and it can therefore get crowded in high season. Still, if you make it to Lumbarda you'll be able to sample its famous golden wine – *Grk* ('Greek') – which is reason enough for going (but, be warned, it's pretty potent stuff!).

If you have the transport (though car hire here is really not worth the money) you can head off to see some of the interior of the island. BLATO is worth a visit. This is the largest town on Korčula situated inland, and has to its credit several buildings dating back to medieval times. Its **castle** is now the town museum containing artefacts found in the nearby Roman villa of Junium. If you're in Korčula on 23 April make a special effort to get to Blato as that's when they hold their pageant play to celebrate the day in 1944 when the island was liberated.

From Blato the road continues on to **VELA LUKA**, the second main holiday resort on Korčula. To be frank, as a resort Vela Luka isn't a patch on Korčula town: it is partly industrialized, has no beaches worth mentioning and is very limited in its nightlife, but if you're a keen naturist it's worth considering as there are frequent boats out to the islands of PROIZD and OŠJAK. (For those looking for a quiet time it is also suitable.) The harbour at Vela Luka is very attractive, and the hotels do make an effort to provide entertainment and sporting facilities, including windsurfing.

Nearby islands worth visiting are PELJEŠAC, separated by a narrow channel from Korčula, LASTORO, a quiet little fishing island just south of Korčula, and MLJET.

PELJEŠAC is a peninsula linked to the mainland by a strip of land, but it's usually thought of as an island with ferry connections to either end of the peninsula: TRPANJ and OREBIĆ. The most beautiful place on the peninsula is **OREBIĆ** which is situated opposite Korčula. If you don't take the ferry but drive the forty-five miles' length of the peninsula from the mainland, you pass the beautiful old village of STON with its incredible hillside fortifications and remarkable old buildings. These include the Gothic **Chancery** of the Republic of Dubrovnik, the **Sorkočević Palace**, the sixteenth-century **Bishop's Palace**, **St Nicholas's Church** and the Gothic **Franciscan Friary**. It's worth taking the road just to see this village. If you fancy stopping off, the **Hotel Adriatic** is acceptable.

If, however, you take the ferry from Korčula or Dubrovnik straight to Orebić, you will find a tranquil, picturesque village, notorious for its seafaring past. Set amid the lush vegetation are numerous villas belonging to retired sea-captains; so many in fact that Orebić has earned itself the name 'town of the sea-captains'. There's a **Maritime Museum** here with old navigation aids, nautical maps and charts, and pictures. More nautical material can be found in the private collections of the Župa and Fisković families which are open to the public. (Matko Župa is the Maritime Museum's Director and an expert on nautical matters.) Beaches in Orebić are poor and have no sand, but the hotels – **Bellevue**, **Orsan** and **Rathaneum** – are very pleasant and lie about a mile from the town. In Orebić you can see the fifteenth-century **Franciscan Friary**, the Gothic **Church of the Mother of God** and the ruins of the **Rector's Palace** from the days when the Pelješac peninsula belonged to the Republic of Dubrovnik (1343–1806), when the Rector lived in Orebić.

The energetic could consider a climb up the mountain range which runs through the peninsula, but with the height going up to 3000 feet an early morning start in summer is strictly essential. The path up to the summit of Sv. Ilija takes just under four hours. There's an overnight mountain hut at the top from where at dawn the sunrise over Dalmatia is breathtaking.

A holiday based in Orebić would suit those interested in history, sightseeing and relaxation. Essentially it would result in a quiet time as there is little in the way of nightlife, but the scenery and setting is more than enough compensation.

There is also a hotel in Trpanj (owned by the Czech government and consequently full of holidaying Czechs) but that village has little to recommend it. Naturists can take the daily boat to the islands of VELIKA STUPA and MALA STUPA.

MLJET

The island of Mljet is well worth visiting as a daytrip from the Split and Dubrovnik regions, and for those seeking a relaxing holiday amid remarkably beautiful scenery it is an ideal base for a week or two's holiday. It is not the right location for the smart set as there are no beaches or trendy places worth mentioning. In fact the whole island (or island within an island, as it turns out) is designated a National Park, which should give you an idea that it is a rather special place and an ideal base for the 'outdoor sort'. (Ironically, back in

Roman times the Emperor Septimus Severus used Mljet as a place of exile for offenders.)

In the twelfth century the island was given to the Benedictines from Apulia, and it was they who established their base on the islet in the inlet of the sea, known as Veliko Jezero. Their twelfth-century abbey today houses a small hotel. The other main accommodation is to be found in the **Odisej holiday complex** which is modern, compact and has watersports facilities.

At the north-west end of Mljet are two lakes – VELIKO JEZERO and MALO JEZERO. They run into the sea via a channel 33 feet wide and 8 feet deep which, not surprisingly, has a very strong current. This is the area of the National Park – all twelve square miles of it – and walks and picnics in the pine woods make for memorable excursions.

On the island of Veliko Jezero is the unusual **Church of Our Lady** which belonged to the Benedictine abbey when it was still functioning. The other main sight is at Polače, the old port, where the remains of a **Roman palace** are to be found. But it is the sights of the natural world which make Mljet worth a visit: the mongeese which freely roam the island (these were introduced from the Far East to curb the snake population); the caves near the village of BABINO POLJE where remarkable stalactite formations can be seen; and the freshwater depressions in the interior of the island.

From Korčula the boat journey to Mljet takes around two hours, and from Trstenik on the Pelješac peninsula about an hour. It's offered as an organized daytrip from most of the resorts on the Dalmatian mainland and islands such as Hvar and Brač.

LOPUD

The last of the islands in this area, lying just off the coast of what brochures refer to as the 'Dubrovnik Riviera', is Lopud, the most developed of the Elaphite Islands – the name given to the chain of islands just six miles north-west of Dubrovnik. A holiday on the island of LOPUD will have to be based in the village of that name as it is the sole resort – and harbour – on the island. There is less going on here than on most of the larger Dalmatian islands, so only base yourself here if you want to have a quiet time. Ruins of castles, villas and a monastery show the past importance of Lopud from the time it was under the control of the Republic of Dubrovnik in the fifteenth century. Lopud was given its own Rector in 1457 and to this day you can see the ruins of his house. Other sights are the **Church of St Elijah**, and the **museum** next to the church's presbytery. Here all the artefacts of local historical interest have been housed under one roof.

Of the hotels in Lopud, the **Lafodia** is the pick of the bunch, though the position of the **Hotel Dubrava Pracat** is preferable, being right in the centre of the village. There is ample scope for naturist bathing on Lopud – a 30-minute walk over the hill from Lopud village brings you out in the second bay of the island which is reserved for naturists.

The two other main islands of the Elaphite Archipelago are KOLOČEP and ŠIPAN. There are excursions from Dubrovnik which take in all three islands as a daytrip. In Koločep see the parish church in the village of DONJE ČELO. Yugotours run to Donje Čelo now. Their Hotel Villas Koločep provide a perfect setting for a quiet family holiday. Facilities are few but the peaceful setting and spectacular scenery make this a favourite with those keen to unwind.

In ŠIPANSKA LUKA, the main village on Šipan, see the **Rector's Palace**, the **parish church** and, en route to the village of Sudjurad, the remains of the Bishop's summer residence which dates back to the sixteenth century. Once at SUDJURAD there is a **sixteenth-century castle** and a **watch tower** to see before returning on the two and a half mile-long footpath to Šipanska Luka. You will find these islands refreshingly unspoilt and scenically very beautiful, but their holiday potential is strictly for the peace-seekers.

SLANO is well worth getting to. This village in the area just north of Dubrovnik takes a bit more time to get to if you're based on the islands, but it is well within reach if you're in Dubrovnik. It lies at the head of a sheltered bay fifteen miles north of Dubrovnik, and though it is a popular holiday resort, it is still relatively quiet even in peak season because, as yet, the package tour operators have not moved in. Of the three hotels the **Admiral** is the best, but there is no shortage of accommodation to be had as private rooms are available in the village. Slano has an excellent setting for a family holiday: the beaches have gentle inclines and because of its position the water warms up more quickly than in the open sea. Nightlife, such as it is, centres on the attractive harbour, but mainly consists of cafés and restaurants. In short, Slano is a good place for a quiet and relaxing holiday. For naturists, there is a special centre at the **Hotel Osnure.**

The main sight is the **Rector's Palace** which dates back to the fifteenth century, though much of what you see today is nineteenth-century. (Slano was the seat of a Rector, or governor, when under the control of the Republic of Dubrovnik from the fifteenth century.) The other main sights are: the **Franciscan Friary** with its early Christian sarcophagus; the **Franciscan Church** of 1420; the **Mansion House** of the Ohmucević; and the **Parish Church of St Blaise** which was built in 1758.

If you're anywhere in the area of Slano on 2 August be sure to make it to the village to see the fair at which villagers dress in traditional costume and perform their local dance – the *lindjo.*

From Slano an excellent excursion is to the village of TRSTENO, eight and a half miles away. As you enter the village you come across two plane trees, now in their fifth century, one with a circumference of 36 feet. The sixteenth-century botanical gardens close by have other attractions of the natural world: a wealth of Mediterranean and exotic trees and flora, and in the former summer villa of this old estate a museum tells of the other people to have visited this beautiful place before you, with names ranging from Titian, the artist, to the poet Lord Byron. Another park to see is that belonging to the Villa Gozze.

Dubrovnik and Southern Dalmatia

This next section looks at Yugoslavia's most famous and popular holiday resort – Dubrovnik, and the area surrounding this town. The resorts of Mlini, Plat and Cavtat, all served by Dubrovnik airport, are also highlighted in this chapter, but most of it concentrates on the historic city of Dubrovnik – the pearl of the Adriatic – which is justifiably considered to be one of the great medieval cities of Europe. Often, basing your holiday in a major tourist attraction is a bad idea – there is no escape from the crowds of tourists and daytrippers; the

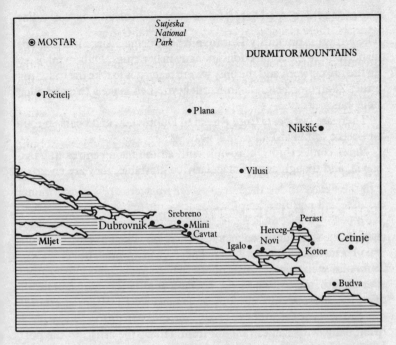

prices are inflated; and one tends to meet more fellow visitors than locals – but in the case of Dubrovnik these criticisms cannot all be levelled. Certainly prices are marginally higher than in the more remote parts of the country, and the ancient city is undeniably busy in July and August, but by way of compensation you have on offer nightlife unrivalled anywhere else in Yugoslavia, and you get a chance to see the city in all its glory at the quiet times of the day – early mornings and late evenings, when the daytrippers have departed, and the locals have time to chat. Also, because many hotels are located on wooded peninsulas and on the Babin Kuk holiday complex just outside the city, it is still possible to retreat back to the swimming pool and find a quiet corner away from the visitors, so really you can enjoy the best of both worlds.

Regular buses ferry you to and from Dubrovnik enabling you to take advantage of the good shopping and restaurants and, of course, to see the numerous beautiful buildings which make up the sights of the city.

COMMUNICATIONS

The *airport* is obviously Dubrovnik and, being a large international airport, there are connections to many major cities. Dubrovnik is not on the *rail* network and the only way to reach it is to take the train from either Zagreb or Belgrade to Kardeljevo, then make a two and a half hour bus journey.

There are fast *boats* from Rijeka to Dubrovnik, and boats en route to Greece call in at Dubrovnik also.

Buses connect up Dubrovnik with all the main centres in Yugoslavia, and though not spectacularly comfortable, they are cheap.

TOURIST INFORMATION

Atlas is the state tourist agency in this region. Their headquarters is at Pile 1. Open daily 8 a.m.–8 p.m. There are many other travel agencies but Atlas will provide you with all the excursions and info. needed. For simple information or for booking private accommodation, the Tourist Information Centre is at Poljana Paška Miličevića 1, just inside the west gate. They supply free maps etc. Open 9 a.m.–9.30 p.m. daily.

CLIMATE

To miss the worst of the crowds, go in late June when the weather is wonderful and there is still a freshness to everything. If you can't, be prepared for temperatures in the 90s in the following two months. Spring is very pleasant, as is autumn, though by October the daylight fades away too quickly to get the most out of your sightseeing time. If you do go in July or August at least you have the benefit of the Summer Festival from 10 July to 25 August.

CULINARY SPECIALITIES

Dalmatian specialities are served in this region (see page 180). The restaurants and cafés in Dubrovnik itself do tend to be more expensive than elsewhere in the country.

WHERE TO GO FOR WHAT

Being based a matter of a few miles outside Dubrovnik is no bad thing and it makes for a far more balanced and relaxing holiday than if you were to be constantly in the centre of things. For those who want just that, though, it is possible to stay in a hotel in the heart of the city, and the inexpensive **Dubravka** is a good bet, but you won't get much quiet sunbathing in. Ironically the nightlife is actually at its 'hottest' in the Dubrava complex at Babin Kuk, for as with everywhere else in Yugoslavia, the tourists are more determined on organized nightlife than the locals are. As a holiday resort, then, Dubrovnik can offer most things to most people. Keen *sightseers* and *historians* will love it, the *beach set* will be happy with the natural beach located near the Excelsior Hotel and the potential to visit nearby islands (the beaches here are better than further north in Yugoslavia, but, as already mentioned dedicated sun worshippers will have to head for the south of the country); and the *sportsman* should find what he wants if he's based at the Dubrava centre. It's not the best location for the get-away-from-it-alls, and the nature lovers are going to have to work that bit harder to get out into the 'natural' sights, but then Yugoslavia is positively bulging with plenty of alternative destinations for these people.

Dubrovnik

HOTELS AND RESTAURANTS

Not surprisingly, Dubrovnik has an impressive choice of hotels, but from our research the best overall are the **Libertas**, the **Villa Dubrovnik**, the **Argentina** and the **Imperial**. The **Belvedere** is also very good, and on the Babin Kuk development the **Hotel President** is the most luxurious hotel on offer. Be very careful (a surprising amount of people are not) that you select a hotel in the right location. If you want to spend more time strolling the old streets, soaking up the atmosphere and aren't too bothered about organized hotel-based nightlife, choose a hotel in the Ploče or Pile districts of the city (the Pile gate area is much busier), near the old town walls, then you're within strolling distance of the city centre (the **Argentina**, **Excelsior** and **Villa Dubrovnik** in Ploče, or the **Imperial** in Pile are your options here).

The Lapad peninsula lies about two miles from the old city and is served by a regular bus service, though in peak season the buses can get crowded and become an obstacle for the elderly or those with young children. The holiday complex there is tastefully done; many of the hotels are set in tranquil gardens; and with the Petka mountain dominating the skyline the overall effect is very scenic and pleasant. This is where you'll find the comfortable **Dubrovnik Palace** – a favourite with many tour operators and which also features a naturist beach. Near the public beach of Sumratin on Lapad is the **Kompas**, **Park** and **Sumratin** hotels, of which the Kompas is best. It's important to check that the hotels out here have their own pools as Sumratin beach gets uncomfortably crowded in July and August.

The Babin Kuk complex is farthest out, situated right at the end of the peninsula. Allowance has been made for the fact that you are further out of Dubrovnik here, and as a result there is a shopping precinct with excellent boutiques, cafes and restaurants. In fact it's almost better being out here than in Lapad as so much is laid on for the tourist, yet you're still, really, within easy reach of the city. This is the location of the **Dubrovnik President**, the **Tirena** and the **Argosy** – all very good hotels, though for the 'little touches' the **President** makes that bit more effort to live up to its 'luxury' classification. As previously stated, the nightlife is at its best at Babin Kuk, as are the sporting facilities, so if you're that way inclined it would be possible to spend a lot of your time on the hotel complex without ever getting bored. Further out still is the **Dubrovnik Marina**, situated on the river at Komolac. This beautiful old patrician house has a few rooms to let out and good sports facilities.

Those travelling independently and seeking a bed in Dubrovnik are in for a tough time in high season. The room capacity is well exceeded by the number of tourists in July and August, and at this time it becomes strictly a seller's market. If you simply can't book ahead, make for the harbour where you'll find old ladies bargaining fiercely with luggage-laden visitors for the price of letting their spare room. Prices average 9380D per person, which is a good bargain, but those unprepared for the haggling involved will end up paying four times that. If that doesn't appeal, the young could try the **Youth Hostel** at Put Oktobarske Revolucije 25, in the west of the town (tel. 23241). To get there, follow Maršala Tita from the bus station to the triangular park, then take the stairs uphill two streets, and head left till you see the sign. Alternatively, try the **Dvorac Rašica** youth centre at Ivanska 14 (bus 2 or 4 from the bus station). Advance booking is essential (tel. 23841). Both are cheap (around 7035D).

Private hotels worth a look are **Hotel Gruz**, 61 Gruška Obala (tel. 24777), which is located up the hill opposite the Jadrolinja office at the pier. Doubles for around 14070D including breakfast; **Hotel Stadion** at Maršala Tita 96 (tel. 23449), near to the bus station, is also reasonable. If you're really stuck you can always camp at the attractive site at **Kupari** – six miles out of the city on bus route 10.

As for restaurants – there are plenty to choose from, and tourists' menus abound. Prices are slightly higher than elsewhere in Yugoslavia, though still relatively cheap, and VISA is often accepted at the more expensive ones. A few recommendations are: the **Jadran** at P. Miličevića 1, set in a former monastery; the **Prijeko** on Prijeko 14, which does excellent fish specialities; **Riblji** at Široka 1, which specializes in Dalmatian cuisine and is situated in an attractive part of the old city; and the **Dubravka** at Brsalje 1, near the Pile gate – a nice place to watch the world go by. **Minoza**, Maršala Tita 27, is hard to beat – local specialities are served on an ivy-covered terrace to the sound of folk music in the evenings.

In order to find your way round and locate any of these, get hold of a map from the **Tourist Information Office** at Poljana Paška Miličevića 20 (open Monday to Saturday 8 a.m.–8 p.m.; Sunday 9 a.m.–noon, 5 p.m.–7 p.m.), located by the west gate. **Atlas**, the local state travel agency for this region (see 'Practical Information'), arrange excursions, windsurfer rental, etc., and organize private accommodation for independent travellers.

HISTORY

To help you get the most out of your time in Dubrovnik and to enable you to interpret the buildings and monuments of this historic city, here is a potted history highlighting the main events which shaped the city of Dubrovnik. In no way is this a comprehensive account of

Dubrovnik's past, but if you require more detail, take one of the many guided tours on offer – your guide will give a full account as you walk round the sights.

In the seventeenth century Slavs and Avars were settling in this area, taking the land by force. They came to the Roman town of Epidaurus (today's holiday resort called Cavtat) and as they moved in, the locals were forced out. Many of these survivors from the sacking of Epidaurus settled on an islet a few miles up the coast at Lave. The channel between this islet and the mainland filled up in the Middle Ages and so the settlement spread on to the mainland as well, and rapid development ensued. This settlement became known as Ragusa. It was thought until recently that this was the time when Dubrovnik (as it later became called) was founded, but it now seems that there was life on Lave before the seventh century as an early Christian capital was discovered on the cliff here.

Whatever the case, the town was ruled first by the Byzantines, then, from 1205 to 1358, by the Venetians, and under the Peace of Zadar in 1358 it became part of the Hungaro-Croatian kingdom. Their rule was however fairly loose and Dubrovnik was only obliged to provide ships and pay tribute to the King. By the fifteenth century the city had attained the status of an independent state. Its own currency had been minted since the fourteenth century, but the zenith of this autonomous city state was the fifteenth and sixteenth centuries. It was a democratic society which abolished slavery, established social services and maintained diplomatic links with foreign powers. Due to its strategic position the city enjoyed a unique status as a link between East and West, and the trade which resulted made the little republic a strong force. The arts and sciences flourished and it was in this period that most of the impressive buildings you see today were erected. Decline followed, however, first in the form of the demise of Mediterranean shipping; then in 1667 the town suffered a disastrous earthquake which killed around 5000 people and destroyed many of her finest buildings. The city never fully recovered, for by this time trade was declining and there was not the money to rebuild and restore all that had been before. This date of 1667 is accepted as the division between the heyday and the decline of Dubrovnik.

In 1806 the French, under Napoleon, entered and occupied the city. The democratic republic of Dubrovnik was abolished in 1808 by the French Marshal Marmount, and Dubrovnik, together with most of Dalmatia, became part of Napoleon's Illyrian Provinces. Its role as pawn in the game of foreign imperial powers had begun. Just nine years later, in 1815, under the Congress of Vienna, Dubrovnik was handed over to the Austrians, under whose control it remained until 1918. Thereafter its fate followed the rest of the country's.

What you see today and what you will find being stressed by the Yugoslavs is the heyday of this city republic, and rightly so, for Dubrovnik did achieve remarkable feats, and in many ways was far ahead of its time. By the thirteenth century it had organized urban development and such sanitary considerations as quarantine. A medical service was introduced in 1301 and the pharmacy you will see (the second oldest in Europe) was open and operational in 1317. Orphanages, old people's homes, a freshwater supply – all these things were present by the fourteenth to fifteenth centuries in Dubrovnik – well before the rest of Europe had such services.

In the arts, too, the republic of Dubrovnik was a flourishing centre. In the golden era of the fifteenth to sixteenth centuries there was a renowned school of domestic painting, and in literature, drama and academia the city played an important role within Europe. The famous Scots architect, Robert Adam, visited Dubrovnik to see the architecture and gain inspiration in the eighteenth century. Bear all this in mind while wandering round the monuments of this remarkable city. If you're keen on history and wish to learn more about Dubrovnik's past there are numerous excellent publications available from the official tourist shops or tourist offices.

SIGHTS

It's really quite impossible for a daytripper to see all the sights of Dubrovnik – even just the main ones – in this short space of time, but if this is all the time you have, be sure to get a guided tour so you are taken to the right places and you see as much as you can. If this does not appeal to you, head for the first suggestions listed in this section, as these are the 'not to be missed' places. Fortunately, though, Dubrovnik, like the famous city it resembles in many ways, Venice, is a wonderful place just to wander in, soaking up the atmosphere, and coming across unexpected sights. Even if you miss half the sights you 'ought' to see, you'll still be left with the overall impression of the place, for the whole of the old walled city is a monument and sight in itself.

Those fortunate enough to be based in Dubrovnik have the opportunity to get to know the city in depth. As an added bonus the whole of the old town is a pedestrian-only zone, which restores sightseeing to a leisurely and pleasurable affair.

The most obvious place to begin in a tour is the **Pile Gate** – one of four original gates to the medieval town of Dubrovnik. Each night people not resident in the town had to leave by a given time, when the drawbridges would be raised to ensure that plague and the criminal element was kept at bay. Walk across the drawbridge at Pile, decorated with statues of the patron saint of Dubrovnik – St Blaise – and take a good look at the town walls – the remarkable fortifications which defended the city in medieval times: up to 20 feet thick and reinforced with numerous towers and bastions, they are one of the world's most impressive medieval defensive systems. They date back to the twelfth to seventeenth centuries, with some fragments from the tenth century, but what you see today is really from Dubrovnik's golden era – the fifteenth and sixteenth centuries. For a small sum you can walk along the walls for a closer look at the fortifications and a clear view of the town below. The best view is from the highest of the fortresses – Minčeta.

The main street of the town is the one you immediately come across when entering by the Pile Gate – the **Placa**. This wide, impressive street, with its network of narrow little lanes and alleys leading off, is built over the sea channel, which until the Middle Ages divided the city into island and mainland. The people of Ragusa, as it was then called, built the street in 1468 after a fresh-water supply system had been laid under the roadway. The earthquake of 1667 destroyed all but the ground floors of the houses either side of the Placa (pronounced 'Platsa'), but they were all rebuilt in the same style of Baroque architecture, giving the pleasing uniform style you see today. The ground floors were restored and today act as the main shopping thoroughfare for tourists, and the venue for the evening promenade.

Just inside the Pile Gate on the right is **Onofrio's Large Fountain** – a domed, sixteen-sided reservoir with water outlets on each face. It dates back to 1438 and is named after the Neapolitan architect who built the city's elaborate water system in the fifteenth century. Though damaged by the 1667 earthquake, it is still an attractive feature, and a popular meeting place for the young.

Just opposite the fountain, to the left of the gate, is the **Church of the Saviour**, a beautiful chapel which escaped destruction in the earthquake. Its mixture of Renaissance and Gothic styles (typical of Dubrovnik because of this changeover era when much of the city's building was underway) gives it a unique beauty. Right next to this church is the **Franciscan Friary** – an extravagant Gothic creation from 1499; look out for the fifteenth-century Pietà above the doorway in the church. Wedged between the church and the chapel is the entrance door to the beautiful **Lower Cloisters**. The capitals of the columns in the cloistered walkway are all different – each one depicting a comic or tragic scene. Here you'll see an original **Middle Ages Chemist's Shop** – the oldest in the Balkans, dating back to 1319, perfectly intact and preserved right down to the mortars and pestles used. This was part of the health service operated by the town as early as 1301.

Back out to the Placa the eye takes you down to the Luža Square, at the far end, where the clock tower stands. Though the 1445 tower was rebuilt in this century (1929) the bell dates from 1506 and the bronze figures who strike the hours are from 1478 when the clock was constructed. Near to here is another of the city's fountains – this time one known as **Onofrio's Small Fountain** which is still in working order despite the fact it's around 450 years old.

The column in the centre of Luža Square is **Orlando's Column** where, in the Middle Ages, criminals were flogged and public decrees were proclaimed.

To the right is **St Blaise's Church**, rebuilt in the Baroque era of the early 1700s. Just beyond is the sixteenth-century **Sponza Palace** – a beautiful building of Gothic and Renaissance architecture which served as the republic's Customs House, and later as the city's Mint. Today it contains archives from the days when Dubrovnik was an independent republic and houses the **Museum of the Socialist Revolution**. The arcaded courtyard here is exceptionally beautiful.

Straight ahead a lane leads you through a passage which goes under the town walls to the old harbour. Off to the left is the **Dominican Friary**, worth visiting to see its beautiful fourteenth-century cloister.

In the church are several fine works of art; notably the painting by Titian on the altar to the north. Beyond the Dominican church is the second of the city's main gates – the **Ploče Gate**. The bridge over the former moat takes you out at Fort Revelin and passing through the outer gate you reach the Ploče quarter of Dubrovnik where some hotels are located. To the right is the Old Harbour – another popular venue for the evening *korzo*.

Retracing to Luža Square (those pushed for time should not leave it, but stay there after viewing the Sponza Palace), look opposite St Blaise's to the **Rector's Palace** – the finest building in Dubrovnik. The palace was built between 1435 and 1451 by the Neapolitan Onofrio Giordana della Cava (of fountain fame), and it was from here that the republic of Dubrovnik was governed.

The Great and Lesser Councils sat here, and here lived the Rector of the Republic – a member of the local aristocracy, for they took it upon themselves to rule in turn. If you get a chance to hear the Dubrovnik Symphony Orchestra performing in the wonderful setting of the courtyard of the palace, take it: the acoustics and setting make for a memorable experience. Today the council chamber and civic halls house the **Museum of Cultural History**, which has displays showing what life was like in the republic of Ragusa. The Rector's office and bedroom are also open to the public. The inscription above the door of the hall where the Great Council met – 'Obliti privatorum publica curate' – means 'Forget your own affairs and concern yourself with civic matters'. (Regretfully the palace is closed at present for restoration and all that can be viewed is the courtyard.)

Right of the Rector's Palace is the city's **Cathedral**, which was rebuilt in Baroque style after the 1667 earthquake. There are some fine paintings here, but it is the **Treasury** which is most remarkable. Some of the relics date back to the ninth century, and the extent of the collection of gold and silver is most impressive. The most prized possession is the skull of St Blaise wearing a twelfth-century Byzantine crown. Also of interest is the Flemish triptych which envoys from Ragusa used to carry with them on their missions to foreign countries and use as a portable altar. (Currently the city cathedral is closed for restoration.)

To the right, beyond the cathedral, is the **Bishop's Palace**, and further on again is the lane which brings you out at **Fort St John**, the main defensive building of the town, which today is a combined maritime museum, aquarium and a museum of ethnography.

Vrata od Pente is the name of the gate, located between the Rector's Palace and the cathedral, which takes you out at the **Old Harbour**. Today only small pleasure boats and the odd fishing boat dock there, but before the sixteenth century this was the main port and shipbuilding base on the eastern Adriatic. They had a very clever way of protecting their harbour and blocking off the entrance to unwelcome visitors – massive chains were stretched between the numerous fortresses which worked with the breakwater to block off entry.

Gruž is Dubrovnik's **New Harbour** ('new' being post-sixteenth century) about two miles west of the old town. This is where today's cruise ships stop en route to Venice, and where the large freighters bring their cargo. Excursion boats leave from here to Lokrum and the Elaphite Islands, and there's a frequent bus service from Gruž to Pile for those arriving there.

Many of the guided tours end their day taking their visitors up Mount Sergius by cable car for the view over the city. The photographic possibilities from 1352 feet are certainly great, and the French Fort from 1809 is worth a look, but it is preferable to make this excursion on your own to avoid the crush and give yourself a chance to appreciate the view in your own time. Early morning or late afternoon bring the most rewarding views.

EXCURSIONS

There are numerous interesting daytrips to be made from Dubrovnik; possibly more than from any other base in Yugoslavia. This is due to your proximity to the south of the country with its fascinating Muslim towns and good sandy beaches, and to the scenic Dalmatian islands, such as the beautiful islands of KORČULA and MLJET. All the places 'not to be missed' are given a separate write-up in their geographical position within this guide, so check the index for the relevant pages. As a rough guide, the most interesting daytrips are to be found in:

MOSTAR, a Turkish-influenced town with its famous old bridge, mosques and souvenir bazaars.

SARAJEVO, the oriental capital of Bosnia-Herzegovina and the town which was the setting for the events which led to the First World War.

CETINJE, the capital of Montenegro, reached at the end of the breathtakingly beautiful drive round the Bay of Kotor.

KORČULA, the charming medieval walled city of Korčula on the island of the same name which has long since been a favourite with British visitors.

MLJET, the forest-covered island, part national park, which will delight those interested in fauna and flora and the natural world.

The Elaphite Islands and the islands of Lokrum are also of some interest, but do not quite rank with the five suggestions listed above, all of which are well worth seeing.

Resorts South of Dubrovnik

Kupari, Srebreno, Mlini, Plat and Cavtat are the resorts on the stretch of coast just south of Dubrovnik. The latter four are developed for package holidays, while the first four lie on the bay of Župa. There is nothing of particular interest in Kupari except the two kilns which stand as a reminder of the tile industry which once flourished in the village. Just south of Kupari, about ten miles from Dubrovnik, is the resort of **SREBRENO**. This tiny village lies in a wide, sheltered bay, protected by the mountain ridges, and now has two large hotels and a few cafés and shops to show for its main industry. It is an attractive setting for a holiday, but, in honesty, Mlini has a lot more going for it, unless you're after a particularly quiet time. Frequent buses link Srebreno to Dubrovnik so you needn't have too quiet a time if you don't want to. The beach is pebbly and gets fairly crowded in high season. Of the hotels, the **Orlando** is preferable.

MLINI, just round the headland from Srebreno, is an attractive little village in a rural setting. Its sheltered bay and wooded slopes make it one of the more picturesque villages in this area, but its main beach is pebbly, busy and has polluted water (there are too many tourists for the present sewerage system in high season – particularly in the naturist section of the beach). It's better to head off for the more remote coves which have gently curving slopes, suitable for children.

There are four hotels in the village, of which the **Mlini** and **Astarea** are the most attractively furnished and best equipped. Waterskiing is available, and the hotels put on entertainments in summer. As well as that there are several attractive tavernas down by the harbour where a pleasant evening can be passed. The name Mlini means mills, and the village was so called because of the mills built at the point where several streams flow into the sea. Today these waterfalls and streams power a small hydroelectric power plant.

Near the main beach is the **Church of St Hilary**, which was rebuilt in the late seventeenth century after an earthquake destroyed its original fifteenth-century structure. Other local sights are the Roman remains on the road to Cavtat. As an excursion TREBINJE makes an interesting day out. This old town lies in the hills twenty miles inland and has as sights an old castle, two mosques and a clock tower.

From the Adriatic Highway there is a fine panoramic view over to Dubrovnik, the Elaphite Islands and Mljet.

The resort of **PLAT**, ten miles from Dubrovnik, is basically a rather uninspiring holiday complex based around the tiny village, near the hydroelectric plant. This, however, does not disturb the peace, and a restful holiday atmosphere exists. You can expect your holiday to be very much hotel-based here, with frequent trips into nearby Dubrovnik for sightseeing and nightlife. The **Hotel Ambassador** and the **Hotel Plat** complex are both good, with organized nightlife, comprehensive sports facilities and their own pebbly beaches. (The Ambassador has more facilities and is slightly grander.) It's a suitable base for a family holiday and its proximity to Dubrovnik ensures activity for those who want it, though for people who find the journeys to and from Dubrovnik a problem (i.e. those with very young children or those averse to using crowded public transport) it may be better to choose a hotel within Dubrovnik.

CAVTAT, however, is a resort worth going to in its own right. It lies in a beautiful bay nine miles south of Dubrovnik, has good hotels, a superb climate, and enough in the way of sights to hold the interest for a couple of weeks, but unfortunately it does have some disadvantages too: it lies directly on the flight path to Dubrovnik and as a result the noise in some hotels can be annoying, its beaches tend to be overcrowded in high season and the water at that time becomes polluted due to an insufficient sewage system. (It also attracts hordes of Germans!) The young, however, will enjoy Cavtat despite this as it's a lively resort with good sports facilities and a nightlife as active as you'll find in Yugoslavia: bars, discos, casinos, nightclubs, bowling alleys and restaurants vie with the laid-on entertainments at the hotels, making Cavtat an ideal under-thirties location. The luxurious **Hotel Croatia** and **Hotel Albatros** are beautifully kitted out, the Croatia proving hard to beat in any sphere: food, service, entertainment and hotel facilities. Several tour operators run to these hotels and the other four within the resort. The hotels cater for the fact that it's essentially a young person's resort, but all offer good value and high standards.

Cavtat (pronounced 'Tsvavtat') was the site of the ancient city of Epidaurus, whose inhabitants fled from the Slavs and Avars in the seventh century and went on to settle in Dubrovnik. The Greeks and Romans have both lived here, though little remains from their times. What does remain from an earlier era is the reconstructed eighteenth-century **Parish Church of St Nicholas**; the **Franciscan Friary** with a beautiful Renaissance cloister dating from 1483; and the former residence of the Rector, which houses the **Municipal Museum**. On the hill overlooking the town is the **Mausoleum of the Rašić Family** (1920–2) by the famous Yugoslav sculptor Ivan Meštrović. This unfortunate family, headed by a sea captain from Cavtat, was wiped out by an epidemic of Spanish flu.

Excursions to several of the small surrounding islets are on offer, but SUPETAR is probably the most interesting. DUBROVNIK, of course, is an easy daytrip, and the Turkish town of MOSTAR is also within reach. The BAY OF KOTOR is almost worth the exorbitant price of car hire to be able to take your time. If your budget is not that elastic, though, try to get to see CETINJE and the Kotor Bay by an organized tour. It's an experience well worth the lumps in your throat as you climb the hairpin bends up the 8–10 per cent gradients.

Montenegro

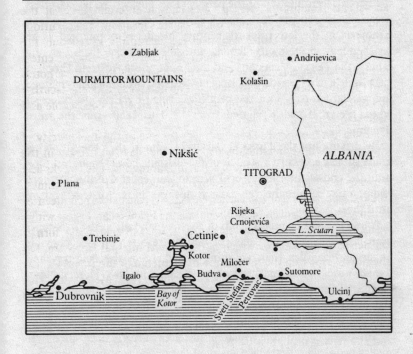

Surrounded by Bosnia-Herzegovina, the Dalmatian coast of Croatia, Serbia and Albania, Montenegro is the smallest of Yugoslavia's six republics: a rugged land of dramatic scenery with inaccessible treacherous mountains ('Montenegro' is the name the Venetians gave the area, meaning, literally, 'black mountains'), large glacial lakes and green valleys. The people are darker, their history more turbulent, and the life generally harder than in the rest of Yugoslavia, and often Montenegro is likened to the Highlands of Scotland where the remoteness and inhospitable landscape has shaped the people's strong sense of independence – until just a century ago Montenegro was an independent state.

What makes Montenegro's history different from the rest of the country today known collectively as Yugoslavia is the fact that for centuries it managed to resist domination by foreign powers. Partly this was due to the inaccessibility of the land, but also it had to do with the fierce determination of the people. The Turks tried on countless occasions to capture this area, but under the leadership of Ivan Crnojević in the late fifteenth century Montenegro emerged as an independent principality which withstood attacks from, among others, the Turks, Venetians and the might of the Austrian Empire.

Despite a brief period of support by Russia, Montenegro remained independent throughout the centuries, ruled by Bishop-Princes of whom Peter II, who reigned from 1830 to 1850, was the most dynamic.

By driving out the Turks at Bar and Ulcinj in 1878 the Montenegrans gained access to a stretch of the Adriatic coast, though it took until the end of the First World War to gain control of the northern end of today's Montenegran coast as this was under Austrian control until then.

Along the eighty-mile stretch of coast which falls in the Montenegran republic lie some excellent holiday resorts, with beaches far larger and sandier than anything elsewhere in the country, and temperatures consistently higher: Bečiči, Budva, Herceg-Novi, Miločer, Sveti Stefan, Petrovac and oriental Ulcinj. The magnificent Bay of Kotor is the introduction to this stretch of coast – a fjord-like gulf which ranks among Europe's most remarkable natural features.

The tragic earthquake which hit this area in April 1979 killed over ninety people and destroyed many of the region's cultural treasures. From the tourist's point of view, though, most of the damage has been repaired and it will certainly not interfere with your enjoyment of the region.

COMMUNICATIONS

Titograd and Dubrovnik are the two main airports used for organized holidays in Montenegro, and from the rail network's point of view there is a service from Belgrade to the port town of Bar.

The region's state travel agency is 'Montenegroturist' whose head office is in Budva. They will organize excursions, book car hire for you, etc.

THE CLIMATE

The weather is very hot in summer on the coast, but inland in the Durmitor mountains it cools down considerably at nights, so take a jacket.

CULINARY SPECIALITIES

The main regional speciality is a whole sheep cooked in a cauldron of milk, over a charcoal fire.

WHERE TO GO FOR WHAT

Inland Montenegro is as fascinating as the coastline, a place where you still get the feeling you're on an adventure rather than just holidaying. Remote villages where time seems to have stood still for centuries are not hard to find, and in the DURMITOR NATIONAL PARK where more than twenty mountains have summits above 6000 feet, you will find resorts such as ŽABLJAK which has great potential for activity and skiing holidays. The Durmitor National Park is also *the* destination for those interested in the natural world. Among the list of things to do is a 'visit to the TARA RIVER CANYON, second in depth only to the Grand Canyon, Colorado', and a trip to see the 'richest concentration of alpine flowers in Europe'. Hunting and fishing holidays are a good idea in northern Montenegro.

The glacial lakes near Žabljak are known for their trout (apply at the town hall of the nearest town for a fishing permit), and fishing is also good in the upper parts of the Zeta, close to Nikšić. To use the state-run hunting reserves of this area, apply in Titograd to the Secretariat for Agriculture (preferably well in advance of your dates).

Places to which tour operators offer holidays are given most space in this section, for, particularly in Montenegro, travelling on an independent basis really is difficult, and definitely not to be recommended for the faint-hearted. There are only a few centres developed for tourism, and hotels are often scarce.

As a basic rule, when choosing your resort in Montenegro, the more exotic and less northern Europe you want your resort to be, the further south you should go. ULCINJ, right down in the south, next to the Albanian border, is almost oriental in character, and around Lake Skadar in the south you feel you've left twentieth-century Europe behind. The mountain resort and former capital – Cetinje – is a good compromise between the comforts of an organized holiday and the unfamiliar, but if you've been used to high-class beach-based holiday resorts, SVETI STEFAN and BUDVA should please you. The mountain resorts should only be considered by active outdoor types, for whom they represent excellent value.

The Coast

 THE BAY OF KOTOR

On approaching Montenegro from the coastal road in the north, you come to the magnificent bay of Kotor. It appears unexpectedly, after travelling through the barren Sutorina valley, and is reminiscent of a Norwegian fjord. It is in fact a broad sea inlet consisting of an outer bay and an inner bay and two straits, but because it penetrates so deep into the high Karstic mountains, the effect is extremely dramatic. It has a micro climate all of its own because of the height of the mountains, making it colder and often more stormy than the surrounding countryside.

The strategic positioning of this land formation has meant that many races endeavoured to capture it, but thanks to the narrow entrance of the bay not all succeeded, and significantly the Turks were kept out; never managing to capture the town of Kotor, at the south-east end of the bay. The first town in the bay is that of **IGALO** – a tourist resort and health spa, famed for its cures of rheumatism through using radioactive mud, mineral water and sea water. It is an attractive town with a good beach and hotels located in the now-united town of Topla. In fact this area is now all part of the tourist complex of **HERCEG-NOVI**, the thriving holiday resort offered by several tour operators.

The mild climate of Herceg-Novi (average temperature in January is 50°F/10°C) is one of the big attractions of this large (by local standards) town, which is situated in Topla Bay. This is one of the towns which was badly affected by the 1979 earthquake, but the damage is being repaired and the town is a popular year-round resort. Lush gardens on the slopes by the Bay of Kotor are a feature of this resort, and overall the town provides a good base for a relaxing holiday, with some excursions available. Of the hotels the **Plaza** is the best on offer. This large hotel, just outside Herceg-Novi, lies in parkland and is as impressive inside as its all-glass exterior would make one think. It specializes in water sports and all its facilities are of a very high standard, except, unfortunately, for the beach, which is pebbly and concreted. Its other lack is an outdoor pool. The **Topla** complex consists of pavilion-type villas, and is a good medium-category hotel.

The sights of the town are, in the market square, the fifteenth-century **Clock Tower** and the **Karadja Fountain**. The fortresses which defended the town are also interesting: the **Venetian Forts** protect the harbour – the upper one has now enterprisingly been turned into an open-air cinema; while another is the venue for open-air theatre. Until the 1979 earthquake the Spanish Fort on top of the hill could be viewed, but now all that can be seen from the summit is the good view of the environs. The **Archaeological Museum** is in the west of the town, while to the east in the woods above the town is the Serbian Orthodox **Monastery of Savina** which is worth finding to see its two churches (though it suffered a lot of the damage in 1979). The older of the churches goes back to the eleventh century and boasts a splendid treasury of religious artefacts, while the newer church is late eighteenth century and an interesting mixture of Byzantine and Baroque styles.

The evening *korzo* venue is inevitably down by the waterfront, on the promenade which used to be the narrow-gauge railway track.

All along the coast are unexpected ancient monuments and historic buildings. Tourism has taken over as the main industry in the resorts favoured by the tour operators, but the villages either side of the built-up resorts are still unspoilt. While on the coastal route, stop off at BIJELA to see the fourteenth-century frescoes in the church. Also take in the second-century Roman mosaics in RISAN; and the beautifully preserved town of PERAST, home of a prestigious naval academy in medieval times, which is worth a couple of hours' wanderings to soak up the atmosphere.

KOTOR, the favourite daytrip from resorts all around Dubrovnik and Montenegro, is tucked away in the corner of the most remote bay in this Gulf. Until the 1979 earthquake this was one of the most beautiful towns in Yugoslavia – a walled medieval settlement of narrow lanes and old churches where cars are banned, and the scenery is incredible with the sea below and the mountains above. Sadly it was badly hit and many of its buildings are closed until restored (and indeed are dangerous due to falling masonry, so do not venture into them). Despite this it's still well worth visiting as the atmosphere remains, and it's possible to see some of the monuments from the past which make this such a special place. **St Tyrphon's Cathedral** is one such place. It was begun in 1116 and rebuilt in different styles throughout the centuries. The towers are of the Renaissance era; the Treasury houses a rich collection which is open to the public, and as its *pièce de resistance* it has the silver-gilt bas-relief (1440) by Hans of Basle – a wandering artist who ended up in Kotor to escape the wrath of his numerous bigamous marriages! Soon to reopen is the Church of St Luke – a twelfth-century Orthodox basilica in Byzantine style. The **Maritime Museum**, reached from the cathedral via the lane passing the Drago Palace, is housed in the eighteenth-century **Grgurina Palace**, and should be of interest to nautical types and historians. In Trg Oktobarska Revolucije stands the modern town hall and the unfinished Venetian palazzo (the Venetians ruled Kotor from 1420 to 1797, when the Austrians took over).

The present **town walls** date from the era of Venetian rule, though originally they go back more than a thousand years, and it is thanks to them and defensive buildings such as **Fort St John** at the top of the town that Kotor managed to withstand the many attacks made on the town by the Turks.

For those wishing to base themselves in Kotor there are hotels outside the town on the road to Muo and Prčanj.

From Kotor it is almost obligatory, having got this far, to make the journey up the mountains to the ancient capital of Montenegro – CETINJE. Getting there involves a journey up Mt Lovćen (5738 feet summit) and encountering twenty-six hairpin bends on the road from Kotor to Krstac (the space of about ten miles). The view is worth the stomach cramps: no one should miss the opportunity to see the

Adriatic coast spread out beneath them. For obvious reasons the road is known as 'the Serpentine'). (For details on Cetinje, see page 239).

The highly developed area of **BUDVA** owes its popularity to its good beaches and sophisticated hotels. Unfortunately the old walled town of Budva, whose beautiful Venetian buildings acted as a magnet for visitors over the years, is now a ghost town and stands desolate and abandoned after its destruction in the 1979 earthquake.

Entry to the crumbling buildings is forbidden, and though there are plans to restore the town to its former glory it will be some time before there is a semblance of normality about the place. Those lucky enough to be based in the Hotels **Slovenska Plaza** or **Avila**, however, will find plenty to do and what with the facilities on site and the excursion opportunities the wreckage of the town seems irrelevant to the holidaymakers (unfortunately this disaster will never be 'irrelevant' to the locals for many were killed, and hundreds of buildings were destroyed). The facilities here for children are of an exceptionally high standard.

Tourism has spread now to the hotel resort of BEČIČI, about two miles south of Budva – the best beach in the area. Bečiči is the destination for the beach bum. The beach of multicoloured, gravelly sand is known as the 'mosaic beach'. The hotels are nicely landscaped, but, though good, are all ultra-modern and not as luxurious as those offered in Budva. Not surprisingly water sports are good and widely available. The lack of the town of Budva is felt, but hotels put on their own nightlife and in peak season the rush of Northern Europeans makes for a lively atmosphere.

MILOČER is the next resort down the coast. This ex-summer residence of the Yugoslavian royal family is truly a beautiful resort. It faces the tiny island of SVETI STEFAN and its beautifully kept hotels lie within gardens and parkland leading on to the sandy beach. For many this is the best resort in Yugoslavia, combining good beaches with beautiful scenery and de-luxe hotels – the **Hotel Sveti Stefan** on the island opposite Miločer uses the island's old houses as holiday accommodation giving the occupant the feeling of living in their personal villa, not a hotel (no one but tourists actually lives on Sveti Stefan). All the hotels offered by tour operators in Miločer are of a very high standard, and the sports facilities and nightlife are equally impressive.

The summer palace of the royal family in Miločer is now a hotel (the **Hotel Miločer**). It is situated in parkland, with the beach stretching out in front of it; this and the Sveti Stefan are the sort of places where honeymoons should be spent, and although these hotels are that bit more expensive than average, the present favourable exchange rates make it the sort of luxury that more people can now afford.

In Miločer seek out the little monastery of **Praskavica** with its frescoes. It dates back to 1050 but was damaged in the 1979 earthquake. It is reached via the park of the Miločer Hotel. The town's other churches were badly damaged and cannot be visited. Excursions to LAKE TARA and LAKE BIOGRAD (see page 243) are on offer from this resort, as is a daytrip to DUBROVNIK, which, as I'm always saying, is worth the effort to get to from any resort.

Turning now to look at **SVETI STEFAN**: this old fishing village is today the showpiece of the Yugoslavian tourist industry. It opened as a 'hotel town' back in 1960 when its 80 houses were restored and converted into 110 apartments and tourist facilities such as the high-class restaurant which overlooks the Adriatic, and the casino and assorted night clubs were opened.

The fifteenth-century **Church of St Stephen** was damaged in the earthquake but the seventeenth-century **Transfiguration Church** is still open to the public. Tourists actually have to pay to visit the island, which is open from 10 a.m.–12 noon, and 3 p.m.–6 p.m. (It's just as well for the visitors living in Sveti Stefan for the perpetual flow of daytrippers becomes tiresome, and only at night can the peace and beauty of the island be properly appreciated.) The beaches are actually part of the narrow causeway which links the island to the mainland, and non-residents have to pay to bathe here. They are very good beaches and are worth the effort and entrance fee.

Historically the island's strategic position ensured it escaped Turkish domination, though the Turks were in force only forty miles down the coast, at Ulcinj. Originally the island was linked to the mainland by a drawbridge; then a sandbar developed. Today a walkway links the island to the mainland.

Six miles south is **PETROVAC**, reached after the great crag to the west of the resort, called Skoči Devojka ('maiden's leap'), so called because of the legend of a young girl, Ruža, who, running from the invading Turks, threw herself over the highest crag into the sea to avoid being unfaithful to her fiancé. Petrovac therefore is situated in front of the Paštrovići mountains which rise to heights over 3000 feet. The resort is off the motorway and therefore does not fall prey to passing motoring tourists. It is a popular family holiday base, with a three-quarter-mile sandy and pebbly beach backed by hills and forests. Overall the resort is attractive, but it is suitable only for those seeking a quiet time. Of the hotels, the **Castellastava** and **Palas** are to be preferred. The harbour by the old castle is the busiest part of the town. The **castle** dates back to the sixteenth century and was erected by the Venetians. Some Roman remains can be seen behind the Church of Sv Ilija (mosaics from a summer villa built here in the third or fourth centuries).

SUTOMORE is the next resort on the coast, set in a shallow bay which is often exposed to strong south-west winds. The main sight of this area is the eighth-century **St Thecla's Chapel**. This is a very modern resort, most of it having been built since the 1979 earthquake. The beaches are the big attraction here, and it's a good base for the keen sun-tanner.

The motorway leads next to BAR – a major port and city of strategic importance for internal travel within Yugoslavia. A ferry between Bari in southern Italy and Bar runs three times weekly and there are services linking Bar with Corfu, Igoumenitsa, Rijeka and Dubrovnik.

Bar is also the end of the line of the new Belgrade–Bar railway. From the tourists' point of view there is little in Bar to induce one to linger. The ruins of the old town – Stari Bar – make a depressing trip, though if you visit it on Friday the colourful market will brighten the picture of this ghost town, cruelly hit by fate on numerous occasions. Explosions, wars and earthquakes have all taken their toll and there are few sights left. Look out for the eleventh-century **St Mark's Church** and the fourteenth-century **St Catherine's Church** in the lower part of Stari Bar, if you're there for an excursion.

Novi Bar (the new town) has nothing to commend it at all. The blocks of high rises hold no fascination for the tourist.

The beaches, however, are a different story, and dedicated sun worshippers should make for this part of Yugoslavia. The long sandy beaches here are not crowded, even in high season. Base yourself in Sutomore for strategic use of the best beaches.

On leaving Bar the road passes ancient olive groves and on closer inspection it becomes obvious, even to the uninitiated, that some of the olive trees are incredibly ancient; one is reputedly 2700 years old! At the end of the coast lies the fascinating city of **ULCINJ** down by the Albanian border. This is a destination for the adventurous and those who crave an exotic location combined with good sandy beaches.

Unfortunately Ulcinj was another victim of the 1979 earthquake which destroyed much of the lovely old town, and the modern town is not attractive. This makes it a resort for those who want limited sightseeing, but are keen on good beaches and a 'different' feel to their holiday. The oriental Muslim influence here is still very strong, and the Minarets and Turkish bazaars add something special to a holiday. The transfer time from Dubrovnik or Titograd is considerable, so bear this in mind if this sort of thing bothers you.

Most of the hotels are clustered in the Lido complex one and a half miles out of the town, near the excellent Velika beach. The **Hotel Galeb** is the pick of the bunch, with an excellent situation on a promontory overlooking the Adriatic. The **Olympic** is also 'A' class, though with less charm, while the **Bellevue-Borik** is popular with families. The disadvantage of the hotels being situated out here is the obvious one of making the guests remain 'on campus' as the walk into the town is exhausting and local transport is not great. **Velika beach** is the big pull to this area, and it must be considered one of the best beaches in the country. It shelves gently into the sea so is suitable for children, and it's big enough to avoid crowding; the only slight snag is that it tends to catch the wind due to its exposed position. The beach is said to have medicinal qualities good for rheumatics, and it stretches for seven miles, going on to the Albanian border. The larger naturist centre on the island of Ada has a good beach, with chalets as accommodation.

As for Ulcinj itself: despite the recent destruction the character of the town remains – the uneven streets; the narrow alleyways; the crumbling houses; the mosques and the minarets which dominate the skyline. Even the people look different from the rest of Yugoslavia; their skins much darker and their customs much more Eastern. (The town's significance in the slave trade is said to account for the preponderance of dark people among its inhabitants.)

The history of Ulcinj is based on piracy and trade – it being the main port between Italy and Albania – and in its time it has been occupied by numerous powers, including the omnipresent Romans, Venetians and Turks. All that is left to see today is the Citadel and the Friday market where you still see the locals in traditional peasant costume.

South of the town below the **Hotel Albatros** is a beach with an underwater sulphur spring. Bathing in it is said to cure infertility in women, hence this cove is reserved for women only, though these days it seems to have become a naturist beach for both sexes.

Nightlife and excursions are both limited (neighbouring Albania does *not* provide a daytrip!) and most of the restaurants are to be found in the town centre. The **Stijena** enjoys a beautiful setting in the rocks overlooking the bay.

Inland

CETINJE in inland Montenegro is a popular excursion for tourists staying anywhere in the vicinity. This strategic little town is the old capital of Montenegro and played an important part in not just Yugoslavia's history, but Europe's also. When Montenegro was recognized as an independent republic, palatial houses and embassies (as many as fifteen) were established in the capital, and the town became one of the most important in this region of central Europe. It is set on a plateau surrounded by the craggy limestone mountains, and undoubtedly its harsh climate accounts for some of the hardiness of its people – the other Yugoslav republics still regard Montenegro as backward and peopled with a barbaric and uncivilized lot (mind you, they were still publicly displaying the heads of their Turkish victims just over a century ago!).

Tour operators do not base holidays in Cetinje but there are a few places to stay for independent travellers, though tourist facilities in the town are not great, as it too suffered in the 1979 earthquake. The

Park Hotel though not cheap is good. It is located in the Castle Park and has been restored after the damage it incurred in 1979. The **Grand** is an alternative. This wood-built hotel dates back to the heyday of Cetinje when it was used as the meeting place for diplomats on business in the capital.

The sights you will see on a daytrip here will include the following historic monuments: the **Biljarda Palace** (meaning 'Billiards Palace' because it had the only billiards table in Montenegro) in Trg Maršala Tita which was the official residence of the Montenegran rulers. It was built in the nineteenth century and today houses three museums and an interesting relief map of Montenegro made by Austrian soldiers between 1916 and 1918. Adjoining it (to the west) is the **Monastery of the Mother of God** where the Prince Bishops who ruled Montenegro from the fifteenth century lived. The building you see today dates from 1785, all previous ones having been destroyed in the almost continuous raids by the Turks. The round tower close by is the **Tablja Tower** from the top of which the heads of the Turks were exhibited. To the east of the Palace is the **National Museum** with its impressive array of memorabilia and weaponry from the days when King Nikola ruled Montenegro. This building is the former King's house and little has changed from the days when the monarch lived here, until his abdication in 1918. Among the exhibits on show are artefacts from the British Royal Family, Kaiser Bill and President Roosevelt. The **History Museum** and **Art Gallery** are found in another of the ex-buildings of state – the Parliament House. The zenith of Cetinje has certainly passed, but the atmosphere of faded glory remains, and in its unique, secluded setting the town in conjunction with the drive round the Bay of Kotor makes one of the best daytrips available in Yugoslavia.

From Cetinje the bus tour invariably makes the trip up nearby Mount Lovćen where Petar II, or more precisely Petar Petrović-Njegoš, is buried. He was the most famous of Montenegro's rulers; a Prince-Bishop, poet and notorious warrior who did much to improve the lot of his countrymen by introducing democratic laws based on common rights, and a fair system of taxation. The mausoleum is open 8 a.m.–6 p.m. and is worth the 400 steps climb up. The sculpture is by Yugoslavia's most famous sculptor – Meštrović.

Continuing on the road from Cetinje to Titograd, the ancient to the modern capital of this region, you come to a village well worth a stop-off: RIJEKA CRNOJEVIĆA. This little fishing village on Lake Scutari (an excellent area for fishermen – no permit required and rich in birdlife) can be reached from Cetinje or the road from Virpazar – the main village on the shores of Lake Scutari. At this unsuspecting place with its square houses and old arched bridges the first book in Cyrillic script was printed; in the monastery of Obod in the late fifteenth century. Unfortunately literature was sacrificed in the great cause of survival and only ten years after the printing press and type had arrived from Venice it had to be melted down to make bullets to fend off the Turks. The main street of Rijeka Crnojevića is flooded every spring when the snow on the mountains melts making the level of the lake rise dramatically.

LAKE SCUTARI has a total area of 143 square miles (86 square miles of which are Yugoslavian; the remaining 57 square miles lie in Albania) which means it is the largest lake in the Balkans. The backdrop of the mountains and the abundance of the fish (thirty-five recorded species) and waterfowl make it a paradise for the outdoor type craving an activity holiday. Spring is the best time to visit here; when the waterlilies are in bloom and the long light nights allow you to gaze at the calm water reflecting the black mountains until bedtime. Keen fishermen and ornithologists should seriously consider a holiday at Lake Scutari, though invariably you will be advised to go with a group as there are no regular ferry services running on the lake (excursions only). Enquire through the Yugoslav Tourist Authority in this country, or from travel agencies in Titograd or in the Adriatic resorts. If you are travelling to this part independently, remember you have the option of taking the train; using the Belgrade–Titograd–Bar line. VIRPAZAR is the best place to base yourself for a holiday on the lake. The hotel and restaurant are well used to fishermen, and boats can be hired from here. Alternatively, if you seek more in the way of action as a contrast to your quiet days on the lake, it's quite possible to stay in Titograd and bus it to the lake.

TITOGRAD is essentially an ugly industrial city with little to recommend it to the tourist. Of the few buildings that survived the

Second World War most were destroyed in the 1979 earthquake, so sightseeing is a non-starter. Before it was devastated by wartime bombing, the city – known as Podgorica until 1946 – had numerous reminders of its 400-year Turkish occupation, but now you have to really look for the bits left standing: the **Fortress of the Nemanjić** (the medieval Kings of Serbia) at the junction of the Zeta and Morača rivers; the sixteenth-century **clock tower** and the **House of Paša Advović**. Also on the banks of the Zeta are the Roman remains of the ancient town of Dioclea (known now as 'Duklja'), which include law courts, a forum, temples and fragments of the Roman baths. (Take the old road to Nikšić, then take a right to the Radovče road to get there.)

As for accommodation: the **Podgorica** on the banks of the Morača is about the nicest hotel in the city; alternatively try the **Zlatica**. Ask **Tourist Information** on Ulica Slobode for maps, information on Lake Scutari, and restaurant suggestions.

 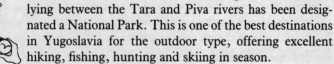 Much of the beautiful mountainous region of DURMITOR lying between the Tara and Piva rivers has been designated a National Park. This is one of the best destinations in Yugoslavia for the outdoor type, offering excellent hiking, fishing, hunting and skiing in season.

Those keen on natural history, geology, etc., should also consider this area, as the glacial lakes, canyons and caves make for interesting analysis. The highest point of the Durmitor range is 8275 feet – Bobotov Kuk – and from the main resort of **ŽABLJAK** it is about a six-hour climb (only experienced climbers should attempt summits like this as there are no huts in the National Park in case you get stuck, nor, even more importantly, is there a mountain rescue service). The mountain streams and lush pastures, lakes filled by the melting glaciers, and painted chalets are reminiscent of an alpine scene (as are the temperatures which are appreciably lower than on the coast), and the overall effect is very dramatic and very picturesque.

'Crno Jezero' or 'Black Lake' is the most visited lake in this region. Linked to it higher up is a smaller lake and dominating the horizon is the Medvjed ('Bear') mountain with a summit of 2300 feet. There is a camp site here and the road from Žabljak to Crno Jezero is good.

Skiing is fast becoming a year-round money-earner in this region and though there are only four tows at present at Žabljak, more are under way. The height of the mountains means that there is enough snow to ski even in the summer months. Instructors and guides reside in the village; just ask at the hotels or at Montenegroturist. A slalom event is held every summer, and skating and tobogganing are also on offer.

As a resort the village of Žabljak is rather dreary, though the hotels are of a high standard, and they do try to introduce some evening entertainment to compensate for the fact that there is little to be found elsewhere (the après-ski is hardly on a par with that found in Switzerland or Austria, but then to compensate there is no commercialism and the prices are very low). Of the choice, the JEZERO is to be preferred for its location, though as an alternative for independent travellers many of the villagers let out rooms in Žabljak at reasonable rates (ask at Tourist Information).

Interesting excursions from Žabljak include a three- or four-day raft trip down the River Tara, camping en route – an unforgettable experience and one for which it's not necessary to be super-fit, only determined – ask Montenegroturist for further details. Other possibilities are to see the incredible gorges of the Tara canyon; or to go hunting for bear, boar, wolf, deer, fox, rabbit, chamois, black cock, partridge, geese or duck. Hunting in northern Montenegro is among the best in Europe. For a permit, apply to the Secretariat for Agriculture in Titograd. ANDRIJEVICA, a small town on the River Lim, is a good base for a hunting and fishing holiday.

For fishing, the River Tara is excellent, or try the Biograd Lake near to the village of KOLAŠIN, at the heart of the National Park. In the village see the Turkish fortress and make an excursion to the MORAČA RIVER GORGE – a place of extraordinary beauty.

Bosnia-Herzegovina

The four-century rule of the Turks is clearly seen in every town and village of Bosnia-Herzegovina. Mosques, minarets, Turkish-style

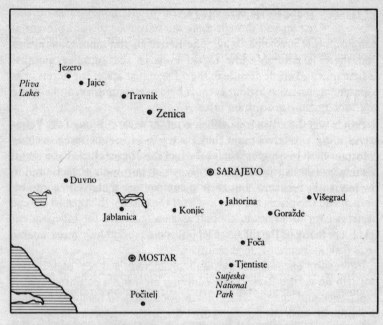

houses with courtyards, gardens and overhanging balconies dominate the scene, and Turkish-style costumes give even the people an oriental look. The Christian villages can be spotted by their different architecture – the European-style houses, broad streets and church steeples replace the narrow alleyways, public wells and minarets of their Muslim neighbours, but in the new concrete jungles, built since the Second World War, no style predominates, and it is impossible to tell anything of the inhabitants by what you can see. The tourist towns are therefore easy to isolate and concentrate on.

COMMUNICATIONS

The main airport for holidays in this area is Sarajevo, which enjoys links with the airports of most major Yugoslav cities.

For those travelling by train, Mostar and Sarajevo are on direct lines from Belgrade and Zagreb. The main 'A' road in this region climbs the Neretva and goes through Mostar to Jablanica, then east to Sarajevo where it connects with the Zagreb–Belgrade motorway.

TOURIST INFORMATION

The state travel agency is Unis Turist, and their main office is at Morića Haru, Sarač 77, Sarajevo.

CLIMATE

Weather-wise, Bosnia has more extremes than the coast of Yugoslavia, and it does tend to get colder at night. Herzegovina can swelter (Mostar is reputedly the hottest place in the country), and as a result it's unpleasant in July–August. Spring and autumn are good, and in the mountain areas the long light nights are particularly rewarding.

CULINARY SPECIALITIES

Bosnian food shows the Turkish influence of spices and seasoning. Try the main course dish of *kapuma* – a delicious blend of mutton, onion and spinach in a yoghurt sauce – or *sarma* which is minced beef rolled in vine leaves.

Bosnian sweets, like Turkish ones, are *very* sweet and sticky, but delicious in small quantities. *Baklava* or *Kadaif* are syrupy pastries, while *tokum* turns out to be a Turkish delight.

Žilavka is the best white wine, but only if the grapes come from the village of Blagaj; and Blatina is a pleasant light red.

WHERE TO GO FOR WHAT

Travelling independently in Bosnia is not easy. Communications are poor and good hotels few and far between. Herzegovina is an ideal place for an outdoor activity holiday. Skiing, hunting, mountaineering, fishing and walking holidays are all possibilities, and because of its inland position most of the holidaymakers to this republic are looking for this type of holiday. The two main tourist towns of Bosnia-Herzegovina are SARAJEVO – the capital of this dual republic – and MOSTAR. The majority of visitors to these centres are daytrippers from coastal resorts and few people base themselves in these towns. Other places of interest are JAJCE, TRAVNIK and BANJA LUKA, the old capital of the Turkish Viziers; the artists' colony of POČITELJ; the beautiful PLIVA LAKES; and the SUTJESKA NATIONAL PARK.

For real *Boys' Own* adventure stuff, take a raft or kayak down one of the rivers (book through Unis Turist), or if you're prepared to lug your own equipment take up a bit of fishing – permits from tourist offices. The rivers suitable for both these sports are the Drina, Tara, Una, Neretva and Vrbas.

Unis Turist are the people to contact for hunting, too. The potential is enormous: Bosnia-Herzegovina boasts some of the best natural habitat for bear, wolves, boar, deer, wild cat and fox. Holiday accommodation is in the designated hunting zone – in peak season it should be booked ahead.

Skiing is the big pull to Sarajevo these days. Because this was the location for the 1984 Winter Olympics, a considerable amount of money has been invested in facilities here, making it one of the best equipped, yet least expensive places in Europe to take a skiing holiday. The main ski resorts are JAHORINA and BJELAŠNICA, while nearby IGMAR is the base for a cross-country skiing holiday.

HISTORY

A potted history of this region shows the influence of Bosnia's strategic location between East and West. Back in the days of the sixth to ninth centuries it meant Bosnia became the frontier between Catholic Croatia and Slovenia, and Orthodox Macedonia and Serbia; later it resulted in the power struggle between the Ottoman and Austro-Hungarian Empires. In the centuries between, Bosnia was ruled by Serbia; was affiliated with the republic Duklja (later Montenegro); and was then allied to the Hungarian crown. It was by this move that later in the fifteenth century, Herzegovina as a separate duchy was added to the republic. By the end of the twelfth century the 'Bosnian' Church or Bogomil faith (considered heretical by the official religions) was taking hold, and after 1463, when under Sultan Mohammed II the Turks occupied the country, it was Bogomilism and Islam which dominated the religious scene.

The Turks ruled in Bosnia-Herzegovina for four centuries, to 1875, when they were ousted by the combined forces of Bosnia, Serbia and

Montenegro. The fate of Bosnia was then put in the hands of the Great European Powers, all trying to gain a foothold in the Balkan Peninsula.

The Austro-Hungarians took control in 1878, despite native rebellion against it, and by 1908 Bosnia and Herzegovina were annexed by Emperor Franz Josef to become part of the mighty Habsburg Empire. This move had major repercussions, unseen at the time, causing friction between the opposing European alliances of Germany and Austria-Hungary on the one hand, and France, Britain and Russia on the other. The end result of this situation was the assassination of Archduke Franz Ferdinand – heir to the throne of the Austro-Hungarian Empire – by a member of the secret Bosnian student society in Sarajevo in 1914, and, as we all know from our history books, one thing led to another, the alliances were called into play, and the First World War resulted.

After the war Bosnia-Herzegovina became part of the new Kingdom of Yugoslavia and one of the country's six provinces. During the Second World War Bosnia was one of the main strongholds of Tito's partisans. The significance in world history of this small area of middle Europe far outweighs its size, and for those interested in history Bosnia's past will make a fascinating study.

SARAJEVO

Sarajevo is the main holiday destination within Bosnia-Herzegovina, in winter for skiing holidays, in summer as a daytrip from one of the coastal resorts. It is the capital of the republic, and from the tourist's point of view the old town is the place to concentrate on – the new being the usual conglomerate of concrete, with rows of housing to cater for the town's growing young population. There is plenty to see here on a day's excursion, but it's not what most people are looking for on a larger holiday.

However for value as a ski resort, Sarajevo is hard to beat. The facilities found at Jahorina and Bjelasnica (about an hour from Sarajevo) are new (having been built for the 1984 Winter Olympics which were held here) and the Slavs are working hard to step up the service and nightlife on offer which, until now, were the only let-downs of a skiing holiday here.

In town the **Hotel Bristol** is the top end of the market, while those on a more restricted budget would try the **Central**, the **National**, or the **Stari Grad**. There are campsites at **Ilidža**, left of the Sarajevo–Mostar road, and at **Djure Djackovića** 22 on the road to Belgrade (better). There is no shortage of accommodation as many new hotels were built for the 1984 Olympics; alternatively private accommodation can be booked through Unis Turist: Morića han, Sarač 77.

The nightlife is good now, reflecting the largely young population of the city. The Hotels Bristol and Europa have dancing, etc., and one of the best bars is the Hamam at Maršala Tita 55 – a converted sixteenth-century Turkish bath! There are numerous good restaurants of which **Morića Han** at Sarači 66 and **Daira** at Halači 5 are the most atmospheric. If you're on a budget there are plenty of cheap self-service places, and cafés and bars abound. The **National Theatre** is located at Vojvode Stepe Obala and is worth checking to see what's on (opera and ballet present no linguistic problems!) or ask at tourist information if there are any folk evenings coming up. **Tourist Information** is at Jugoslovenske Armije 50. Open Monday to Saturday 7.30 a.m.–8 p.m., Sunday 8 a.m.–12 noon, and the main **Post Office** is at Obala V. Stepe 8.

As for the sights of Sarajevo, it seems a bit ironic that each year tourists flock in their thousands to visit the Turkish mosques and buildings from the Ottoman era in towns such as Sarajevo and Mostar, given that when the Turks were here the Slavs hated them, but they now realize it makes good touristic sense, and the Turkish influence is therefore what one comes to see. The old town – the Baščaršija quarter – lies on the right side of the Miljacka River between the castle and Ul. Maršala Tita. The buildings show clearly the two major influences the town has experienced: the Turkish and the Austro-Hungarian Empires. The mixture of these architectural styles is pierced alternately by the minarets of the mosques and the steeples of the Orthodox and Roman Catholic churches.

To complicate matters further there is even a Jewish population – originally from Spain – in Sarajevo, so a synagogue adds a further dimension to this extraordinary town. The tourist area where excursions will lead you is the site of the old market place, which today is the location for the Turkish bazaar where handicrafts such as copper pans, jugs, coffee sets, jewellery, carpets, handmade shoes and other souvenirs can be bought. Bartering is crucial unless signs to the contrary are displayed. This is *the* location for photography (it's also *the* location where you're more likely than normal to be taken for a mug, so bear that in mind).

At the end of this exotic square is the **Husref Bey Mosque** – a huge structure built in the early sixteenth century for the Turkish governor, Husref Bey. In the courtyard is his mausoleum and an observatory, and also outside the mosque is the fountain for the ritual washings necessary for the faithful. Inside is a riot of ornate decor, Arabian carpets and one of the earliest copies of the Koran. By the mosque is the clock tower with the hours of prayer marked on the clock face in Arabic numerals.

Facing the mosque is the **Kuršumli Medresa**, a theological High School restored in 1910, and close by is the **Imaret** and **Musafirhana** where the poor could be fed and sheltered. This early form of municipal charity benefacted impoverished students and travellers respectively, who were at liberty to claim the right to free food and shelter for three days, paid for out of the fund set up by the wealthy citizens of Sarajevo.

Another place worth a visit is the sixteenth-century Brusa Bezistan at the north end of the Baščaršija quarter. This **Municipal Museum**, containing Bosnian crafts and costumes, is in the building where the merchandise waiting to go north in the next caravan trip was stored. On the left bank of the River Miljacka, near the city centre, is the **Imperial Mosque** which was built by the Sultan Suleiman in 1566. Close to the Imperial Mosque is the former residence of the Turkish vizier, the **Konak**, which today serves as Parliament House to the republic of Bosnia-Herzegovina.

The last mosque not to be missed on a daytrip is the **Ali Pasha Mosque**, with its beautiful garden and its fine sixteenth-century Turkish architecture. There are several **old Turkish houses** kept in traditional style and open to the public, and also worth a look is the house of an eighteenth-century Bosnian merchant – **Despić House**, located down by the river.

In Liberation Square is the **Orthodox Cathedral**, but more interesting is the little **Orthodox Church** in Ulica Maršala Tita with its wall to hide from the Turks the faces of those who attended it. The Regional Museum may be of interest to see the changes this area has gone through, or for those who prefer getting the feel of the place from its old buildings the districts of **Benbaša** and **Dariva** on the hill will be rewarding.

While in Sarajevo most people will want to see what brought this town to the attention of the world in 1914: the spot where Archduke Franz Ferdinand was shot. Opposite Princip Bridge is the **Young Bosnian Museum** which contains a plaque marking the spot where Princip stood when he shot the Archduke and started the chain of events which led to the First World War.

From Trebević mountain (5345 feet) the view over Sarajevo is superb. A cablecar takes you up the mountain from its starting point on the left bank of the River Miljacka. The restaurant up there has one of the best views in Yugoslavia but is touristy and priced accordingly.

WINTER SPORTS

The JAHORINA RANGE and Mount Bjelašnica provide the base for skiing holidays in Sarajevo. New hotels, ski towns, chair lifts and roads were built for the 1984 Olympics and, combined with the snow depth on Mount Jahorina of around 10 feet from November to April, these make Sarajevo one of the best ski resorts in the country. Equipment to hire is much cheaper than in most other skiing countries, and there are slopes to suit all levels of proficiency.

Hotel Jahorina, seventeen and a half miles from Sarajevo (regular bus) is the best place for young active types. The nightlife is good and the prices reasonable. That bit more luxurious and quieter is **Hotel Bistrica**, with sports facilities such as a gymnasium, sauna and indoor pool.

Mount Bjelašnica is the other ski location at Sarajevo – the venue for the Nordic skiing events for men and women in the Winter Olympics. **Hotel Igman** is a well equipped hotel located here, and equally well situated for Mount Igman (for cross-country skiing) and Mount Bjelašnica. Sarajevo itself is within reach for the odd disco, meal out or sightseeing trip.

EXCURSIONS FROM SARAJEVO

JAJCE – find the Tourist Office opposite the road bridge over the River Pliva and you're right in the heart of sightseeing territory. The famous **waterfall** (up to 100 feet high) can be seen from viewpoints either side of the river. Also here, on the right bank, is the **Museum of the National Struggle for Liberation**, which is located in the actual hall Tito used to chair his 1943 Liberation Council. Just up from your starting point is the entrance to the old town – the Pliva Gate. Once inside, there are well preserved old Bosnian houses and the **Esme Sultanija Mosque**. There is also a touristy area, akin to that found in Mostar and Sarajevo, where Turkish-style souvenirs can be bartered for in the bazaars.

The belfry of St Luke (early fifteenth century) is the 100-foot tower you see from all over the town. This church, located within the town walls, is of particular historical interest as it was converted from a church to a mosque by the Turks and its campanile used as a minaret. Another sight to seek out is the **Mithraic Shrine** in the Roman fortress under the present street level (ask at Tourist Information for a guide to show you this). The **catacombs** (entrance near the round 'Bear Tower') were built in the fourteenth century by the same Grand Prince who built the castle.

Historically Jajce is an important place in Yugoslavia: it was here that the last King of Bosnia was executed by the Turks in 1461, and it was also in Jajce that a siege lasting one and a half years was acted out by the Turks, eager to gain control of the town. The Hungarians were then in control and it took until their absorption into the Austrian monarchy, after the Battle of Mohács (1526), before the Turks took hold of the town. More recently Jajce played an important role in 1943 when the foundations of the present-day state of Yugoslavia were laid down in the hall opposite the Tourist Office.

The PLIVA LAKES generally form the second part of the daytrip excursion to Jajce, and this is the location where most of the tourist facilities for Jajce are to be found. This area is about five miles from the town, on the road to Bihać, and the main settlement is at JEZERO. The scenery is beautiful, the fishing very good, and rowing and canoeing competitions are held around here. The hotel for fishermen's holidays in this area is the **Sokočnika**, further upstream at ŠIPOVO.

Outdoor types will enjoy the scenery and open spaces at LAKE BALKANO (twenty miles from Jajce) where the walking potential is great and peace and solitude is guaranteed, even in mid-summer.

If you're independently mobile, make the effort to get to TRAVNIK at the foot of Mount Vlašić. This was the seat of the Bosnian Governors from 1700 to 1852 and though many of its fine buildings were burned down in a fire in 1903 enough remain to make this Turkish town an interesting afternoon's sightseeing. Don't miss the **Coloured Mosque**, the **Hadži Ali Bey Mosque**, and the view from the castle. Mount Vlašić is today an expanding winter sports development and a centre for game-hunting.

MOSTAR

The old town of Mostar provides a popular daytrip for holidaymakers from Dalmatia and Montenegro, and it's one well worth making for it shows a side of Yugoslavian life completely different from that found on the Adriatic coast: the influence of the Turks is still strongly felt and the mosques and souks give an exotic Oriental feel to the town. The old town is the only part of Mostar worth visiting; the new is the usual modern array of concrete, but there's plenty to keep your camera clicking and hold your interest for a day in the narrow streets, bazaars and historic houses of the tourist centre.

Few visitors actually stay in Mostar, but if you're travelling independently and want to base yourself here, consider the following hotels: the modern, large **Ruža**, close to the bridge and the old town; the **Neretva** across the river; or the **Bristol**. Private rooms are to be found one block left of the bus station at Ul. Mladena Balorde. Look for '*sobe*' signs. For food and nightlife try the **Labrint Restaurant** where you can eat on a terrace overlooking the Neretva River, or the **Stari Most**, located by the bridge.

There's no way of avoiding the throng of tourists in the summer months if you're tackling Mostar as a daytrip, and throngs there certainly are – in fact the main sight of the town, the old bridge, is positively lethal as a result of the number of visitors' feet which have worn the cobbled paving stones down to a surface akin to a sheet of glass (those in leather-soled sandals, be warned!). Many tours whisk you round the sights in record time, leaving you only a few minutes to absorb the craftsmanship of centuries. If yours is like this, return to the shady mosque gardens and Turkish houses when the guide leaves you for your excessively long lunch break, and soak up the atmosphere while the busloads are munching their *čepvaččiči*.

Most buses park at the Hotel Ruža, where they'll recommend you to take lunch (don't), as this is close to the entrance to the old town. The **Old Bridge** is invariably your first stop. This beautiful old construction was built over the Neretva in 1556 by the Turks. The town's name derives from the bridge (*most* means bridge; *stari* means old), and it certainly is the focal point of visitors' attention.

The story goes that the Sultan of the time swore to execute the architect if this bridge, like his previous attempts, collapsed. Not feeling too confident of the guaranteed success of his project, the architect took to his heels on the day the supports were to be removed. He was eventually found digging his own grave, but the news was not what he expected – the bridge stood, and to this day continues to stand as a reminder of his excellent engineering. For the tourists, and a small fee, the local lads will dive the 65 feet from the bridge into the Neretva.

Close to the bridge is the **Mosque of Karadjoz Beg** in Ul. Braće Fejića. This is the largest of Mostar's twenty-four mosques; it dates back to 1557 and is a splendid example, complete with a *medrese* (religious school) and a fountain for the ritual Muslim ablutions in the courtyard. While in Mostar you're bound to hear one of the five daily calls to prayer. These days, however, they're not chanted by the muezzin, but have a more twentieth-century feel, being relayed from the minaret by a public address system! Near to here you'll find the **Mehmed Paša Koski Mosque**, finished in 1618, towering up from the river. The view from its minaret gives a classic view over the town. Another is from the top of the little hill outside the tourist office, looking over to the bridge.

The **Old Serbian Orthodox Church** of 1833 is interesting because of the fact that it lies below ground level and contains some beautiful icons and European works of art. Traditional **Turkish Houses** are always included in an organized tour of Mostar. These old merchants' dwellings are still occupied and the inhabitants, dressed in Turkish garb, serve Turkish coffee to the tourists. Those wishing to find out more about the way of life in these parts should visit the **History and Ethnographic Museum**, located near the bridge. The bazaars of the old town are colourful and will provide souvenirs for everyone, but barter!

Excursions from Mostar to the surrounding countryside prove very rewarding. Perhaps the best daytrip is to BLAGAJ, a village six miles from the town, and the source of the River Buna – a tributary of the Neretva. The source erupts suddenly and dramatically from the bottom of huge cliffs, and the effect is quite spectacular. Also here are the ruined remains of the **Fortress of Stjepangrad** built on the site of the Roman town of Bone.

After 45 minutes travelling south from Mostar to the coast, you come to the village of POČITELJ – an artists' colony and 'living museum' which transports you back to the days of Turkish rule, giving you, more than any other place, an idea of what life was like here centuries ago. Independent travellers have the opportunity to stay in one of the private houses here (arrange this through the Tourist Office). The main sights are the **Ibrahim Pasha Mosque** and the ruined castle which affords a wonderful photo location from the top.

The whole village, however, is very photogenic and Počitelj must be taken as a whole, not a collection of separate sights. It is a beautiful little place, a million miles away from commercialism and organized tourism, and a wonderful place to spend a few relaxing days.

TJENTIŠTE AND THE SUTJESKA NATIONAL PARK

This is the location for countryside enthusiasts and the outdoor type attempting an independent holiday. The National Park is located around an area of pristine natural forest (it was not planted by man, nor has it been much interfered with) at PERUĆICA, and other highlights of this National Park are the glacial lakes in the Zelengora Mountains and a 240-feet waterfall at Skakavac. Bosnia's highest mountain is here – Maglić (7832 feet) – making it popular with climbers. TJENTIŠTE is the place to stay: there's a large youth hostel plus a few basic hotels.

Fishermen may like to consider FOČA or GORAŽDE as holiday bases. Both are known for the exceptional trout and salmon caught in the River Drina. The **Zelengora Hotel** in Foča or the **Gradina** in Goražde would do nicely as your base, and there's plenty to keep you amused in the old town of Foča. This is the location for enjoying a raft trip on the River Drina, and it's also a convenient base for those taking climbing or fishing or hunting holidays in the Sutjeska National Park or in the Durmitor Range.

Sights in Foča include the **Aladža Mosque**, the **Market Square**, and the **Municipal Museum** with displays of local costumes, art and household items, but it is the original atmosphere of Foča which is the main attraction. The two-day raft trips which start at Foča end up at the beautifully positioned town of **VIŠEGRAD**. The **bridge** over the Drina is the only real sight of the town.

Slovenia

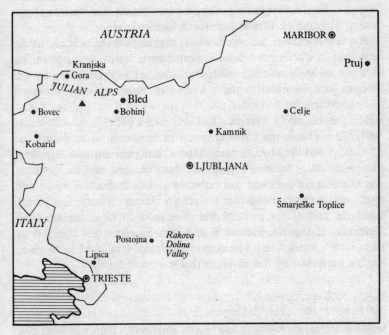

The beautiful alpine region of Slovenia lies between Italy and Austria and is a haven for peaceful walking, climbing or, in winter, skiing holidays. Considering the scale of its beauty and its relative cheapness compared to neighbouring Austria or Switzerland, Slovenia ranks as one of Europe's best kept secrets. In the north lie the Karawanke mountains, the natural boundary with Austria; to the west are the popular mountain resorts of the Julian Alps – Bled, Bohinj and Kranjska Gora; eastwards the land slopes down into the fertile plains which stretch all the way to Hungary; and in the south, Croatia is the neighbouring territory. Slovenia has only a small share of the Adriatic coast – its main resorts are Koper, Piran and Portoroz (see page 150), all of which are great favourites with daytripping Austrians and Italians, and holidaying Germans.

It is the mountains of Slovenia, however, which draw the foreign tourists to this beautiful region. The unspoilt beauty of the Alps is carefully conserved and the clear glacial lakes and thermal spas act as a magnet for those who delight in a healthy alpine holiday. The added incentive here is that these pleasures come to you at a fraction of the cost of a similar holiday in Austria or Switzerland.

A quick history of this region shows that its position next to Austria and Italy has accounted for its comparative wealth and power. Its location on the road to the Adriatic coast led to domination by the Roman Empire which made it one of its most powerful colonies. Neighbouring Austria ruled this area for over a thousand years, and while the rest of Yugoslavia was dominated by the Turks, Slovenia, under the Habsburgs, was engaged in the fight to stave off the Ottomans and the Muslim faith. After a brief period under Napoleon (1809–13) the Austrians regained control, but by then strong nationalistic feelings had been aroused and both the Slovenians and the Croatians worked together to curb the Habsburg influence. It took until the end of the First World War to oust the Austrians from Slovenia, and in the Second World War Slovenia was annexed by Hitler and Mussolini. (The occupying Italians in 1941 were given such a hard time by the Slovenes that they withdrew!)

COMMUNICATIONS

On a practical note, this is one part of Yugoslavia where independent travel is easily possible. Communications and tourist facilities are of a standard comparable to that found anywhere in Western Europe and tourists are warmly welcomed. Guest houses (*gostilna*) abound, making accommodation-finding easy. The standards in the hotels used by package tour operators in Slovenia are generally higher than those further south, and generally things run more efficiently.

The airport used by tour operators flying package tourists to this region is Ljubljana (forty minutes from the centre of town), and for those coming by rail Ljubljana connects with Zagreb, Belgrade, Niš and Skopje on express lines.

TOURIST INFORMATION

The state tourist agency is Kompas at Prazakova 4, Ljubljana, or alternatively there's Globtour at Šmartinska 130, Ljubljana. The main Tourist Information Office in Ljubljana is at Titova Cesta 11. Open Monday to Saturday 7 a.m.–10 p.m.; Sundays and holidays 8 a.m.–noon; 5 p.m.–8 p.m.

THE CLIMATE

Weatherwise, Slovenia has a typical alpine climate, so remember to pack a waterproof and take a jumper for those cooler nights. June until October is the summer season. Spring is particularly beautiful, and late September to early October, just as the leaves are turning, is another magical time to visit the mountains.

CULINARY SPECIALITIES

Regional dishes have a strong Austrian influence – Wiener Schnitzel and delicious pastries are widely available, and in the Kranjska region würst, akin to those found in Germany, are eaten. Magyar influences can be detected in the dishes found in northern Slovenia ('gypsy roast' – *cigansko pečenje* – is a favourite). Ask for *kmečka pojedina*, *krvavica*, *pečenica* and *zelje* and you'll be given the traditional Slovenian dish of sausage, black pudding, sauerkraut and buckwheat, which, after a long hill walk, washed down with the smooth red Refosk wine, is all one could ask for.

Wines are excellent and cheap. In hotels you will be charged appreciably more, so do most of your experimenting in wine bars. Ljutomer and Jeruzalem are good whites, but remember, just because we don't see many Yugoslav reds at home it doesn't mean they don't exist or aren't good: Refosk and Teran are both excellent. If you ask for house wine you will usually end up with a strong rosé wine, served in carafes, called *civček*.

WHERE TO GO FOR WHAT

The Kamnik Alps and Pohorje Mountains offer more peace and quiet than the Julian Alps, but they have fewer tourists' facilities and no package holidays. Although Bled can be busy in high season, few of the alpine resorts feel anything other than quiet as there is simply so much space to lose oneself in. What this effectively means is that even if you are after a real 'peace and quiet' holiday you will still find it in the resorts of Bled, Bohinj, Bovec or Kranjska Gora: you needn't go out of your way to find more remote places for a restful time as these resorts are all quiet.

The excursion in this region is to POSTOJNA to see the caves: a huge underground labyrinth of fascinating rock formations, of interest even to those not remotely geologically minded.

Walking and mountaineering holidays are only two possibilities; there are numerous other outdoor pursuits which Slovenia can offer: boating, kayak trips, golf, and in winter skiing, to name a few. Slovenia is, in fact, a superb location for the outdoor type.

For a climbing holiday the Trenta Valley – based in Bovec or Kobarid – is ideal; alternatively there's excellent climbing around Bled, Bohinj, Kamnik town or Kranjska Gora. To escape the crowds completely, try basing yourself in Jezersko (take the bus to Kran from Ljubljana and change) or Solčava. For boating, Bled is the best location, and for more details on the kayak trips contact Kompas travel agency in Ljubljana. Golf is available in Bled at Yugoslavia's one and only course, though it is not cheap.

For a sample of what Slovenia has to offer in terms of hillwalking and spectacular scenery, take the daily 08.25 bus from Bled to Pokljuka in the Triglav National Park. Get off at the terminus and begin a walk up Debela Peč via Lipanca. At Pokljuka take the signs to Lipanca. Once you have passed through the spruce woods and the larch at higher altitude you enter the big gorge under Lipanca. From this landmark there are signs to Lipanca in a northerly direction. From there you reach the main ridge and upper dome of Debela Peč, with its fine views of Triglav, Yugoslavia's highest mountain.

In total the ascent will take around two hours and at the top you stand 6000 feet up, face to face with the mountain sacred to all

Yugoslavs. There are no superlatives sufficient to describe the splendours of the alpine scenery up there, and in total this rewarding walk will only take three hours maximum of your day. The return bus to Bled is at 11.30 a.m. daily and at 4 p.m. on Fridays and Sundays.

Winter sports are excellent at Kranjska Gora where facilities are good and prices low. The après-ski gets livelier each year as this resort becomes more internationally renowned. There are slopes to suit all stages of expertise. Bohinj is an alternative for the serious skier, while the Pohorje Mountains (close to Maribor) are cheaper, quieter and more suited to beginners. The Pokljuka Plateau (Zatrnik) is another ideal place to learn, or for the super-fit wanting to stretch themselves there's an Olympic ski-jump at Rateče Planica, not far from Kranjska Gora. The best thing to do if you're considering a skiing holiday in Yugoslavia is to gather all the brochures together and spend a bit of time analysing exactly what your requirements are in terms of skiing facilities and après-ski, then choose your resort accordingly. Money is being invested each year in skiing facilities in Slovenia as the Yugoslavs realize how much of an income-earner winter holidays are, consequently facilities are always improving.

Skiing begins at Christmas and carries on until Easter. There is a bob-sleighing competition in late March each year at Kranjska Gora which draws the crowds and fills the hotels, so bear this in mind if you're looking for peace and quiet.

It is perfectly possible to be based in Bled (where most of the activities are to be found) and still have a skiing holiday, thus combining skiing with a winter holiday.

If you have a party with mixed skiers and non-skiers, this would be your best bet as sleigh-rides, boating, sightseeing, shopping and numerous other activities can all be enjoyed here, while the skiers can take the half-hourly ski buses to Zatrnik, where the nearest skiing is to be found. Skiers in Bled have the choice of several places: Pokljuka, Bohinj, Kobla, Mount Vogel, Kranjska Gora, Krvavec, Zelenica and Španov Vrh. All are accessible by coach.

A spa holiday is offered by Yugotours in **ŠMARJEŠKE TOPLICE**. For a healthy break, the facilities offered here are virtually impossible to beat. The surrounding countryside is beautiful, and in comparison to similar resorts in Austria and Germany the cost is extremely low.

The Mountain Resorts

Bled, Bohinj, Bovec and Kranjska Gora are the big names as far as tour operators are concerned.

BLED ranks as one of *the* sights in Yugoslavia. It lies on the lake of the same name and is a spa town which attracted the elite in the days of the Austro-Hungarian Empire, and today caters for tourists all the year round, still of a fairly affluent class. Dozens of tour operators offer Bled as a resort on its own, or as part of a two-centre holiday, so there is a choice of tours and hotels. Its setting is spectacular: standing 1500 feet above sea level, dominated by Mount Triglav, and with views all around of the Julian Alps.

The island in the middle of the lake, with the old Baroque Church of St Mary, adds the final touch to this fairytale setting, and it can be rowed out to from the shore for visits. This is quite a regular occurrence on Sundays when the locals row out to attend Mass in the church, singing hymns and traditional songs as they go.

Modern, comfortable hotels now fill Bled and tourism is the town's main industry. Of the hotels on offer, the **Park**, **Grand Hotel Toplice** and **Golf** are the most luxurious (the Toplice is particularly beautiful: well fitted out and with an incomparable view over the lake from the lounge) and are those generally used by tour operators. The **Jelovica**, with its skittle alley and location near the lake, is a good, medium-priced hotel as a cheaper alternative, or for those on a tight budget the **Pri Mari Pension** could be considered. Independent travellers prepared to rough it a bit will be interested in the Youth Hostel, just around the corner from the Jelovica Hotel. Alternatively there is a well appointed campsite at the west end of Lake Bled. Most British tour operators (especially Yugotours) manage to get their clients into these 'A' class hotels for very reasonable prices, making holidays in this area excellent value for the facilities offered.

Staying with the tourist facilities on offer – the nightlife here is livelier than in most of the other mountain resorts as there are always more people in Bled than elsewhere, so the hotels put on live entertainment, and discos and cafés have sprung up to cater to this demand.

Having said all that, nightlife is still pretty tame by Northern

European standards and you'll be limited to the Yugotours Holiday Club (top floor of Park Hotel) if you're with Yugotours; the disco in the Park Hotel; or going out for a drink or meal. The **Gostišče Mlino** in Mlino, half a mile west of Bled when walking round the lake, is a good fish restaurant, and **Dnevni Café Bar**, up from the horse and carriage taxi rank, is a good place to have a drink or snack meal. It's open 10 a.m.–8 p.m. Like many cafés and bars in rural areas of Slovenia, it does not keep late hours, for the very good reason that people start work at 6 a.m. each day, so go to bed early.

In summer wealthy Northern Europeans and Americans tend to make up the bulk of visitors to Bled. The young crowd do not arrive until the winter, for the skiing. Because of the glut of rich Germans, shopkeepers and restaurateurs feel justified in charging prices which further south in Yugoslavia would be considered ridiculous. It is still cheap, however, even for the Brits.

Sights within the town include the **Castle of Bled**, which stands on a crag above the lake, and dates back to medieval times, though today's façade is Baroque. This was the home of the Counts of Bled and still houses furniture and artefacts from their time. Visit the museum and castle chapel to see the original frescoes. Remember to take your camera along as there are spectacular views over the surrounding countryside. To get up there, take the road from the Jelovica Hotel until you see the sign saying 'Grad'. Follow this up the steep slope until you approach the drawbridge.

The parish church of **St Martin** is the only other sight in Bled itself. On the island in the lake is the seventeenth-century **St Mary's Church**, and there is a **regatta complex** at Lake Bled where national championships are regularly held. The walk around Lake Bled is particularly beautiful. It takes in the grounds of Villa Bled – Tito's old summer house – and in total takes about one hour.

EXCURSIONS

It is the countryside around Bled which makes it one of the country's best loved holiday resorts. Organized excursions (through Globtour and Kompas) are to LJUBLJANA; the POSTOJNA CAVES; the LIPICA STUD FARM; VENICE; KROPA – a wrought-iron centre; the TRENTA VALLEY with its beautiful botanical gardens; a tour of the JULIAN ALPS; the mountain resorts of BLED, BOHINJ and KRANJSKA GORA; and, as part of the Bohinj tour, the VINTGAR GORGE AND WATERFALLS. Each one of these excursions is interesting and will take you through spectacular scenery. If you're pushed for time a good choice would be the POSTOJNA CAVES – which really are quite something and considered to be one of the natural sights of Europe; VENICE, which is definitely one of the great sights of the world; and a tour of the JULIAN ALPS.

Obviously if you're keen on flora and fauna you'll be tempted to take all the excursions into the mountains. Particularly worthwhile then is the trip to the Trenta Valley. These excursions are offered from the other Slovenian mountain resorts too.

Whether you do it independently or on an organized excursion, a trip to BOHINJ through the valley of the Sava Bohinjska is well worth making. The scenery is spectacular and on arrival at Bohinj you are greeted with a quiet, beautiful little village lying in the shadow of the Julian Alps, with a selection of good hotels for refreshment. Mountaineering excursions in the Triglav National Park begin from Bohinj as well as Bled. Carry on about three and a half miles from the end of Lake Bohinj to the hotel, then, leaving your wheels behind, walk up to the dramatic source of the RIVER SAVA. From the hut at the bottom turn right across the bridge on the north bank of the stream, following the road towards Zlatarog, and follow the signposted path to get to the Seven Lakes and deep into the Julian Alps. Although this path is steep walking, it is not difficult as it is well laid out.

Walking and climbing in the JULIAN ALPS is both popular and rewarding. There are walks suitable to all skills and ages, and for peace and solitude in beautiful surroundings you'd be hard pressed to find a better location anywhere in Europe.

The highest peak in the Alps is also the highest in Yugoslavia (9394 feet) – MOUNT TRIGLAV (pronounced Triglow, to rhyme with 'now'). 'Triglav' means 'three-headed' and the locals tell you one head looks to the past, one to the present and the third to the future. A great deal of folklore is attached to this mountain which is regarded as the sacred mountain of the Slovenes. It is believed to be the home of the mountain spirit, Zlatarog, or Golden Horn – a white chamois with golden horns.

There are several routes to the peak: the most scenic starts at the

Sporthotel in Pokljuka (take the road from Bled to Zatrnik through the forests to the Pokljuka plateau where you'll find this popular winter sports hotel). Buses run from Bled. See 'An Alpine Guide', free from Tourist Information, Bled. Alternatively this route can be approached via the west end of Lake Bohinj (see previous page). This is not the shortest way to the top, but it allows you to enjoy some spectacular views on the way up (approx. seven hours).

A different approach is from the village of NA LOGU in the Trenta Valley. Take the road up the Zadnjica Valley (the side road before the climb up the Vrsic pass). Cars must be left at the Zadnjica Valley from where it is a five-hour climb.

The village of MOJSTRANA is another starting point (take the marked road off the Kranjska Gora–Jesenice road). The car must be left at the mountain inns of Aljažev Dom from where the two marked paths to the summit begin. This is a famous meeting place for climbers assembling to tackle the peak. These climbs rank as difficult and should you decide having got this far it's all a bit ambitious, there is the opportunity to go for the second highest peak in the Alps – Škrlatica – from Aljažev Dom (8983 feet). This will take a good five hours, and should not be attempted by the inexperienced or those without proper climbing gear.

A mountain hut network exists on Triglav offering basic overnight accommodation for climbers. From the Aljažev Dom ascent, there is a hut at 7800 feet open in summer.

If you're the lazy type (or haven't brought the right equipment) you can get a good look at Mount Triglav from the car by going to Mojstrana and taking the narrow road off to the right for about eight miles, then three miles out of Mojstrana you will come to the Pericnik Waterfall.

For details of this and all the climbs in this area either buy the booklet on the Triglav National Park, or better still ask Tourist Information in Bled for a copy of the excellent free leaflet, 'An Alpine Guide'.

After Bled, **BOHINJ** is the next most popular Slovenian mountain resort. Quieter than Bled, it tends to attract more serious walkers and away-from-it-all types than its livelier, more cosmopolitan neighbour, and it is an ideal location for families with young children. Several tour operators run to Bohinj, and two-centre holidays are available with Bohinj as one of the options.

Bohinj is five miles south-west of Bled and the holiday area, known collectively as Bohinj, is based around the village of Bohinjska Bistrica and Lake Bohinj. The hotels congregate around the lake, most of them built on slopes above it, giving magnificent views from lakeside balconies. The **Zlatarog** is the exception to this. This alpine chalet-style hotel lies at the end of Lake Bohinj, near to the cable car which takes you up the mountainside of Mount Vogel. Facilities in the Zlatarog are the best in Bohinj and nightlife is laid on by the hotel. Boats for rowing on the lake can be hired here, as can bicycles for the fit who wish to pedal up and down the countryside exploring the terrain.

The hotels **Jezero, Kompas, Bellevue**, and **Pod Voglom** are all comfortable and provide a range of sporting facilities. The Kompas has a disco which attracts the young in both winter (when it acts as a ski hotel) and summer. On the Mount Vogel plateau, about 3300 feet above Lake Bohinj and reached by cable car, is the **Ski Hotel** – another busy venue in winter. Three chalet-type **Pensions** are available on Mount Vogel for those wishing to economize, but in the case of Yugoslavian skiing holidays a package deal makes much more sense and invariably works out cheaper in the long run. Skiing facilities in Bohinj are better than average (though not as good as Bovec), and cross-country and ski trekking are available.

As for Bohinj itself – beside the bridge over the River Sava is the small **Church of St John** in which there are beautiful, if gory, fifteenth-century frescoes. It is the landmark of the village and if by chance it is not open ask for the key at Tourist Information. Taking the road past the church towards Bled you come to the quaint little village of **Stara Fužina** (Old Furnace) where a farming museum is located. It has exhibits which aim to show life in the dairy farms of this area.

The impressive SAVICA FALLS have a drop of 200 feet at their extent. To reach them, take the road that winds its way beyond the south side of the lake till you come to a dead end where the walk up begins. From here you can walk up to the falls or to the mountain refuge hut of Dom Savica. Also here you can walk up to the Black Lake – an invigorating climb with spectacular views, taking around four hours.

KRANJSKA GORA is Yugoslavia's most developed ski resort. In winter it comes to life and offers excellent skiing and the liveliest après-ski to be found in Yugoslavia. Several companies provide holidays here, and there are now many good hotels available. The **Kompas** is the top of the range, though the B-grade **Larix** and **Alpina Kompas**, **Lek** and **Prisank** are all equally comfortable and close to the slopes.

Here are all the facilities you'd expect in an international ski resort – chairlifts, ski tows, a skiing school, cross-country tracks and ice rinks for skating and curling (though these sports can equally well be enjoyed on the lake on the road to Vršič).

The ski tows to MOUNT VITRANC (5352 feet) – the highest ski station in this area – begin behind the hotels and the journey down takes you through the forests of spruce, larch and beech. Five miles from Kranjska Gora are the three world-class Planica ski jumps, where the current world record was achieved.

In the summer months Kranjska Gora is filled with climbers and hill walkers, keen to take advantage of the spectacular alpine terrain. There is a system of mountain huts in the alps here so that serious walkers can spend days climbing the peaks. The 'Alpine Guide' – free if asked for in the Tourist Information Office (open Monday to Saturday 8 a.m.–3 p.m., closed Sundays) will describe some of the possibilities. Particularly worth climbing (or driving, as there is a road built by Russian prisoners of the First World War) is Vršič. On the way up to the summit of Vršič (5236 feet) is a small Russian Chapel, built to commemorate the four hundred Russians who lost their lives in an avalanche while building this road.

The Sava Valley also offers walking (of easier standard) and magnificent scenery. The 'Julian Alps' organized excursion by any of the local travel agencies covers this area in great depth.

Yugotours run to **BOVEC**, as both a summer and winter resort, though the village only really comes to life in winter when experienced sportsmen come to enjoy the challenging conditions and take advantage of this well-kept resort. It is relatively unknown at present, but it won't be for long as in 1992 it is due to be developed into Yugoslavia's leading winter sports resort. Because of this, facilities are in the process of being developed.

The skiing takes place in the Kanin range (8481 feet at the summit) which because of its high altitude receives a lot of snow until as late in the year as May. The two hotels at the moment (many more are planned) are the **Kanin** and the **Alp,** both B category, though the Kanin has the added facilities of a sauna and indoor pool.

The village of Bovec in the Trenta Valley is an ideal summertime haven for those really wanting to get away from it all. There is nothing much to see except spectacular scenery, and nothing much to do except walk and take the excursions on offer, but for those looking for a complete rest and a change from polluted urban living this could be the absolutely perfect resort.

There are four ways to get to Bovec: (1) from Tarvisio in Italy, (2) from Ljubljana via Logatec, Idrija and Kobarid, (3) from Jesenice to Vršič; or (4) over the Predil Pass from Italy to the Lake of Rabelj and Sella Navea.

Fishing and canoeing are available, and there is a scenic drive to be enjoyed up the Trenta Valley to the picturesque alpine village TRENTA NA LOGU where there is a folk museum. Also worth seeing is the source of the River Soča – take the track off just as the road begins to approach the VRŠIČ PASS. There are no sights as such in the village of Bovec but all the excursions available from Bled and Bohinj apply to Bovec too, so there is no shortage of things to do.

All the sights are covered in the 'Julian Alps' excursion which from Bovec takes you up the mountains to the Predil Pass and into Italy. The scenery is spectacular and every effort should be made to get to this outer limit of the Triglav National Park.

 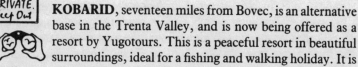 **KOBARID**, seventeen miles from Bovec, is an alternative base in the Trenta Valley, and is now being offered as a resort by Yugotours. This is a peaceful resort in beautiful surroundings, ideal for a fishing and walking holiday. It is totally unspoilt and uncommercialized in package terms, and until the development of Bovec is likely as an ideal location for a quiet, relaxing holiday amid wonderful scenery. Entertainment is extremely limited, but the hotels are comfortable, particularly the **Matajur.**

THE POSTOJNA CAVES provide a popular excursion for holiday-makers from all the Istrian and some Dalmatian coastal resorts, as well as those close by in the Slovenian mountain resorts. It is deservedly popular as these caves with their incredible stalagmite and stalactite formations rank as one of *the* natural sights of Europe. They are of sufficient novelty value to merit visiting even if you're not into geology or natural history; historically they're of interest as during the Second World War parts of the caves were used as storage for German supplies of oil and petrol. The Yugoslav guerrillas discovered this and set up a time bomb which destroyed around 10,000 tons of essential fuel, hence the scorched, black appearance of parts of the caves.

In total the Postojna Caves are 12 miles long, though your visit will only go in as far as 4½ miles, which is as far as there is electricity. For the first 1½ miles of your underground adventure you are transported on a cable railway; thereafter you explore around 2½ miles on foot. The temperature is at a constant 46°F/8°C so take a jumper (alternatively, cloaks can be hired out there). A guide will take you to the most amazing of the rock formations and trot out the stereotyped names which man has given to these incredible forms since discovering them around 170 years ago. Hence you will see 'The Leaning Tower of Pisa', 'The Cathedral' and 'Paradise Grotto', to name a few.

What is interesting is the rather grotesque little creatures, specially adapted to underground life, which inhabit the lower levels of the caves. Their biological name is 'Proteus Anguineus', and they resemble salamanders: eyeless, colourless and with gills for breathing in water and a lung for breathing in oxygen when on land. These incredible amphibians are mammal and fish at the same time, and have a life span almost as long as man's. They can be viewed in the aquarium of the 'Great Hall', close to the visitors' shop.

Other caves in this area are the ŠKOCJAN CAVES (fifteen miles south-west of Postojna) which are less touristy, more dramatic and altogether more pleasant in high season; the PLANINSKA JAMA CAVES, and the KRIŽNA JAMA CAVES. The latter two can be visited with a guide on application.

While in this part of Slovenia it is worth finding your way to the NATIONAL PARK OF THE RAKOVA DOLINA VALLEY. Here you can stumble across still unexplored caves and areas of great unspoilt beauty, ideal for walking and picnicking.

Close to the border with Italy, at **LIPICA**, is the stud farm of those beautiful animals famed from their use in the Spanish Riding School of Vienna – the Lippizaner horses. Excursions are organized from most holiday resorts in northern Yugoslavia to visit this centre and see the horses being put through their paces. It is an unusual and interesting excursion, and for those of an equestrian bent, an absolute must! This breed, a mixture of Andalusian and local stock, is noted for its intelligence and longevity, and their grace of movement can be confirmed by watching one of the displays open to the public twice daily. Interestingly, the foals are all black. It is not until maturity that these horses turn to their characteristic white colour. The organized excursion includes a tour of the stables, 'meeting' the stallions, watching a dressage display and, occasionally, riding the horses, knowledge and confidence permitting.

LJUBLJANA

The very attractive *old district* of Ljubljana comes as a pleasant surprise after driving through the sprawling suburbs of this expanding city. Just as one begins to despair of the place and put it down as another twentieth-century concrete jungle the old town emerges – a haven of mellow Baroque buildings, Venetian-style bridges and elegant boulevards, dominated by an old castle which in centuries past housed the feudal lords of the town. The air of opulence in this regional capital, where the *per capita* income is greater than in any other Yugoslavian town, is apparent, and one can't help noticing the similarities between this town and the major cities of neighbouring Austria. Certainly it has more in common historically, architecturally and atmospherically with Vienna than it does with Belgrade. The university here ensures an active nightlife. A daytrip gives you just about enough time to see all the sights of the town, but if you're travelling independently and have transport at your disposal a stay of a few days in Ljubljana can be a rewarding experience and gives you an ideal base from where you can enjoy the pleasures of the Julian Alps and the Karavanke mountain range. Hotel suggestions within the town are the luxury class **Holiday Inn** and **Hotel Lev**; in a cheaper category the **Kompas** (close to the station); or for motorists, **Motel Tikves**. **Tourist Information** will fix you up – they're at Titova Cesta 11. Open Monday to Saturday 7 a.m.–10 p.m., Sunday and holidays 8 a.m.–noon, 5 p.m.–8 p.m. The main Post Office is at Cigaletova 15, but often handier is the one at Titova Cesta 8 (next to Tourist Information and the station). Open Monday to Friday 8 a.m.–8 p.m., Saturday 8 a.m.–2 p.m.

Restaurant suggestions are: Maxim's at Trg Revolucije 1 – an authentic Slovenian restaurant with live music – and Pri Vitezu at 20 Breg, which is worth finding for its excellent fixed-price lunch, and Emonska Klet at Plečnikov Trg, located in a cellar. South of the three-bridge area is a glut of reasonably priced and good restaurants by the riverfront.

The sights are all located in the medieval town on the banks of the Ljubljana River. What you see today is not medieval but Baroque as the town was rebuilt in the late seventeenth and eighteenth centuries. The **Town Hall** in Mestri Trg is an impressive sight, as is the fountain close by which represents three Slovenian rivers: the Sava, Krka and Ljubljanica. The town hall and clock tower were begun in the fifteenth century and altered in the eighteenth century. Taking a right from here you come to the massive structure of the **Cathedral of St Nicholas** – a riot of Baroque architecture and ornate decoration. Behind this is the old **Episcopal Court and Seminary** where Napoleon stayed during his time here; the courtyard is particularly attractive.

To get to the castle take the square beyond here – Vodnikov Trg – and to the right of this square (opposite the statue of the Slovene poet after whom the square is named) you find the steep (very steep!) old street of **Studentovska Ulica** which will take you up to the castle – the oldest building in the town, originally dating from the twelfth century. As there is a large reconstruction programme currently in progress, the castle has no rooms open to the public nor interesting buildings (except a restaurant), but the wonderful panoramic view from the top over the surrounding countryside and the Julian Alps is worth the strenuous climb.

The **Franciscan Church** overlooks the centrally located Prešernov Trg (in the heart of the old city; by the river) and dates back to the mid-seventeenth century. This Italian-style church contains a high altar by artist Robba who created many works of art for the town in the early eighteenth century, including the fountain in Mestri Trg.

The **National Museum** on Herojev Trg is particularly fine. (Turn on to Titova Cesta from the Franciscan Church; take Šubičeva

Ulica, and Herojev Trg is off that.) The collection in this museum is one of the country's finest – don't miss the bronze urn from the fifth century BC. Also located in this area, on Cankarjeva, is the **Modern Gallery** and the National Art Gallery. If, by now, your feet are weary, head for the park on Tivoli Hill which surrounds a château. This is the venue for the Ljubljana Fair, held annually.

The KAMNIK ALPS are close enough to beckon any visitor to Ljubljana. Even an afternoon is enough to show you some of their dramatic beauty, and if you have no car, there are excursions arranged by Kompas and other local travel agents.

Stopping points tend to be KAMNIK and CELJE, which are about 32 miles apart, and between them lies some of the country's most attractive scenery. If you're going it alone, get a good map of this region and trace your route so it zigzags through the alps to the Valley of SAVINJA and to the source of the River Savinja, where the scenery is spectacular and the driving dramatic!

MARIBOR

Celje lies halfway between Ljubljana and Maribor, the second city of Slovenia. The scenery on this route is not terribly special, so if you're planning to visit or stay in Maribor you're as well making this part of your journey of the non-stop type. Few holidaymakers, other than those touring the country, journey to Maribor as it is largely an industrial town, but because of its proximity to the Pohorje Mountains and the excellent excursion potential of the town, you might consider using it as a base from which to explore the surrounding countryside. It is situated between the Pohorje and Kozjak hills and lies on the River Drava – the old town on the left bank; the new on the right.

For those looking to stay in Maribor the **Hotel Orel**, **Hotel Habakuk** or **Motel Jezero** offer good standards, while for those on a budget the **Zamorec** is a good choice.

Historically Maribor was built as a Christian bastion to stave off the advances of the Muslim Turks, though in 1529 and 1683 the town was completely destroyed by the enemy en route to take Vienna. The Thirty Years War of 1614–48 and plague in 1680 brought destruction to the town – note the large Plague Column in Glavni Trg, the main square of the town. Maribor was an Austrian town from the twelfth century right up until 1918 when it was handed over to the new state of Yugoslavia by the defeated Austrian side of the First World War. Today's expanding town makes its money from textiles and the metal industry.

The sights of the town are relatively few: the **town hall** from 1565; the **Plague Column** and **St Aloysius's Chapel** all stand in the main square – Glavni Trg. Walking through the pedestrian precinct, you come to the town **cathedral**. What you see today is largely from the seventeenth century though the original structure dates from 1150. Central to the old town is the fifteenth-century **Castle** which today houses the interesting Municipal Museum in some of its halls. If you've time, other sights worth a look are the **Venetian House** near the Drava Bridge and **St Barbara's Chapel** on Calvary Hill close to the **Municipal Park**.

A bus from Maribor takes you the three miles to the start of the cablecar which climbs three and a half thousand feet into the POHORJE HILLS. Hotels are located here, and the view over the surrounding countryside is spectacular.

Another excursion, this one an absolute 'must', is to the medieval town of PTUJ. Wandering through the narrow old streets you see well preserved buildings from all eras, from the twelfth century on, and it is easy to see why the whole of the old town has been designated a national monument. Ptuj also produces some of the best wine in the country, so take advantage of this fact while you're here by visiting the large wine-tasting house, open to the public; then, suitably inspired, pay a visit to the **Wine Museum** in the old Water Tower, by the bridge over the Drava.

The main sights of the town (all of which you will see if you take an organized excursion from Maribor) are: the **Orpheus Pillar** from AD 194, erected to honour Emperor Septimus Severus, but used in medieval times as a pillory; the **City Tower**, originally part of the town's defensive system; the thirteenth-century **Dominican Monastery**, and dominating the scene, the **Castle**, where you can find the Municipal Museum. Outside the old town on the opposite side of the Drava are the remains of **Mithraic Temples** dating back to Roman times.

Tourist Information will assist you for accommodation or sightseeing particulars. They can be found opposite the Post Office, close to the bridge over the Drava.

(The coastal resorts of Slovenia – Portoroz, Koper and Piran – are covered under Istria.)

Inland Croatia

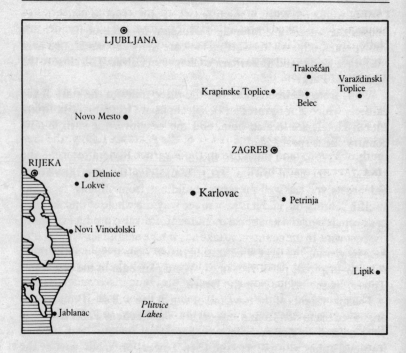

The fertile, rolling countryside of inland Croatia is rarely seen by most package-holidaymakers who happily stay in the resorts on the Croatian littoral, yet the contrast is striking, and excursions into the interior of this region of Yugoslavia are invariably rewarding. Geographically Croatia stretches from Istria on the Adriatic coast to the Dinaric Alps, with the Rivers Drava and Sava running through the republic. The regional capital is Zagreb, an impressive city with a distinctly central European air to it, reminiscent of the cities of Austria, Hungary and Germany. In fact eastern Croatia has a distinctly Teutonic feel to it, which is not surprising when one learns that this area was settled by German peasants in the latter half of the nineteenth century.

Industry has made Croatia one of Yugoslavia's most prosperous regions and today the traditional corn-earner, agriculture, is being replaced by aluminium working, chemical industries, the oil business and tourism. The tourist industry's prize spot inland is the PLITVICE LAKES, which lie south of Zagreb toward the coast. This series of mountain lakes linked by waterfalls and surrounded by forest lies in a National Park and is a deservedly popular location for tourists seeking a restful holiday in unspoilt countryside, and with daytrippers making it an excursion from their coastal resorts.

For the purposes of this section the following places are highlighted: the city of ZAGREB; the hilly area north of the city called ZAGORJE; the area just inland from Rijeka and the Istrian coastal resorts – GORSKI KOTAR; the resort of the PLITVICE LAKES; the area south of Plitvice and inland from the Kvarner Riviera resorts – the LIKA VALLEY; and, briefly, the largely industrial area known as SLAVONIA.

HISTORY

To summarize Croatia's history is no mean feat, but the key events which shaped her destiny were as follows. By 925 the various Croat tribes were unified in their fight against the Hungarians under the rule of King Tomislav. In 1102 Croatia joins in union with Hungary and increasingly becomes dependent on the old enemy. In 1527, when the Turks force their way into Hungary and Croatia, the Croatians transfer their loyalties to the Habsburgs of Austria. While allied to the Austrians there followed a period of feudal warring when the peasants rose against their powerful nobles, only to be harshly countered. In 1779, finding the increasingly centralized policies of Vienna unacceptable, the Croats again united with the Hungarians.

In 1848 the Croats rise against the dominant Hungarians. The nobility lose some of their power and a more democratic society begins to emerge. The Prussian defeat of the Habsburgs in 1866 created, two years later, the dual monarchy of Austro-Hungary which gave control of Croatia to Hungary. Under the Croatian-Hungarian compromise, Croats were allowed to control their own internal affairs.

Thus encouraged, the Croats determined to achieve full independence and a political movement got under way. Despite various pan-Slav movements to achieve independence and unity, it took until the end of the First World War in 1918 and the collapse of the Austro-Hungarian monarchy before this could be achieved. On 1 December 1918 Croatia became part of the newly formed Kingdom of Serbia, Croatia and Slovenia. Internal conflict paralysed the development of this Parliament and after the murder of the Croatian peasant leader Stjepan Radić in 1928 it collapsed.

In 1929 King Alexander declared the state should be known as the Kingdom of Yugoslavia. His assassination in Marseilles in 1934 by the extreme nationalist party known as the ustaše sparked off a decade of extreme instability during which time, in 1941, the ustaše seized power and proclaimed the independent state of Croatia. In 1944, after the surrender of the Yugoslav army to the Germans in 1941, the federation of Yugoslav republics was declared and, under Tito, a more stable future assured.

COMMUNICATIONS

Zagreb handles airport charter and schedule flights, and there are frequent air connections between this city and Yugoslavia's other main centres.

By train: Zagreb is a major junction and lies on the route to Belgrade, Niš and Skopje. There are also connections to coastal resorts such as Split and Zadar.

By car: there is a motorway from Ljubljana to Zagreb (continues on to Belgrade), and there are good roads from Zagreb to Rijeka. Some spectacular mountain roads link the coast with the interior, and generally the roads in Croatia are of a good standard, making independent touring easily possible.

TOURIST INFORMATION

The state tourist agencies in Zagreb are:

Atlas, at 17 Zrinjevac
Croatiaturist, 17 Tomislav Trg
Dalmacijaturist, 16 Zrinjevac
Generalturist, 18 Zrinjevac
Kompas, 6 Gajeva St
Putnik, 6 Preobraženska St
TD Novi Zagreb, 15e Trnsko

All offer excursions, money-changing facilities and general tourist information (for the official Tourist Information Centre in Zagreb, see page 277).

THE CLIMATE

All you have to watch for are the extremes in temperature. Inland it can get very hot in July and August, while in spring, autumn and winter the evenings can be surprisingly bitter, so pack accordingly.

CULINARY SPECIALITIES

For details of culinary specialities, look under the chapter of the coastal region you are closest to. 'Croatia' includes resorts covered in Istria, Kvarner and Dalmatia, so the cuisine varies accordingly.

WHERE TO GO FOR WHAT

Nature lovers and recluses will find perfect destinations in the Plitvice Lakes and the spa resorts of Varaždinske Toplice, Krapinske Toplice and Stubičke Toplice. The villages of Zagerje are a different world from our urban sprawls, and places like Trakošćan and Varaždin provide havens for those wishing to get away from it all and enjoy beautiful countryside, historic monuments and a simple way of life. The Lika Valley is ideal touring and camping country and remains a well kept secret, so peace is assured.

Winter sports are available in the mountains of the Gorski Kotar region. Platak and Delnice are two of the main centres.

Fishing is good on the Rivers Kupa, Korana and Mreznica, where kayaking is available too. Slavonia provides a rich hunting ground for deer and wild boar. Ask about the hunting reserves of Croatia at Tourist Information, 14 Zrinjevac, Zagreb.

Tour operators currently offering the Plitvice Lakes as an organized tour are the two Yugoslavian specialists: Yugotours and Phoenix.

ZAGREB

Package tourists are only likely to encounter Zagreb very briefly as they are taken from the airport to their coastal resorts, on the Istrian or Kvarner Rivieras, or if they are on one of the city holidays offered by a couple of British travel agents. Because of this, and the fact that few independent travellers stay long here either, Yugoslavia's second city is not known as a major tourist centre, yet it has more to offer than first impressions might suggest, and a stay of two or three days would not be too long to get round the major sights and attractions of the town. If you're there the last week of July you'll fall into the annual 'International Review of Original Folklore' which adds colour and life and brings festivities on to the streets.

Accommodation is plentiful and covers all categories. In the deluxe range is the large **Hotel Inter-Continental Zagreb** at 1 Krsnjavoga Street with casino, nightclub, etc.; the **Dubrovnik** at 1 Gajeva Street is less plush, more central and very acceptable; also worth a mention is the **Palace Hotel**, close to the railway station at 10 Strossmayeror Square. For those on a strict budget the **Central**, opposite the station, at 3 Branimirova Street, is a safe bet. Private accommodation can be arranged via Croatiaturist, Generalturist and TD Novi Zagreb (see page 275 for addresses). Students and under-26s can book up cheap beds through the Studenski Center Turist Buro at Savska Cesta 25. There's camping on the north bank of the River Sava at Horvćanski Zavoj. Take tram 14 towards Savski Most to its terminus to get there.

Suggestions for restaurants are hardly necessary in a city where the choice is so plentiful, but a couple of ideas are: the centrally located **Kaptolska Klet** at 5 Kaptol; or **Gornji Grad** at Meldoska 2. Picnics can be easily assembled from the open-air market near Trg Republike.

As for the sights of the city: head first to the Tourist Office at Zrinjevac 14, bordering on to the west side of the parks. Here you will find free maps, leaflets on all the cultural happenings and all the help you need.

The city is divided into three main areas: the Upper Town, dating from the thirteenth century; the Lower Town, which is nineteenth century; and the modern, postwar New Zagreb. Concentrate your efforts upon Upper Zagreb and head for **St Mark's Church** with its works by Yugoslavia's most famous sculptor, Ivan Meštrović, and the coloured arms of Croatia and Zagreb on the roof. Also in the Upper Town are several fine old houses including the mansions of the **Jelačić Palace** and the **Oršić Palace**. The Kaptol district, or churchmen's town, lies to the east of the Upper Town and here you'll find the **Gothic Cathedral** and **Archbishop's Palace**.

Down in the **Lower Town** the galleries and museums are to be found. These are generally open all week except Mondays and Sunday afternoons. The **Archaeological Museum** at 19 Zrinjski Square is worth visiting to see the Egyptian mummy with its lengthy text in the Etruscan language. The **Strossmayer Gallery** with its collection of old masters is at 11 Zrinjski Square; and the **Ethnographic Museum** is at 14 Mažuranić Square.

The parks and gardens of the Lower Town provide a pleasant haven for the footsore visitor. If you're keen on Yugoslavia's Native Art, visit the gallery at Cirilmetodska 3 (open daily 11 a.m.–1 p.m.; 5 p.m.–8 p.m.). In the evenings during the International Folklore Festival (see page 276) there are free performances at Trg Katerina at 8 p.m. and in Trg Republike at 9 p.m.

If you tire of museums and galleries, consider an excursion to MAKSIMIR PARK – a forest close to the city centre with a zoo, ideal for relaxing walks and picnics. Other excursions are to the mountainous area of Medvednica. This particularly attractive district is reached by taking trams 14 or 21 from the city centre to Gračani, where the cablecar which takes you up to this area starts. Beyond Medvednica begins the ZAGORJE district with its rolling hills, historic castles and famous spa towns, such as Krapinske Toplice and Stubičke Toplice.

THE ZAGORJE

If you're touring here the following places are the highlights of this area.

THE SUTLA VALLEY – this begins just west of the city of Zagreb and reaches its climax at the Zelenjak Gorge where the river pushes through the rocks in a most dramatic way, making this one of the most beautiful places within striking distance from Zadar.

The spas of the Zagorje district date back to Roman times and are still used today for the benefits of Yugoslav citizens and tourists wishing to take a cure, or indulge in the fine facilities at affordable prices. KRAPINSKE TOPLICE lies at an altitude of 525 feet and has hot springs of 104°F/40°C; and VARAŽDINSKE TOPLICE lies at 650 feet and its hot springs are of 130°F/58°C. If you're interested in taking a spa holiday, write for the leaflet on the wide selection available to the Yugoslavian Tourist Authority, 143 Regent Street, London W1R 8AE.

The castle at TRAKOŠĆAN is worth every effort to get to. The castle, restored in the nineteenth century, lies on the edge of a lake set picturesquely among woods, and today serves as a museum with an impressive collection of medieval armoury.

The village of BELEC near Zlatarn, officially in the region of Ivančiće, has to its credit a medieval castle and two churches of interest; one medieval, one Baroque. The interior of the latter is the most interesting: a riot of gold and silver and extravagant sculptures and ornamentation – true unashamed Baroque.

In the north of the Zagorje is the historic town of VARAŽDIN. The Baroque seventeenth-century architecture of this town, combined with its French-style 'château' and cemetery based on the layout of the gardens at Versailles, make it one of the most interesting centres in this region, and if you are looking for a daytrip in the country to see a way of life different from that lived in the city, this is an ideal location. The castle today is a museum, and the cemetery lies opposite it.

The final place of interest in this region perhaps means more to the Yugoslavs than to tourists: it is the birthplace of Marshal Tito, at KUMROVEC, five miles from Klamjec in the Sutla Valley. His birthplace is now a museum containing memorabilia from his childhood.

GORSKI KOTAR

One area inland from the coastal resorts of Istria and what's termed in the brochures as the Kvarner Riviera is known as the Gorski Kotar. Only a matter of a few miles from Rijeka, on the E96 road you enter the picturesque district of Gorski Kotar with its forests, meadows, streams and mountains. Some of the peaks reach heights of over 5000 feet and skiing is possible. PLATAK is a resort on a side road off the E96 at the foot of Mount Risnjak (5013 feet) and Snežnik (5893 feet) popular with winter sports enthusiasts. DELNICE and LOKVE are two other very attractive winter resorts for skiing in this area. If you have transport it is actually possible to combine a skiing and beach holiday by staying at a resort near Rijeka and travelling in to ski. The month of May is the time of year when this is possible as there is sufficient snow and sun to permit both activities.

One highlight of this region is the waterfall of ZELENI VIR, close to the town of Skrad, where water throws itself down 300 feet in a dramatic gesture. The town of **KARLOVAC** is an historic landmark, not far from the Gorski Kotar. It lies off the E96, 27 miles from Zagreb, and in the late sixteenth century was selected by Archduke Charles of Habsburg to become a garrison town to curb the advance of the Turks. A fortress and moat were built and the town, as well as the nearby castle of Dubovac, was strengthened sufficiently to withstand any attack. As it happens, when the Turks did arrive in 1683, en route to capture Vienna, they by-passed Karlovac and the town's military significance waned. In the early eighteenth century it became a trading post, and in 1776 Empress Maria Theresa granted it the status of a 'royal free city'. Today the **burghers' houses**, **Baroque Church** and the **Municipal Museum** are the attractions of the town, and bear witness to its significant past.

If you intend to stay in Karlovac, the **Korana Hotel** is a good, medium-priced choice. Alternatively there's camping at Korona campsite on the road to Plitvice, or at the other end of the scale there's luxury accommodation at Dubovac in the **Castle Hotel**. DELNICE is probably the most attractive place to stay, though, if you're more interested in the countryside, in which case the **Delnice Hotel** is a good choice.

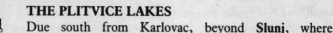

THE PLITVICE LAKES

Due south from Karlovac, beyond **Slunj**, where Napoleon's troops were installed in the castle, lie the sixteen lakes of Plitvice, set in the National Park of the same name. This is definitely one of the most beautiful yet underestimated areas of Europe. The National Park comprises of 19,200 hectares of which 13,500 are forested. Some of the trees found here are as much as 160 feet high and extremely old. The lakes are all positioned on different levels, connected by cascades and waterfalls, and the overall effect is one of remarkable beauty. For those looking for a 'different holiday' which seems a million miles away from the hustle and bustle of the coastal resorts and which engulfs you in spectacular scenery, this destination is well worth considering. The lakes are offered as a day's excursion from many coastal resorts, but in the 2–3 hours which you have in the National Park you can do no more than glimpse some of the natural wonders. It's certainly better than not going at all, but if you're really interested in fauna, flora and natural history you will find the thousands of gawping tourists rather off-putting in this beautiful setting, and be able to do no more than scratch the surface of the sights. As a base for a walking holiday Plitvice is ideal, and the lakes provide excellent fishing too. For a small fee trout fishing is available in Lake Kozjak, Lake Ciginovac and Prošćansko Jezero, and boats can be hired.

Holiday accommodation has been available in this area for nearly a century now as Plitvice first became a favourite with Austrian officers in the days when they ruled the region. Of the hotels available, the **Jezero** and **Plitvice** are the two top choices, both class 'A' and with facilities of very high standards. The **Bellevue** is also good, though it offers fewer frills. Yugotours and Phoenix both run packages to the Jezero and Plitvice hotels, and excursions to the lakes and picnics in the National Park.

The lakes divide into two groups – the Upper Lakes and the Lower Lakes. The largest is Lake Kozjak which is about 2 miles long and 151 feet deep. Motor boats link the lake to trains and take visitors on a panoramic rail ride through the park. The other lake of a comparable size is the Prošćansko Jezero; all the other lakes are much smaller. This is the highest of the lakes, over 2000 feet above sea-level. The lakes receive their water from the Rivers Bela and Crua which meet south of Prošćansko Jezero. The lowest lake flows into a national dam at the foot of the 'watersmeet' waterfall, where it forms into the River Plitvice.

For the scientifically minded, leaflets are available at the lakes and from the Yugoslav Tourist Authority before you go, which provide great detail on the make-up of the lakes; their interesting 'rauhwacke barriers' and the calcareous mud on the lake bottoms which give off the different colours depending on the angle of the sun's rays. A diverse wildlife population is supported by the park: bears, wolves, foxes, badgers and deer, to name a few. Hunting is not permitted.

THE LIKA VALLEY

The area around the town of Gospić in the valley of the River Lika is one of great scenic beauty. The Velebit Ridge lies on the seaward side and it is here that the dramatic landscape is at its best. From this 50-mile ridge the views over the Kvarner Islands are exceptional, and the 5000-feet high mountain creates a totally different climate from that found on the coast only 25 miles away. As the Lika approaches Dalmatia, which officially begins at Obrovac, you come to the Halan Pass from where the views are spectacular.

SLAVONIA

The area between Zagreb and Belgrade, known as Slavonia, is not one of particular beauty and has little to offer from the tourists' point of view. This flat, fertile land supports farming and heavy industry, and its towns and cities, such as Osijek, having nothing to commend them. The spa of LIPIK is the only place worth a commendation It lies in the attractive Pakra Valley, on the road south to Bosnia-Herzegovina. For further information on spa holidays, apply to the Yugoslav Tourist Authority.

Serbia

Most of eastern Yugoslavia is taken up by Serbia: from the Rivers
Sava and Danube in the north to the Kapaonik mountain range in the
south; and the mountains adjoining the Balkans and Transylvanian
Alps in the east, to the Dinaric Alps in the west. There are two
autonomous regions within Serbia: the Vojvodina in the north and
Kosovo in the south-west. Hungarians and Albanians make up the
respective racial groups in these regions, giving Serbia a real mix of
blood, culture and history. Serbia does not really feature in the
package holiday market and the industrial, unattractive cities do not
draw independent travellers either, but there are places of great
natural beauty and historic interest to be found. The Gornjak Gorges
in the east and the Iron Gates of the Danube in the north, where the

river plunges into a deep narrow gorge dividing Yugoslavia and Romania, are two outstanding examples. The scenery is extremely variable: the flat fertile plains of the north are interrupted by villages where life has changed little in the past century. Belgrade, the capital, is the main city of Serbia and Yugoslavia, and gateway to central south-eastern Europe. Southern Serbia, however, is a mountainous region, distinctly different from the north. Albanians are a significant racial group in the south and the Albanian and Turkish languages are heard. Historic fortresses and beautiful medieval Serbian monasteries and churches are some of the highlights of this republic, and travelling here can still be classed as an adventure.

Covered in this chapter are the following areas: western Serbia; the autonomous regions of the Vojvodina and Kosovo where in recent years protests for independence have broken out; the city of Belgrade; the Iron Gates and Danube Valley; the area south of Belgrade – Šumadija and the Ibar and Morava Valleys; and finally the area down to the border with Macedonia.

Serbia is a vast region and a book on this area alone would be perfectly possible, but from the average package holidaymaker's point of view this region is a non-starter. Only a few packages are offered: to Belgrade city, a tour of the monasteries, and to the Kapaonik mountains (Yugotours). Independent travel is possible with a lot of pre-planning and organization, but it is really only advisable for the experienced traveller as the going can get quite tough in rural areas where facilities are few and English is not spoken.

HISTORY

The proud nationalistic Serbian state dates back to the ninth century and until the mid-fifteenth century this region was an important independent state. At this time the richly adorned monasteries you see were built along the Ibar River, and Serbia was at her zenith. In the fourteenth century Serbia was split into several small states which due to their lack of strength could not put up a sufficient fight to curb the Turkish advance.

By the 1370s Serbian states were captured, and after their defeat at the Battle of Kosovo in 1389 the Turks were able to advance through into Europe. The capture of Smederevo, the Serbian capital, in 1459 marked the end of the independent Serbian State. By the late sixteenth century a resurgence of national feeling occurred in Serbia, and the Turkish influence began to wane as the movement for national liberation gathered momentum. From the 1690s to the 1720s tens of thousands of Serbs were forced to live in southern Hungary and the depopulated area was taken by Albanian immigrants. The seventeenth century saw virtually constant uprisings against the Turks and the governing Pashas. The cruelty with which they were crushed was considerable and the massacre of leading Serb figures in 1804 led to a national revolt in which Belgrade was captured by Karageorge, who became the national leader. This did not last long, however, as friction between the leaders allowed the Turks to take back Belgrade and crush this rebellion. A second insurrection took place in 1815 and from this came the agreement that Serbia would be granted autonomy. In 1878 Serbia received her independence and was granted previously Turkish territory. By 1882 Serbia was a kingdom, ruled by an Orbrenović king. His heir to the throne was killed in 1903 and the Karageorgević dynasty which took the throne ruled until 1941.

In the First Balkan War in 1912 Serbia, Montenegro, Greece and Bulgaria formed an alliance to rid themselves of the Turks. The partition of Macedonia led to the Second Balkan War the following year, and immediately following this came the outbreak of the First World War. The Habsburgs retaliated swiftly to the assassination of their heir to the dynasty in 1914, and the war began.

Serbia put up a brave and valiant fight in the face of the mighty Habsburg Empire, but after Bulgaria's entry into the war she could no longer hold out and was forced to withdraw through Albania to Corfu. In 1918 the Serbs took part in the breakthrough on the Salonica front, and in the Treaty of Versailles the new Kingdom of the Serbs, Croats and Slovenes was declared. The Serbs were the dominant force in this union and virtually all the positions of authority went to Serbs, which, in itself, caused internal conflict. Before the inevitable teething troubles had time to be sorted out, the run-up to the Second World War was upon them. In 1941 they took the decision to side with the Allies, against the Nazis, and during this war around one million Croats, Slovenes and Serbs were killed for the Allied cause. Today's Serbia stands on an equal footing to Yugoslavia's other five republics.

COMMUNICATIONS

The airport used for Serbia is Belgrade which has air connections with all major European cities and New York.

Rail links to Belgrade are very good, with expresses from all major European cities: Ostend, Paris, Basel and Vienna. The Yugoslav network centres on Belgrade from which connections to all major Yugoslav centres are possible.

Cruises also pull in at Belgrade en route to the Danube. They come from Passau and Vienna and stop at Budapest in Hungary.

Within Serbia the roads are average, with a motorway to Zagreb, Niš and the Ibar Magistrala going on to Skopje.

TOURIST INFORMATION

The main state tourist agency in Serbia is Putnik at Dragoslava Jovanviča. The Tourist Information Centre is located at Belgrade Central Station (open Monday to Friday, 7 a.m.–9 p.m.), and in the underground passage by the Albanije building at the start of Terazrje (open daily 8 a.m.–8 p.m.). The youth travel agency is Karavan Agency, Takovska 2: open Monday to Saturday, 8 a.m.–8 p.m.

CLIMATE

It's very hot and dry in the summer and gets very cold in winter, so pack accordingly.

CULINARY SPECIALITIES

Spiced dishes, fish and soups as filling as main courses are specialities in Serbia. The oriental flavour is prevalent and Turkish-style grilled meats are widely available. Try *musaka* or *ražnjiči* to taste the Turkish influence. Serbian cuisine is the richest and spiciest in Yugoslavia.

Negotin is an acceptable wine, as is Prokupac. The most commonly served wines are *fruškogorski biser* and the Danube-grown *smederevka*.

Lunch is the main meal of the day, so don't save up your appetite until nighttime or you may end up with an empty stomach and a great deal of frustration. The set-course lunches are generally extremely good value.

WHERE TO GO FOR WHAT

Historians, art lovers and culture vultures of any description will delight in the Serbian monasteries. To see these enchanting churches, set among the mountains, go to the *Ibar* and the *Morava*. There are also some monasteries of interest in the Fruška Gora, near Belgrade, though these are from later periods.

Sightseers will not be satisfied in Serbia to the same extent as they would be in Dalmatia as the cities are modern and have few sights as such. Apart from the monasteries the main attractions stem from the natural features and beauty of the mountains and countryside. The forests provide ample hunting and the rivers fishing. The Obed swamps and Tara plateau are popular with sportsmen, and in Kaonik a programme of development to turn the area into a water-sports centre is underway. So far the only real resort there is at Kopaonik. Nature lovers will enjoy this destination for the mass of wild flowers and abundance of beautiful walking country surrounding the hotels.

WESTERN SERBIA

The area west of Belgrade stretching in the north to the autonomous region of Vojvodina and to the similarly independent region of Kosov in the south is one of great racial and historic interest. Those touring independently by car should plan their route to take in the following regional highlights: the drama of the TARA PLATEAU, best approached from Bajina Bašta, some twenty miles north west of the town of Titovo Užice; the thirteenth-century **Monastery of Mileševa**, with its magnificent frescoes, located near to Prijepolje at the start of the Lim Valley which runs on to Montenegro; and the **Ovčar-Kablar gorge** on the western Morava River, close to the town of Čačak.

These are the main sights of this vast landmass, but if further detailed touring information is required I suggest you purchase a guide such as Fodor's or Collins's *Complete Guide to Yugoslavia* which covers independent touring in this region in greater detail.

THE VOJVODINA

In the north of Serbia lies the autonomous province of Vojvodina – an area with a population of around two million and with a racial mix more varied than can be found in many other places. Here five languages can be heard: Hungarian, Romanian, Slovak, Serbo-Croat and Ruthenian. Add into this melting pot Ukrainians and other Slav people and you begin to realize why this place must be an anthropologist's dream. Undoubtedly the largest ethnic group is Hungarian. In the nineteenth century around 100,000 Slovaks came from northern Hungary to this area, and the fertile land of this region – known as Yugoslavia's granary – is today being worked by their descendants and by those Hungarians who settled when this was still part of the Austro-Hungarian Empire. The Hungarian-speaking population now numbers around half a million and they have their own schools, newspapers and folklore.

Scenically there is little to keep you in the Vojvodina. The flat fertile plain is broken by two mountain ranges: the Fruška Gora and the Vršački Breg. The villages on the Danube side of the Fruška Gora, particularly Stara Pazoua, are the most interesting and pleasant places to look for a bed.

Bird watchers should head for the OBED MARSH – a marshland haven for migratory birds – and fishermen and hunters will find rich pickings if they base themselves around Bačka Palanka.

NOVI SAD is the capital of Vojvodina; an industrial town whose main sights are the **Old Town Hall**; the **Orthodox Cathedral**; **Petrovaradin Castle**, just outside the city; and the **Bishop's Palace**. Hotels range from the luxurious **Trdjava Varadin** to the medium-priced **Park**, to the inexpensive **Vojvodina**.

A worthwhile trip from Novi Sad is to the FRUŠKA GORA NATIONAL PARK, just south of the city. The rolling countryside skirts the Danube for fifty miles, and within the National Park are interesting old monasteries dating from the days when the woods were a place of refuge for priests. Another trip is to SREMSKI KARLOVCI, an historic town seven miles from the capital. Here in 1699 Turkey signed the treaty which gave Austria possession of most of Hungary, Transylvania and Slavonia. In the town the sights are the **Patriarch's Palace**, the **Cathedral** and the **Town Hall**, all in Baroque style.

The area north of the Danube and east of the Tisa is known as the BANAT, and if you're looking for somewhere completely different, where you will not be able to use English and you will decidedly feel in a foreign land, this is where to go. Real recluses will enjoy the area just before the Romanian border, around Vršac.

KOSOVO

The Albanian-dominated autonomous region of Kosovo lies in the south east of Yugoslavia and can also definitely be classed as somewhere 'different' to go for a holiday. Exotic, 'very foreign' and still unspoilt and undiscovered by Western visitors, this republic is for the hardy, adventurous and daring.

Albanians make up two thirds of the population here, with Turks, Serbs and Montenegrans accounting for the remaining share. The scenery is dramatic and mountainous, and in parts the atmosphere is distinctly oriental. Places to consider staying are: Priština, the capital; oriental Peć; or Prizren. These towns provide basic tourist facilities and make ideal touring bases.

The Turks only left **PRIŠTINA** in 1912 and this is still quite apparent. The feel, look and atmosphere is decidedly oriental and the **Emperor Mosque**, **Turkish Baths** and **Field of Kosovo** are the sights of the town. The battlefield of Kosovo lies a couple of miles from the town and marks the site where the largest battle in medieval Europe was fought out in 1389 between the Serbs and the Turks. The Turkish victory saw the start of five centuries of Turkish domination in the Balkans.

Only eleven miles from Albania lies **PRIZREN**, the most oriental and interesting of all the towns in this region where local costumes can still be seen (especially on Wednesdays when the peasants come in to sell their wares), and the old way of life is very much in evidence. The main sights in the town are the seventeenth-century **Sinan Pasha Mosque**, the **Sveta Bogorodica Ljeviška Church** and the **medieval Pasha Mosque**. Wander in the narrow streets to soak up the atmosphere of the place and barter for some of the silverwork for which the town is famed. High above the town is the ruined castle from where there are good views of the countryside. South of the town the Šar Planina Mountains (with heights up to 9000 feet) mark the boundary with Macedonia. From Prizren the road west runs on to

Albania, but this is not open to tourists. To get to Skopje and Macedonia take the road to Uroševac.

If you're staying in Prizren, **Motel Vlazrimi** is a reasonably priced motel of 50-bed capacity.

PEĆ is the capital of the 'Metohija' or 'church land' – the area in the north west of the Kosovo which was owned by the Serbian Church in the Middle Ages. Again, Peć is a fascinating, oriental destination and the sort of place where the adventurous or those with an eye for the exotic will delight in, but, even to some Yugoslavs it is considered 'dangerous' to travel in. (Tell a Croatian or Slovenian you are travelling independently to the Kosovo and you will instantly be harangued with advice, warnings and stories that all Albanians are thieves and murderers!) Take heart, though, for the end result is worth the effort.

Peć was the home of the Patriarch of the Serbian Church from the fourteenth century, and the Patriarch's residence and monastery can still be seen about a mile out of town, on the road towards Montenegro. The Church of the Apostles here is still occupied by nuns and is an impressive sight, with its rich treasury, fine thirteenth-century architecture and art treasures.

The Patriarchate of Peć can be reached from the Adriatic coast by way of Titograd and Andrijevica, and the incredibly scenic and dramatic CAKOR PASS and Rugovo gorge. So worthwhile is this route that you get value from hiring a car from a resort on the Montenegran coast just to make this trip alone.

If you wish to stay over in Peć, the **Hotel Metohija** on the banks of the Bistrica River is a good choice.

Belgrade

The capital city of Yugoslavia, considered the link between Eastern and Western Europe, is not one of the country's best advertisements for tourism. Its tragic history and strategic position has meant the city has been razed to the ground so often that all that is left from the last century or earlier is one small district. The remaining sprawl is of concrete skyscrapers and unattractive housing schemes.

In package terms the city features as part of a tour and though it must be said this type of stay is actually quite enjoyable as only the best sights and hotels are on the itinerary, the numbers involved are few and independent travellers really only tend to use the place as a stop-over for a few days.

Accommodation in Belgrade is tight, as there are more visitors (mainly on business) than beds, and the prices tend to be higher. Suggestions of differing grade hotels are: at the top end of the scale the **Beograd Intercontinental**; in the A class, the **Palace Hotel**; the **Balkan** is a centrally located, medium-grade hotel; as is the **Park Hotel**. In the budget price range try the **Pansion Centar**, opposite the station; or camp in the bungalows at **Camping Kosutnjak** at Kneza Viseslava. Private accommodation can be arranged through the Lasta Tourist Office, near the Astorija Hotel, or through Putnik.

Belgrade is positioned on the confluence of the Rivers Danube and Sava. The old quarter of the city is near to Trg Studentski; the restored nineteenth-century area is around Ulica Skadarska. **Tourist Information** is in the underpass by the Albanije Building at the start of Terazije: open daily 8 a.m.–8 p.m. There is also an information kiosk in the train station: open Monday to Friday 7 a.m.–9 p.m. *Putnik* – the state travel agent – is at Dragoslava Jovanviča 1, though their offices at 27 Terazije and Požeška 45 are more convenient.

The sights of the greatest interest are: the **National Museum** at the corner of Trg Republike (the main shopping street), which is full of icons, paintings, prehistoric remains, etc. (closed Mondays); **Kalemegdan Park** with its fortress, amusement parks, Serbian orthodox chapels and beautiful views; for art lovers and historians, a trip to the **Fresco Museum** near to Kalemegdan at Cara Uroša 20 where you will find examples of the beautiful and vividly coloured frescoes from the medieval Serbian monasteries and churches (closed Mondays).

Opposite the orthodox cathedral and the café at Sime Marković is an attractive mansion – the **Palace of Princess Ljubica** – which was restored and refurbished in 1978 in its original Turkish-style furnishings (closed Mondays). Across the river in Novi Beograd is the **Museum of Contemporary Art**, of interest to art lovers. There are several more art and history museums in the capital – if you're interested, get details from the Tourist Board.

Excursions to the IRON GATES by hydrofoil operate from March, and this is one daytrip definitely worth making. Other popular excursions are to TOPČIDER PARK to see the Palace of Prince Miloš which today houses the Serbian Museum; and to **Mount Avala**, ten miles south of Belgrade.

Eating out in Belgrade is one of the greatest pleasures of the city. Good restaurants abound and prices are reasonable. SKADARLIJA is the place to go for restaurants and nightlife. The atmosphere here is far better than in the soul-less international hotels with their standardized menus, and if you go to the right places you can be serenaded by singers and gypsy violinists as you eat the sturgeon (and caviar) caught that day in the Danube. Sturgeon is the delicacy of Belgrade and should be enjoyed in all the different ways it is offered.

Restaurant suggestions are **Ima Dana**, a lively colourful restaurant with open-air dancing, good food and music, and **Skadarlija**, which is another along these lines. Those looking for something quieter and less expensive could try **Tri Sesira**, a café at 31 Skadarska: it's certainly less grand and a lot cheaper but the food is every bit as good as that found in the expensive touristy restaurants. Alternatively you can just wander round Skadarlija, stopping as you go to sample various snacks from the carry-outs near the fountain. The *lepinja* (hot bread filled with *kajmak* – a dairy speciality which defies description) is excellent and some of this, some fish, some charcoal-grilled meat and a few glasses of cold beer and you've had a meal as good as any you could find, for a quarter of the price.

One final suggestion outside Skadarlija is **Vuk Restaurant** on Vuka Karadzicaio, two blocks from the Kalemegdan Park – tasty Serbian food at reasonable prices.

If you're interested in going to the theatre, ballet or opera, ask Tourist Information for details of what's on at the National Theatre in Trg Republike. English language films can usually be found playing somewhere in the city, and there is street entertainment in summertime in the Skadarlija district.

EXCURSIONS FROM BELGRADE

THE IRON GATES AND THE DANUBE VALLEY
The 'Iron Gates' are two miles of rapids and gorge on the Danube River, 95 miles east from Belgrade. This treacherous territory marks

the boundary between Romania and Yugoslavia, and the day-long hydrofoil excursion to Djerdap makes a memorable outing. A dam was built in 1972 to control the flow of the river and enable shipping to use this stretch of the strategically important Danube – a film of the construction of the dam and why it was needed can be seen at Djerdap. In the making of this incredibly complicated and much-needed construction whole villages were submerged by the river and the face of the landscape totally changed. For those with an interest in engineering this will undoubtedly be a trip of great interest.

Excursions leave from the Sava harbour in Belgrade at the unearthly hour of 6 a.m. (the Yugoslavs think nothing of rising at this time as a matter of course; holiday or not) from March to October – check specific dates with Tourist Information or Centroturist. The return time is 6 p.m. Centroturist have an office at Bulevar Revolucije 70, Belgrade. They organize this excursion and it is advisable to book ahead as despite its hefty price this is one of the most popular excursions from Belgrade. (Putnik may also be able to book you on to this excursion.) If you're making the excursion on your own and wish to pop over into Romania when you're so close, remember to take your passport.

One of the places of particular interest which you sail past on the trip to the Iron Gates is SMEDEREVO, with its immensely impressive medieval fortress. This massive construction was built back in the 1420s to withhold the advance of the Turks. It was not successful in this mission, however, for by the 1460s Sultan Mehmed was installed in it, and the Turks remained there for a further four centuries. Despite severe damage in 1941 when the German explosives stored in the castle mysteriously blew up, the fortress remains a very impressive sight, with its 16-foot thick walls and 25 defensive towers.

Just before approaching Romania you can see the old castle at RAM. This fifteenth-century Turkish stronghold stands on the right bank of the river, while what you see on the left is Romania. You are now coming to the most scenic section of the trip. MOLDOVA ISLAND is the landmass you see in the middle of the river, and the fortress further on is Golubac Castle which was erected to defend the entrance to the gorge.

Not much further on you come to a place where keen archaeologists will be in their glory – the site of LEPENSKI VIR. The finds made here answered many questions about life in Neolithic times. This little fishing village was 8000 years old when discovered in 1965. Some of the remains can be seen in the museum near Donji Milanovac, just upstream, but most are on display in the National Museum in Belgrade.

The approach to the Iron Gates dam is both impressive and dramatic. The passage through the 'Kazan Defile' (*kazan* means cauldron) is one barely 500 feet wide, with sheer cliffs either side of heights over 2000 feet. Now that the water level has been raised by the dam the surface of the water is calm, not the treacherous swell it once was and which claimed so many lives. The stone sculpture to be seen at the narrowest point of the river is Trajan's Tablet – a Roman carving to commemorate the successful building of a road through the defile in AD 103. This was moved from its original site which today lies below water level to its present position above the river.

Not far from here the hydrofoil docks on the right bank where a bus waits to convey tourists to the Djerdap dam and the power stations. After your tour of the dam the excursion continues by bus to the town of KLADOVO with its sixteenth-century fortress. The local delicacy here is caviar from the Danube. This will probably be the best priced caviar you are likely to encounter, so take this opportunity to sample it.

THE ŠUMADIJA, IBAR AND MORAVA VALLEYS

Leaving Belgrade by the Ibar Magistrala (Route 23), you travel south through the wooded rolling countryside of the Šumadija – a favourite daytrip with the city dwellers and an area of great charm and serenity. Here you will find the interesting village of TOPOLA where the Karageorge family hailed from. (The Karageorge dynasty ruled Serbia and eventually took the throne of all Yugoslavia in 1929.) The family's home has been restored and is open to the public, but the church built as their mausoleum, on the hill overlooking the village, is the main reason for visiting Topola. It contains beautiful mosaic replicas of medieval frescoes, such as are found in the Serbian monasteries.

The Magistrala leads on to the next natural stopping place – the town of KRAQUJEVAC, 25 miles further south. The leader of the Second Serbian Insurrection in 1815 – Miloš Obrenović – came from here, and made this his capital from 1818 to 1842. The city museum is of interest, though really this is an industrial town and begs no more than a short visit.

Travelling south west to the town of KRALJEVO is one of the best bases from which to explore the monasteries of the Ibar Valley. This is the centre of the Old Kingdom of Serbia (called 'Ras'), though today little remains from the past and the town relies on industry and intensive agriculture for its wealth. It lies at the junction of the Ibar and Western Morava rivers and is surrounded by mountains and hills. Several of the Raška School monasteries can be visited on daytrips from here, and if this is your intention the **Hotel Termal** in the town is as good a place as any to be based. Within Kraljevo itself the only place of interest to see is the **Municipal Museum** which is housed in the former governor's residence in the municipal park.

Žiča Monastery is the closest to hand. It lies three miles out of the town, left of the Priština road (Route 22). This fourteenth-century structure with its distinctive red walls and fine frescoes is the place where the kings of Serbia were crowned, and was regarded as the birthplace of the Serbian Orthodox Church.

Carry on for a further 25 miles and take the side road at the town of Ušće for a further seven miles to **Studenica Monastery**, the finest example of the work of the Raška School. Three churches remain at this site: in the largest, the **Church of the Mother of God,** are the remains of Stefan the first king of Serbia and his son. The frescoes in this late twelfth-century church are magnificent, particularly 'the crucifixion' on the west wall of the choir. A collection of treasures can be viewed, including some beautifully illuminated Gospels.

In the smallest of the churches here – **St Nicholas's Church** – look for the painting of the head of St John the Baptist. The last church is the **Royal Church**, built by King Milutin in 1314.

A three-mile walk up from the monastery will lead you to the remains of the hermits' cells, dating back to the twelfth century. Taking the road east from Kraljevo (Route 5) which runs to Kruševac, you can make another tour of monasteries. The first one en route is **Ljubostinja**: twenty miles out of the town take the side road which veers off to the left. This monastery is early fifteenth century and was built by the Serbian Princess Milica who is buried there.

Kalenić Monastery is your second port of call. It is not easy to get to – the road is poor and you have to encounter twenty odd miles of it before getting there, but if you're a keen art lover or historian it will all be worthwhile , for at the other end is a fine ornate fifteenth-century church with well preserved frescoes (they were only rediscovered in 1877 as the Turks had painted over them with whitewash): a classic of the Morava School.

Carrying on the main road east you come to the town of KRUŠEVAC – another industrial town though one with a difference as this was at one time the capital of Serbia (in the fourteenth century). You can still see the ruins of the fourteenth-century castle, and within this stands the beautifully restored **Lazarica Church**.

From Kruševac take the road north to ĆUPRIJA which is the point of entry to the **Monastery of Ravanica**, the last of the absolute 'musts' to visit in this region (though for the real enthusiasts the list could go on and on). Ravanica lies in a valley a few miles north east of Ćuprija (follow the signs for Senje and Ravanica). It is a fourteenth-century monastery lived in by monks and nuns who do farmwork. The restored frescoes are very impressive and the exterior of the church is richly embellished and intricately worked.

These are only some of the main monasteries to see. If you are taking a guided tour of the monasteries your guide will be more expert in the finer points of the art and architecture than any written guide, but if you are making your own independent tour and want only the basic tourist information, this will suffice. For the real experts I suggest buying a specialist guide (available in Yugoslavia) or purchasing an additional guidebook such as J. Cuddon's *Companion Guide to Yugoslavia* (Collins).

Apart from monasteries these regions south of Belgrade can offer quiet relaxing holidays for independent travellers looking to discover the 'real' Yugoslavia. Tourism is not a feature of Serbian life, so don't expect to find the accompanying facilities, but if you're interested in really seeing how the country people live, ask to be put up in some of the farmhouses in the Morava Valley or in Šumadija.

KOPAONIK MOUNTAIN RESORTS

The mountain resorts in the **KOPAONIK MOUNTAINS** are becoming more geared to tourism now. Skiing brings package tourists into the resorts of SUVO RUDIŠTE and PAJINO PRESLO, where Yugotours also offer an outdoor-type holiday on a May to September basis. The hotels they offer as 'Kopaonik' are fine for a recluse or countryside lover, but in honesty outside the ski season they offer very little for anyone else. The scenery here is attractive, but not as dramatic or alpine as in the Slovenian mountain resorts; in every way Kopaonik is much quieter and less commercialized (though it's all relative as even Bled, the leading Slovenian resort, cannot be accused of being brash). In the winter months when skiing takes over, the place is totally transformed. Kopaonik is becoming an increasingly popular winter sports resort, and the après-ski and hotel facilities are most impressive. The **Hotel Srebrnac** is popular with the young, while for a summertime break the **Hotel Karavan** is the best choice.

NIŠ

The city of **Niš** lies on the River Nišava at the crossroads of the routes going on to Greece, Bulgaria and Turkey and as such is an important centre for transport and industry. In tourist terms it is worth a day or two of your time if you're touring this area, though it is actually more pleasant to be based in the spa of NIŠKA BANJA, just outside Niš.

The main sight of the town actually lies outside it – the **Tower of Skulls**. The history of this gory monument is that in 1809, during the First Serbian Insurrection against the Turks, the Turks encircled the Serbs in this tower whereupon the Serbian leader, Stjepan Sindjelić, decided that rather than fall into the brutal hands of the Turks he and his men should blow themselves up. This they did. The Turks then cut off the heads of the suicide victims and the Serbs who had fallen in the battle, filled them with cotton and sent them to Constantinople as trophies. The five-sided tower was built specifically for the purpose of showing the 952 skulls which were set in it to the Serbs to deter them from further insurrection. The Pasha obviously did not understand the Serbian psyche, for all this did was to make them more determined to rid themselves of Turkish rule. Few skulls remain today (many were put in a chapel after liberation in 1877). The Tower of Skulls is situated south of Niš, right of the main road to Sofia.

Other sights are the **Turkish Citadel**, in a park found opposite the town centre on the right bank. This dates back to the late seventeenth century and early eighteenth century and is externally in a good state of preservation. Note the Arabic script over the gate and the heavy defensive system of thick walls and gateways.

Two sites of interest just outside Niš are, first, the remains of the Roman site of MEDIANA where parts of a villa, believed to be that of the Emperor Constantine, can be seen. Fragments of other villas and mosaic pavements are also here and for keen historians this is well worth seeing. Most of the more valuable finds from this site are housed in the **Archaeological Museum** in Niš, located on the left side of the river. Secondly, in the **Jaqodin Mahala** quarter (take the road north as if going to Belgrade, turn right on to the Zaječar road, then sharp left) a fifth-century Byzantine crypt, Roman buildings and the remains of four early Christian churches can be seen.

Hotel suggestions in Niš are the central **Ambassador** and the inexpensive **Park**.

From Niš the road on to Bulgaria is the E5N which provides an attractive drive through dramatic mountainous countryside and runs by rural areas where life has changed little in decades. The road to Macedonia is the E5 to Leskovac then the E5N. Not long after Leskovac the GRDELICA GORGE brings interest to the landscape, and as a place to break the journey there is no better choice than VRANJE with its old Turkish harem palace of Rajif Beg, Turkish baths and its old bridge. The road into Macedonia is one of the country's best and is faster than the alternative from Kraljevo and Priština.

Macedonia

The most southerly of Yugoslavia's six republics is the orientally influenced Macedonia. In many ways this is the most backward region of Yugoslavia, so if you're the type who must have tea and toast for breakfast, and be able to buy yesterday's *Daily Mail* at the local newsagent's then forget a holiday here, even a package to Lake Ohrid. If you enjoy adventure and somewhere that bit different, this is the location for you. Magnificent scenery; exotic old towns of narrow alleys, mosques and medieval churches and the feeling that you left

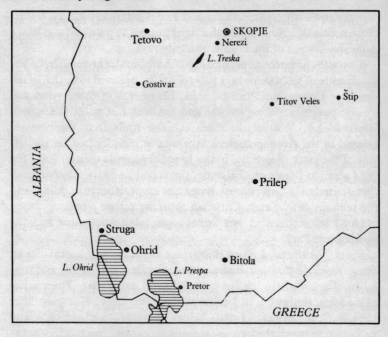

behind the hustle and bustle of the twentieth century at the airport; these are just some of the compensations of travelling to the other side of Europe to Macedonia. The capital – Skopje – is no longer the tourist attraction it once was because of the devastating 1963 earthquake; better to concentrate on Ohrid – a medieval gem – or the lakes – Ohrid, Prespa and Dojran. Tourist facilities are improving and in Ohrid they are of a standard comparable to the rest of the country, but do remember that until the 1920s Macedonia was an unknown place, even to what are now the other Yugoslavian republics. The geographical impossibility of communications assured this, and even today the number of British who have travelled round Macedonia is very low. The Yugoslavian area known as Macedonia is only a part of this once large and powerful province. Before 1919 Thessalonika and part of Bulgaria were part of Macedonia too, but the state was divided following the First World War – when Yugoslavia received the lion's share.

Covered in this chapter are SKOPJE and environs; the road from Skopje over the mountains to the town of Ohrid; LAKE OHRID and LAKE PRESPA.

Packages to Ohrid are offered by Yugotours, but Macedonia is still a region for independent, not organized, travel.

HISTORY

Macedonia endured foreign domination for a period of over two millennia. First it was the Romans, later the Byzantines, then the Turks. It was 1913 before the Macedonians could shake off Ottoman rule, though even today the Turkish influence is strongly felt. Looking way back to its early history and the zenith of its power, you find that the Macedonian Kingdom peaked around the fourth century BC when the most famous Macedonian of all – Alexander the Great – brought the whole of Greece under his control. The glorious days when Alexander successfully ruled over half the globe were to be shortlived and by the middle of the second century BC the Romans had captured and were in command of Macedonia.

The next major force of domination was the Byzantines in the tenth century. After capturing eastern Bulgaria the Byzantine ruler, Emperor Basil II, finally crushed the Slavs under Tsar Samuel and put an end to their independent state by the battle of 1014.

Byzantium ruled until the fourteenth century when the strengthened Serbian state took over, though ironically it took the imposition of yet another foreign power – that of the Turks – to unite the two Slav neighbours. The Turks controlled most of present-day Yugoslavia from the fifteenth to the twentieth centuries.

Despite attempting to overthrow the Turks in the early nineteenth century and later in the early twentieth century (1909), the Macedonians were no match for their well equipped masters and little help for them came from abroad. It took the First Balkan War in 1912 to free Macedonia from Turkish domination.

Following the First World War Macedonia was divided; Thessalonika and its area was given to Greece; Bulgaria received a small share, and Yugoslavia the rest. During the Second World War the Germans gave Bulgaria all of Macedonia but the 1919 boundaries were restored with the German defeat in 1945. Since the war this republic has enjoyed a period of dramatic growth and investment, and formalized social services have been introduced. It is still the least advanced of Yugoslavia's six republics (and there is still an element of resentment among the richer Croatians, Serbs and Slovenians that they are having to pay the price for the advancement of this poor neighbour), but the intention is to even out the disparity of wealth as much as possible.

From the traveller's point of view it is its backwardness, the way it still resembles the nineteenth century, which is its main appeal. This will not change overnight; industrialization, however, is progressing rapidly, so aim to visit Macedonia before the twenty-first century to see this unknown corner of Europe before it's too late.

COMMUNICATIONS

The *airports* used for Macedonia are Skopje and Ohrid, and flights from the other major Yugoslav airports connect up. Packages to Ohrid use Ohrid airport.

Rail links to Skopje from Belgrade are good as the express trains to Greece run via Skopje. In high season, however, this route is packed to capacity and seat reservations are a must if you don't want to spend the day out in the corridor. There are some trains from Belgrade to Bitola. In general the rail network in Macedonia is fairly comprehensive and most places, even small villages, have a rail station. The trains, it must be said, are slow and often run late.

Internal communication within Macedonia has greatly improved in the last decade or so. The main road from Macedonia to Greece is good, as is the new road from Skopje through Tetovo to Ohrid. The alternative route from Skopje to Ohrid is via Titov Veles, Prilep and Bitola, and of the two this is the more attractive and interesting.

Coaches are cheap, go virtually everywhere and are convenient. To counter this, they are often dirty and busy and always overcrowded. The motto is reserve a seat.

TOURIST INFORMATION

The main state tourist agencies in Macedonia are Centroturist,

Kompas, Putnik and Generalturist. In Skopje the Tourist Information Centre is at Kej Dimitar Vlahov 1: open Monday to Friday 7 a.m.–7 p.m., Saturday 9 a.m.–3 p.m.

CLIMATE

Inland the weather is that of a continental climate which means it is extreme: the summers are very hot and the winters very cold. The most consistent good weather is found in the area closest to Greece. Around Lake Ohrid you will always find a breeze because of its height above sea level (over 2000 feet) and its position among the mountains.

CULINARY SPECIALITIES

Turkish and Greek influences can be detected in the local specialities. Vine leaves filled with mince and rice comes out as *sarma od vinivog lišća* and is very reminiscent of dolmades in Greece; *čevap* is the spit-grilled meat found all over Yugoslavia and Greece, and Ohrid trout – *belvica* – is a delicious salmon-tasting fish, unique to this location. In the sweet line, the very sticky Turkish pastries can be picked up for a few dinar from stalls and pastry shops.

Most Macedonian wines are good, very reasonably priced, red and strong. The beer in this neck of the woods is also very palatable when chilled.

WHERE TO GO FOR WHAT

Sightseers should head for Ohrid with its medieval churches and photogenic old town so reminiscent of Turkey. Other dramatic sights of the natural land are to be found at Lake Ohrid, Lake Prespa and Lake Dojran.

Historians may find the ancient Roman and Greek remains of interest. The main site is at Heraclea Lyncestis near the town of Bitola.

The Socialite – or, given the relatively unsophisticated appeal of this region, perhaps it should just read 'the manwatcher' – will find the Ohrid Summer Festival of interest. It lasts from mid-July to mid-August and as part of the attractions folklore performances, singing, poetry and drama events are staged.

The *Great Outdoor* types will find great potential by walking by the lakes or in the spectacular Demir Kapija, Treska or Radika gorges. The Šar Planina mountains, west of Skopje, or Solunska Glava, south of Skopje, are as challenging as most mountaineers could want. The Mavrovo National Park, the Galičica, and the Pelister National Parks all offer wildlife and walking.

The *Recluse* is in heaven anywhere in Macedonia, except possibly Ohrid in high season. Central Macedonia, south of Skopje, or the area bordering with Greece is as quiet, unspoilt, remote and totally undiscovered as you can get anywhere in Europe. Fishing is available on Lake Ohrid and Lake Prespa. Further information on boat hire from the Tourist Office in Ohrid.

Wintersports are taking off at Popova Šapka and on Mount Pelister in the Šar Planina area, close to the city of Tetovo. They have not reached the degree of sophistication of the Slovenian alpine resorts, but for something 'different' or for a family skiing holiday, Macedonia could be an ideal destination.

SKOPJE

Although it's well over twenty years since the terrible 1963 earthquake which destroyed so much of this town, the capital of Macedonia, and killed over a thousand of its citizens, the evidence is still all around you, and even if you didn't know the history you would be able to tell there was something not quite right about this sprawling city. Because of the destruction caused by the earth tremors many of the town's historic old buildings no longer stand – only one restored part of the old town remains – and in their place vast, ugly concrete blocks have been built. These have no special character and are of no interest to the tourist, despite the eulogies showered upon them by the Yugoslav authorities. Practical, modern and convenient they may well be, but attractive they are not. There is, therefore, little real reason to stay long in Skopje. If you happen to find yourself with time to kill there are a few places of interest, but the main attractions are to be found outside the city in its immediate environs.

Staying in Skopje, though, hotels range from the A class **Continen-**

tal and **Grand Hotel Skopje** to the more affordable **Bellevue** and **Jadran** to the campsite and motel seven miles south of the town – Motel Katlanovo – or the youth hostel – Dom Blagoje Šošolcevat 25 Prolet. **Tourist Information** is at Kej Dimitar Vlahov 1: open Monday to Friday 7 a.m.–7 p.m., Saturday 8 a.m.–3 p.m. Ask for free map. For eats try **Pilister self-services** at M. Tito 50.

The sights of the town are all located on the left bank of the River Vardar: the old quarter. After crossing the fourteenth-century Turkish **stone bridge** (the only monument to survive the 1979 earthquake undamaged) from Tito Square to the old town you see, on the right, a huge domed building. This is the impressive structure of the **Daut Pasha Hammam** – the largest Turkish bath house left in all the Balkans. It was built in 1489 and today houses a collection of Macedonian art.

Once in the old town (turn right after Bulevar Goce Delčev) you enter an area of picture-postcard qualities: the oriental **Bazaar** with its stalls selling copperware, silverware, leather goods and souvenirs of all descriptions – very picturesque, very photogenic, and very touristy. Keep going up Samoilova Beogradska to come to the **Church of Sveti Spas** with its wooden tower and inside a beautifully carved bishop's throne. (Closed Monday. Small entrance fee.) Just beyond it is the enormous **Kuršumli Han**, a sixteenth-century caravanserai, now restored to its former glory after the damage of 1963, and housing the Archaeological Museum.

South of here is the **Mosque of Mustafa Pasha**, a beautiful late fifteenth-century building in classical Muslim form. Looking down on the town from its dominating position is the **fortress of Skopje** from where there is a panoramic view over the town. Further north stands the **Museum of Contemporary Art** which has a good collection of international art of the last thirty years.

The **Church of St Panteleimon**, close to the village of NEREZI, is an excursion well worth making if you're interested in art or architecture. This twelfth-century church has some very fine Byzantine frescoes discovered under plaster in 1926, the most famous of which is the 'Bathing of the Infant Christ'. The church is located three miles out of Skopje on the road to Tetovo.

LAKE TRESKA is another daytrip of interest, especially if you fancy combining a walk in some beautiful countryside with a look at fine art and old Byzantine Churches. Head towards Tetovo for about six miles, then take the road which veers off to the left along by the River Treska; two and three-quarter miles from here is **Matka Monastery** which you can wander around. A mile or so further on you come to the Treska River Dam at the end of the road, and half a mile beyond the dam you'll find the beautiful old **Church of St Andrew**, built in 1389 and containing some especially fine frescoes. The Tourist Information Office in Skopje will furnish you with a map and more specific details of a trip out here, should you so require.

OHRID

Ohrid is unique and beautiful and well worth the effort to visit. This town and the lake will delight not only the recluse and nature lover, but also the historian and antiquarian. To get to Ohrid from Skopje you have two realistic options: driving or busing (the train only goes to Bitola and buses do not link up well). Buses take four hours and there are nine daily. When driving, there are two alternative roads, but from a scenic point of view there is only really one – the road via Tetovo, Gostivar, the Mavrovo dam, on to Debar and Struga, and then, at last, Lake Ohrid. The route via Bitola has little to commend it and is not faster. Stop en route in TETOVO to see the **Sarena Mosque**, the **Turkish Baths** and the former Pasha's residence – the **Konak**.

At STRUGA you have reached the northern end of Lake Ohrid. This huge lake, surrounded by mountains, is 19 miles long, 9 miles wide and 938 feet deep. Two thirds of it are Macedonian, one third lies in Albania (don't worry, the frontier is marked by buoys so there's no chance you'll swim away and never be seen again). The water is unbelievably clear and this can best be seen by taking one of the twice-daily boats down the length of the lake from Ohrid to Sveti Naum, beautifully positioned at the south end of the lake close to the Albanian border. An old monastery has been converted into a hotel here and few places in Europe can rival its setting.

Apart from the great beauty of the lake itself, with its changing colours and quite ethereal atmosphere, there are the added bonuses of the towns and villages dotted around the lake's shoreline: the wonderful old town of OHRID; STRUGA (see Palasturist, 13 Kidric, for private accommodation); **Sveti Naum Monastery** with its good beaches; and **KALIŠTA**, near Albania, with its fascinating old monastery where time seems to have stood still for decades.

The lake is an ecologist's dream. Species of fish and primitive forms of life exist here and nowhere else (hence the Hydrobiological Institute).

The very attractive ancient town of **OHRID** is a popular holiday resort with Yugoslavians, consequently there's a fair number of hotels and tourist facilities in the town. This is one resort where sightseeing can be married with sun worshipping as only a couple of miles south of Ohrid, between Hotel Slavija and Hotel Park in Gorica, is a lovely sandy beach currently being developed into a holiday resort.

Good hotels available in Ohrid are: the **Grand Hotel Palace**, the **Metropol** and the **Slavija** (all A class). Also at Gorica (two miles south) are the very attractively situated **Park** and **Inex-Gorica** hotels. For independent travellers on a tight budget there's a youth hostel (take the bus in the direction of Struga and ask to be put off at Hostel Mladost) and a camping site next to the youth hostel. One novel way of getting to the beach here is to ask a fisherman in Ohrid harbour to take you out to the beach where the campsite is located.

The **Tourist Information** in Ohrid is on Partizanska and is open 8 a.m.–9 p.m. daily.

Nightlife centres on the entertainment provided by the large hotels. There's a disco in the Hotel Metropol from May to October, and the tourist agency Palasturist run a disco aboard a hydrofoil with limited success, though it has novelty value. Restaurants in Ohrid tend to reflect the high level of tourism in the town, and inflated prices and tourist menus are the result. The **Letnica Restaurant** is good, but cheaper and more authentic is the **self-service** behind it. The international hotels offer good, though expensive, cuisine in pleasant surroundings. Ohrid trout – a speciality of the town – is not really worth the inflated prices charged for it.

As for the sights of Ohrid itself – the Byzantine churches converted into mosques by the Turks are the main features of the town, and these and the castle which stands on the top of the hill constitute the core of Ohrid's historic monuments.

In Roman times Ohrid was a strategic stopping place on the Roman road – Via Egnatia. The Slavs moved in during the ninth century, and in the Byzantine period were erected the beautifully adorned churches that you see dotted about the town. The Turks ruled here from 1394 to 1912, hence the decidedly oriental feel to the town and the reason why so many Christian churches were converted into mosques.

In the upper part of the town stand the ruins of the castle built by Tsar Samuel of Macedonia. West of it is the **Church of St Clement**: a beautiful building with recently renovated frescoes from the thirteenth century. (For the cognoscenti: these Byzantine works of art are from the Palaeologue Renaissance.) Also here are some impressive thirteenth-century icons (closed Monday). Another thirteenth-century gem is the **Church of St John** in the little hamlet of Kaneo, just around the other side of the hill. From here is the picture-postcard view of Ohrid. The church itself stands on a promontory above the lake, and below it is an attractive (though mobbed) beach. Right in the centre of Ohrid stands the **Cathedral of St Sophia**, the oldest church in the town, with frescoes dating from the eleventh century. During the Summer Festival held here every July and August concerts are given in St Sophia's.

The evening *korzo*, or promenade, takes place in the pedestrian precinct at the end of which a 500-year-old plane tree stands. Souvenirs are sold in the craft shops along Ulica Goce Delčev and the local market day is Monday.

LAKE PRESPA

In southern Macedonia lies Great Lake Prespa, most of it in Yugoslavia, but a little in Greece and also in Albania. Joined to it by a natural channel is Little Lake Prespa which lies almost entirely in Greece. The road from Lake Ohrid to Lake Prespa runs from Trpejca to Carino and climbs in the course of its hairpin bends to a height of over 3500 feet.

This is an area of outstanding natural beauty, and though Lake Prespa can hardly be said to be undiscovered by tourism, it is still refreshingly unspoilt. Mountains surround the lake to the east. The highest point – Pelister at 8534 feet – is a convenient skiing venue for the nearby towndwellers of Bitola, set in the National Park of Galičica. To the west, too, the scenery is dramatic, for the Galičica mountain range dominates the landscape.

The road from Trpejca to Carino is extremely scenic and well worth driving. Tourists can stay in the **Oteševo complex**, just off the main road. The beach here is very crowded but the wide range of sports on offer make up for it. There are numerous hotels in this holiday village and accommodation is rarely a problem. An alternative resort on the lake is **Pretor**, located just off the signposted road to Bitola.

For the outdoor types who do not want to be 'packaged' into a hotel in the holiday complex there is camping available in Oteševo from where you can enjoy hiking, fishing and botany trails in the Galičica National Park. A great diversity of plant species thrive here, including an interesting range of wild flowers in the higher pastures and woods. Hiking is undertaken from the pass road between Prespa and Ohrid. For further information on the National Park contact the Park Office in Ohrid or Tourist Information in Skopje.

Vocabulary

Most tourist-orientated businesses will have among its staff some English speakers which, given the difficulties of learning Serbo-Croatian, is just as well. These few words and phrases therefore are intended for situations where no one can speak a word of English, German or anything useful to you.

One good thing about this language is that words are pronounced just as they are written. There are however some accents unknown to English speakers:

č is pronounced 'ch' as in 'chocolate'
ć is pronounced 'ch' as in 'cheers' *with* the 'e' sound
š is pronounced 'sh' as in 'sheep'
ž is pronounced 's' as in 'pleasure'

English	*Serbo-Croatian*
Yes	Da
No	Ne
Please	Molim
Thank you	Hvala
Good morning	Dobro jutro
Good afternoon	Dobar dan
Good evening	Dobro veče
Goodbye	Zbogom
Excuse me	Izvinite
Where is/are	Gde je/su
When	Kad
What	Šta
How	Kako
Who	Ko
Why	Zašto
I understand/I don't understand	Razumem/Ne razumem
Do you speak English?	Govorite li engleski?
Can I have . . . ?	Mogu li dobiti . . . ?

I would like . . .	Żeleo bih . . .
A single/double room	Sobu sa jednim krevetom/sa dva kreveta
A room with a bath/shower	Sobu sa kupatilom/sa tušem
What is the price per night/ week?	Koliko staje za jednu noć/ nedelju?
It is	To je
It isn't	Da li je to
Is there/are there . . . ?	Ima li . . . ?
There is/there are . . .	Ima . . .
Good/bad	Dobro/loše
Cheap/expensive	Jeftino/skupo
Big/small	Veliko/malo
Where can I get a taxi?	Gde mogu da dobijem taksi?
Take me to this address, please	Odvrezite me na ovu adresu, molim vas
Where's the nearest bank, please?	Gde je najbliža banka, molim vas?
Can you change traveller's cheques, please?	Možete li promeniti putni ček, molim vas?
Can you show me where I am on the map?	Možete li mi pokazati na karti gde se nalazim?

I'm lost	Zalutao sam
Can I have my bill, please?	Molim vas račum?
Where's the ladies/gents toilet?	Gde je toalet za žene/muškarce?
Can I use your telephone?	Mogu li se poslužiti vašim telefonom?
It's urgent	Hitno je
Call an ambulance/doctor/police	Pozovite kola za hitnu pomoć/brzo doktora/policiju
One	Jedan
Two	Dva
Three	Tri
Four	Četiri
Five	Pet
Six	Šest
Seven	Sedam
Eight	Osam
Nine	Devet
Ten	Deset
Sunday	Nedelja

Monday	Ponedeljak
Tuesday	Utorak
Wednesday	Sreda
Thursday	Četurtak
Friday	Petak
Saturday	Subota
Today	Danas
Tomorrow	Sutra
Yesterday	Juče

Katie Wood and George McDonald

Fontana Holiday Guides

No one can afford to take a chance with their holiday – yet people
often do. Whether you want to sightsee or sunbathe, birdwatch all
day or dance all night, the Fontana Holiday Guides tell you all you
need to know to plan the best possible holiday for *you*: which
resort, which tour operator, where to stay, how to travel, what to
see and do.

Easy to read, objective, well researched and up to date, they are
indispensable guides to getting fun – and value for money – out
of your holiday.

Titles available:

Holiday Greece
Holiday Portugal
Holiday Turkey
Holiday Yugoslavia

Holiday Coastal Spain

Katie Wood and George McDonald

No one can afford to take a chance with their holiday – yet people often do. Whether you want to sightsee or sunbathe, birdwatch all day or dance all night, the Fontana Holiday Guides tell you all you need to know to plan the best possible holiday for *you:* which resort, which tour operator, where to stay, how to travel, what to see and do.

COASTAL SPAIN

With its bright summer sunshine, its hugely varied terrain and excellent value-for-money holidays, coastal Spain has become one of the most popular destinations for the holiday-maker abroad. It offers not only the high life and world-famous beaches of the Costa Brava or nearby Canary Islands, but the tranquility and lush green slopes of Majorca, the almost eerie lunar landscape of Lanzarote, or the ancient port of Cádiz, steeped in history.

Be it wide golden sands or desert island shore, Moorish castle or modern deluxe hotel, Spain has something for everyone.

- Every Spanish resort featured in holiday brochures appears in this guide
- Most detailed hotel analysis of any guide on the market
- All relevant tour operators covered
- Inland excursions from the major resorts suggested to show you the other side of Spain

Easy to read, objective, well researched and up to date, this is the indispensable guide to getting fun – and value for money – out of your holiday.

A FONTANA ORIGINAL

Katie Wood and George McDonald

Europe by Train

Every year cheap European rail travel entices hundreds of
thousands of people to sample for themselves the diversity and
pleasures of the Continent.

Designed specifically for students and those on a tight budget,
this is the only guide which looks at 26 countries from the
Eurorailer's viewpoint. It is full of essential, practical information
on:

* Train networks and station facilities
* The best routes
* Maximizing the benefits of rail passes
* What to see
* Where to sleep and eat
* Where the nightlife is

No traveller wanting to see Europe inexpensively can afford to
leave home without this guide.

Ken Walsh

Hitch-Hiker's Guide to Europe

An invaluable guide for anyone wanting to travel cheaply in Europe, including the British Isles, Western Europe, Scandinavia, Iceland, the Eastern Bloc, North Africa, Turkey and the Middle East.

Packed with useful information on:

* What to take	* Routes
* How to travel	* Useful phrases
* Where to sleep	* Emergencies
* What to eat	* Local transport
* Best buys	* Working abroad
* Roughing it	* Currency hints

'Practically researched . . . colossal fun to read'
Observer

Katie Wood and George McDonald

The Round the World Air Guide

The long haul travel market is dramatically expanding and for little more than the price of a return flight to Australia you can now circumnavigate the globe. *The Round the World Air Guide* has been written specifically for the new breed of serious traveller and whether you are on a round the world ticket or using conventional long haul options, it will guide you to the best places and the best prices. It is the only book which covers all you need to know to plan and book your trip *and* acts as a practical guide to the world's fifty major destinations.

Full of essential information on:

* How to cut costs and get the most out of your ticket
* Stop off possibilities and side trips
* Airport facilities around the world
* Where to go and what to see
* Where to sleep and what to eat
* Dining out and nightlife

No frequent traveller can afford to take off without it!

Fontana Paperbacks
Non-fiction

Fontana is a leading paperback publisher of non-fiction.
Below are some recent titles.

The Round the World Air Guide *Katie Wood & George McDonald* £9.95
Europe by Train *Katie Wood & George McDonald* £4.95
Hitch-Hiker's Guide to Europe *Ken Walsh* £3.95
Eating Paris *Carl Gardner & Julie Sheppard* £2.95
Staying Vegetarian *Lynne Alexander* £3.95
Holiday Turkey *Katie Wood & George McDonald* £3.95
Holiday Yugoslavia *Katie Wood & George McDonald* £3.95
Holiday Portugal *Katie Wood & George McDonald* £3.95
Holiday Greece *Katie Wood & George McDonald* £5.95
Waugh on Wine *Auberon Waugh* £3.95
Arlott on Wine *John Arlott* £3.95
March or Die *Tony Geraghty* £3.95
Going For It *Victor Kiam* £2.95
Say It One Time For The Broken Hearted *Barney Hoskins* £4.95
Nice Guys Sleep Alone *Bruce Feirstein* £2.95
Impressions of My Life *Mike Yarwood* £2.95

You can buy Fontana paperbacks at your local bookshop or newsagent.
Or you can order them from Fontana Paperbacks, Cash Sales Department, Box 29, Douglas, Isle of Man. Please send a cheque, postal or money order (not currency) worth the purchase price plus 22p per book for postage (maximum postage required is £3).

NAME (Block letters) _____

ADDRESS _____

_____

_____